When the Spirit Meets the Spirits

Julie C. Ma

When the Spirit Meets the Spirits
Pentecostal Ministry among the Kankana-ey Tribe in the Philippines

2., revised edition

WIPF & STOCK · Eugene, Oregon

Wipf and Stock Publishers
199 W 8th Ave, Suite 3
Eugene, OR 97401

When the Spirit Meets the Spirits
Pentecostal Ministry Among the Kankana-ey Tribe in the Philippines
By Ma, Julie C.
Copyright©2001 by Ma, Julie C.
ISBN 13: 978-1-60899-464-9
Publication date 2/8/2010
Previously published by Peter Lang, 2001

Table of Contents

Acknowledgements 17

Preface 19

Introduction 23
1. Geography 23
    1.1 Cordillera 23
    1.2 Assemblies of God in Cordillera 24
2. Background 24
3. Study 25
    3.1 Purpose 25
    3.2 Structure 26

Part I: History of the Christian Works among the Mountain People

Chapter 1: Sociopolitical Context of the Igorots 31

1. Discovery of the Cordillera 31
2. Origin of the Word "Igorot" 33
3. Political Contact 33
    3.1 Initial Interest 34
    3.2 The Establishment of Civil Government 35
    3.3 Bureau for Non-Christian Tribes 35
4. Constitution of Mountain Province 37
5. Civil Administration in Mountain Provinces 37
6. Social Contacts 38
    6.1 Development of Education 39
    6.2 Development of Hospital Service 41
    6.3 Development of Agriculture 42

Chapter 2: Ministry of Non-Pentecostal Christian Groups among the
            Mountain People 45

1. Roman Catholic Church 45

1.1	Historical Background of the Roman Catholic Church in the Philippines	46
1.2	Historical Background of the Mountain Ministry	46
1.3	Current Ministry in the Mountain Provinces	48
1.4	Contextualization Methodology	48
1.5	Leadership Training Program	48
1.6	Social Works	49

2. The Episcopal Church 51
   2.1 Historical Background of the Church 51
   2.2 Historical Background of the Mountain Ministry 51
   2.3 Current Situation of the Church 53
   2.4 Leadership Training 54
   2.5 Ways of Contextualization 56
   2.6 General Social Works 57
      2.6.1 Brent School 57
      2.6.2 Easter School 59
      2.6.3 Other Works 61

3. The United Church of Christ in the Philippines (UCCP) 62
   3.1 Historical Background of the UCCP 63
   3.2 Historical Background of the Mountain Ministry 64
   3.3 Current Status of Ministry 64
   3.4 Leadership Training 65
   3.5 Typical Ways of Contextualization 66
   3.6 Social Works through Various Institutions 66

4. Southern Baptist 67
   4.1 Historical Background 67
   4.2 Mountain Ministry 68
   4.3 Present Situation 69
   4.4 Leadership Training 70
   4.5 Ways of Contextualization 71
   4.6 Social Works 71

Chapter 3: History of the Assemblies of God among the Kankana-eys 73

1. Historical Survey of the Assemblies of God in the Philippines 73
2. The Ministry in the Northern Philippines 74
   2.1 Elva Vanderbout 74
      2.1.1 The Call of God 74
      2.1.2 Vanderbout's Initial Ministry 76
      2.1.3 Pentecost in Tuding 77

	2.1.4 Building Tuding Church	78
	2.1.5 Evangelism and Power Encounter in Tuding	79
	2.1.6 Salvation-Healing Ministry in Baguio City	80
	2.1.7 Salvation-Healing Ministry in Mountain Province	81
	2.1.8 Establishment of an Orphanage	82
	2.1.9 Development of Children's Ministry	84
	2.1.10 Training Young People	84
	2.1.11 Conclusion of Vanderbout's Ministry	85
2.2	Ministry of Mountain Workers	86
	2.2.1 The Recruitment of Leaders	86
	2.2.2 Leadership Training Program	87
2.3	Works Established by Ministers, 1950-1969	89
	2.3.1 Basic Assembly of God Church	90
	2.3.2 Poblacion Assembly of God Church	90
	2.3.3 Tabuk Assembly of God Church	91
	2.3.4 Takadang Assembly of God Church	91
	2.3.5 Taneg Assembly of God Church	92
	2.3.6 Papasok Assembly of God Church	93
	2.3.7 Longboy Assembly of God Church	94
	2.3.8 Beto Assembly of God Church	94
	2.3.9 Abatan Assembly of God Church	94
	2.3.10 Kaang Assembly of God Church	95
2.4	Works Established by National Ministers, 1970-1990	96
	2.4.1 Tinek Assembly of God Church	96
	2.4.2 Binabulayan Assembly of God Church	96
	2.4.3 Ambiong Assembly of God Church	97
	2.4.4 La Trinidad Assembly of God Church	97
	2.4.5 Sebang Assembly of God Church	97
	2.4.6 Palali Assembly of God Church	98
	2.4.7 Lamut Assembly of God Church	98
	2.4.8 Goldfield Assembly of God Church	98
	2.4.9 Pudong Assembly of God Church	99

Part II: An Anthropological Perspective

Chapter 4: Religous Practices of the Kankana-eys 103

1. Spirit Beings 103
   1.1 Adika-ila 104
   1.2 Kabunyan (gods/goddesses) 104

	1.3 Ap-apo	105
	1.4 Kak-kading	105
	1.5 Anito	106
	1.6 Makedse	106
	1.7 Maeya	107
2.	Data Analysis: Spirit Beings	107
	2.1 Domain Analysis	107
	2.2 Taxonomic Analysis	110
	2.3 Componential Analysis	112
	2.4 Theme Analysis	113
3.	Roles of the Priests	114
	3.1 Manbunong	114
	3.2 Mansib-ok	115
	3.3 Mankotom	115
4.	Data Analysis: Roles of the Priests	116
	4.1 Domain Analysis	116
	4.2 Taxonomic Analysis	118
	4.3 Componential Analysis	118
	4.4 Theme Analysis	119
5.	Ritual Practices	121
	5.1 Thanksgiving Rituals	121
	5.1.1 Teteg	122
	5.1.2 Tolo	123
	5.1.2.1 Preparation	123
	5.1.2.2 Procedure	124
	5.1.3 Potok	126
	5.1.4 Dasadas	127
	5.1.5 Liyaw	127
	5.1.6 Benat	128
	5.2 The Healing Rituals	129
	5.2.1 Bay-yog	129
	5.2.2 Dipat	132
	5.2.3 Pakde	133
	5.2.4 Bosal-lan	134
	5.2.5 Maksil/Dawdawak	134
	5.3 Data Analysis: Ritual Practices	135
	5.3.1 Domain Analysis	135
	5.3.2 Taxonomic Analysis	135
	5.3.3 Componential Analysis	140
	5.3.4 Theme Analysis	140

Part III: Theological Foundation

Chapter 5: Three Encounters 145

1. Power Encounter 145
   1.1 Dark Powers 145
   1.2 Fallen Angels 146
   1.3 Demonic Power 147
   1.4 Satan 147
   1.5 Spiritual Warfare 148
2. Truth Encounter 148
   2.1 God as Source of Truth 149
      2.1.1 Victory of Hezekiah 149
      2.1.2 Victory of Elijah 149
   2.2 Christ as Exemplar of Truth 150
      2.2.1 The Man with Leprosy 151
      2.2.2 Overcoming Satan in the Wilderness 151
   2.3 Truth Encounter in the Book of Acts 152
   2.4 Freedom in Truth 153
   2.5 Role of Truth 153
   2.6 Process of Truth Encounter 154
3. Allegiance Encounter 154
   3.1 Darkness to Light 155
   3.2 Worldview Change 155
   3.3 Growth in Faith 156
   3.4 Maturity 157
   3.5 Commitment 158
4. Relationship of the Three Encounters 159
   4.1 Integration 159
   4.2 Interworkings of the Three Encounters 159

Chapter 6: Power Encounters in Scripture 163

1. Manifestation of Power of God in the Old Testament 163
   1.1 Healing 163
      1.1.1 Naaman's Cure 164
      1.1.2 Snake Bite 165
   1.2 War 165
      1.2.1 Fall of Jericho 166
      1.2.2 Battle with Canaan 166

1.3	Punishment..	167
	1.3.1 Nabal's Death...	167
	1.3.2 Catastrophes upon Egypt...............................	168
1.4	Life and Death...	169
	1.4.1 Elijah Taken up to Heaven	169
	1.4.2 Birth and Revival of the Shunammite Woman's Son..........	169
2. Manifestation of Power of Christ in the Gospels...............		170
2.1	Healing...	171
	2.1.1 Restoring a Centurion's Servant....................	171
	2.1.2 Restoring Deaf and Mute.............................	172
2.2	Life and Death...	172
	2.2.1 Raising the Daughter of Jairus.....................	172
	2.2.2 Raising Lazarus	173
2.3	Nature..	174
	2.3.1 Water Turned into Wine	174
	2.3.2 Feeding Five Thousand People....................	174
2.4	Demoniacs...	175
	2.4.1 Driving out an Evil Spirit	175
	2.4.2 Devils Cast out of a Man	176
3. Understanding of the Power of Christ in Pauline Literature		177
3.1	Power of Salvation...	177
3.2	Power of Love..	179
3.3	Power of Justification and Reconciliation.............	180
3.4	Power of Perfection in Resurrection	181

Part IV: An Ethnological Analysis of Kankana-ey Christianity

Chapter 7: Kankana-ey Understanding and Practice of the Christian Faith.. 187

1. God..		187
1.1	Blessing...	187
	1.1.1 Failure of Crops and Plants in Farming..........	188
	1.1.1.1 Female Respondents	188
	1.1.1.2 Male Respondents...........................	190
	1.1.2 Low Productivity in Mining	192
	1.1.2.1 Female Respondents	192
	1.1.2.2 Male Respondents...........................	193
1.2	Curse	195
	1.2.1 Hatred from Non-Believers	195

		1.2.1.1 Female Respondents	195

```
            1.2.1.1  Female Respondents ..........................  195
            1.2.1.2  Male Respondents ............................  196
        1.2.2  Rejection of the Gospel .............................  197
            1.2.2.1  Female Respondents ..........................  198
            1.2.2.2  Male Respondents ............................  199
2.  The Holy Spirit: Healing .........................................  200
    2.1  Infants' Sickness .............................................  200
        2.1.1  Female Respondents ...................................  201
        2.1.2  Male Respondents .....................................  202
    2.2  Temptation of "Shortcuts" to Healing ......................  202
        2.2.1  Female Respondents ...................................  203
        2.2.2  Male Respondents .....................................  204
3.  Revelation .........................................................  204
    3.1  A Bad Omen ..................................................  205
        3.1.1  Female Respondents ...................................  205
        3.2.2  Male Respondents .....................................  205
    3.2  A Terrible Dream ............................................  206
        3.2.1  Female Respondents ...................................  206
        3.2.2  Male Respondents .....................................  207
4.  Spiritual World: After Death ...................................  208
    4.1  Understanding of Spirits ....................................  208
        4.1.1  Female Respondents ...................................  208
        4.1.2  Male Respondents .....................................  209
    4.2  Perception of Spirit World .................................  209
        4.2.1  Female Respondents ...................................  209
        4.2.2  Male Respondents .....................................  210

Chapter 8:  A Comparative Theological Analysis of Traditional
            Kankana-ey and Pentecostal Practices .................  213

1.  God ...............................................................  213
    1.1  Blessing .......................................................  213
        1.1.1  Native Kankana-eys ...................................  214
        1.1.2  Pentecostals ..........................................  215
        1.1.3  Kankana-ey Pentecostal Christians ..................  216
    1.2  Curse .........................................................  218
        1.2.1  Native Kankana-eys ...................................  218
        1.2.2  Pentecostals ..........................................  219
        1.2.3  Kankana-ey Pentecostal Christians ..................  220
2.  The Holy Spirit: Healing .........................................  221
```

2.1	Native Kankana-eys	222
2.2	Pentecostals	222
2.3	Kankana-ey Pentecostal Christians	224
3. Revelation		225
3.1	Native Kankana-eys	226
3.2	Pentecostals	227
3.3	Kankana-ey Pentecostal Christians	228
4. Spiritual World		229
4.1	Native Kankana-eys	229
4.2	Pentecostals	230
4.3	Kankana-ey Pentecostal Christians	231

Conclusion	233
1. Missiological Implications	233
2. Recommendations	236
2.1 Power Ministry	236
2.2 Mobilization of Laity	238
2.3 Women's Involvement	238
2.4 Contextualization	239
2.5 Social Work	240
2.6 Family Planning	240
2.7 Environmental Issues	241
2.8 Community Services	241
2.9 Cultural Sensitivity	242
2.10 Evangelistic Challenge	242
2.11 Growth in Understanding the Word of God	243
2.12 Missionary Involvement	243
3. Concluding Remarks	244
References Cited	249
Subject Index	259
Scripture Index	265
Appendix	271

List of Figures

1. Taxonomy of Spirit Beings 111
2. Taxonomy of Powers of Spirit Beings 111
3. Taxonomy of the Roles of the Priests 118
4. Taxonomy of Ritual 139
5. Truth Encounter 154
6. Interworkings of the Three Encounters 160

List of Tables

1. Domains of Spirit Beings 108
2. Domains of Power of Spirit Beings 109
3. Domains of Manifestation of Power of Spirit Beings 110
4. Componential Analysis: Characteristics of Spirit Beings 113
5. Domains of the Priests 119
6. Domains of the Roles of Priests and Occasions 119
7. Componential Analysis: The Roles of the Priests 120
8. Domains of Rituals 136
9. Domains of Occasion for Ritual 136
10. Componential Analysis: Rituals 141

Dedicated to
Wonsuk Ma, my husband, a co-worker and true friend,
and Woolim and Boram, my beloved two sons.

Acknowledgements

My mission work with one tribal group of people in northern Luzon in the Philippines helped me to launch on my Ph.D study at Fuller Theological Seminary, Pasadena, California. As I reflect on the process, I cannot help but to recognize many people's assistance, particularly mountain pastors and mountain ministers: Olive Lagman, Tito Inio, John Vicente, and Tita Cayso. They made many visits to mountain churches, collected valuable historical material, and undertook interviews on my behalf. This adds significance to the present work.

My deep gratitude goes to my mentor Dr. Paul Pierson who not only helped me to explore the vast area of historical studies, but also shared his brilliant insights to the history of missions and, in my case, the ministerial history of the Assemblies of God among the Kankana-ey people in the northern Philippines. His valuable suggestions helped me to recover some pertinent and important historical material. My deep appreciation also goes to the committee members, Drs. Charles Kraft and Charles Van Engen. Dr. Daniel Shaw helped me to obtain an in-depth grasp on the anthropological significance of the animistic understanding of "power."

Dr. William W. Menzies, then the president of Asia Pacific Theological Seminary in Baguio City, Philippines, not only served as my external reader, but also encouraged me and my husband in an immeasurable way.

My appreciation also goes to Dr. Prof. Walter J. Hollenweger for approving the publication through Peter Lang, assisting in the process and writing the preface.

My deepest gratitude goes to my husband, Wonsuk Ma, and my two sons, Woolim and Boram who have enormously supported and helped me in many ways. Wonsuk taught an experimental course titled "Philippine Mountain Churches" and this triggered an academic interest on my part in the present topic. The great understanding of my family has been beyond human description. Without their help, and God's grace, it would have been impossible to complete this dream.

Finally, I thank several editors: Mr. Sandy Wilks and Mr. Kwang-jin Jang at APTS and the editorial team of Peter Lang, and their skillful editing and careful reading improved the book drastically.

My prayer is that through this small work, people of God will be encouraged to continue to reach people for God through the living Word of God and the power of the Holy Spirit. May the name of the Lord be glorified!

Julie C. Ma
Baguio, Philippines

Preface

A single female missionnary founded the Pentecostal churches among the Kankana-ey tribes in the northern Philippines. Her name was Elva Vanderbout. In fact, the story reads very much like many other Pentecostal missionary stories in which women played – at least at the beginning – the central role. Elva Vanderbout later married a local pastor and had to leave the ministry of the American Assemblies of God because a marriage between an American missionary and an indigenous pastor was not permissible according to Assemblies of God practices. This incident seems to be a good *parable* of the Pentecostal missionary work in this area. The missionary work led to a marriage between American Pentecostalism and local culture. However, the marriage – although *de facto* consummated – was not officially blessed. That is why the author writes in her original abstract, "there is no sign of syncretism with the old religion." A marriage between Pentecostalism and the local culture is not permissible. This is a debatable statement, for the marriage happened all right but it was hardly theologically and spiritually recognized.

Proof of the marriage is the present dissertation by Julie Ma. It is an amazing piece of research by an amazing and extra-ordinary woman. Julie Ma is a Korean theologian, and wife of the academic dean of the Asia Pacific Theological Seminary, where she also teaches. This seminary draws on students from the whole of Asia, mainly of Pentecostal background. Julie Ma learned the language of the mountain tribes. She lived among them, earned their confidence and has unearthed a wealth of information of texts. She describes how many aspects of Kankana-ey culture and religion reappear in Kankana-ey Pentecostalism. They are "baptized" and belief in "dark powers", "fallen angels" and many other themes reemerge with Pentecostal features. These elements are conceived by Julie Ma as a biblical and Christian way in dealing with forces of nature, sickness, world powers, economic powers, nature catastrophes etc. So, the marriage is a fact – but it is not recognized and publicly named.

I am not sure whether Julie Ma recognizes in the above description the intentions and the kernel of her research. For her the break between the pre-Christian existence and the Pentecostal presence is probably much more marked. I have formulated in the above way in order to give readers of the "Studies in the Intercultural History of Christianity" a clue for understanding an extremely foreign and strange world. If we say that we want to take Third World theologies seriously we cannot only take those parts which we can fit into a Western theology. We have much more to consider those elements which not only look strange but which seem to be out of step with our modern thinking. Spirit and dark powers, miraculous healings and angels are not exactly part and parcel of European theology, although they figure prominently in the theology of the Reformers and in Scripture. But they are not – so it seems – part and parcel of Western scholarship and everyday life.

However, they are part of the everyday experience of the Kankana-ey tribes and of the Korean researcher, Dr. Julie Ma. A Western observer can understand why, in these circumstances, an encounter between Pentecostalism and the mountain tribes of northern Luzon is promising. The worldview of the mountain tribes fits much easier into the Pentecostal outlook of life than - for instance – into a Presbyterian theology.

All in all, this is the report of a not yet recognized but *de facto* marriage between pre-Christian and Christian elements. However, here the questions begin, for instance: What will be the ecumenical standing of this type of Christianity? How does it relate to a more rational type of Christianity? Will the encounter change Pentecostalism and/or the other Christians with whom they are in contact? What will be the effect, for instance, on Asian Presbyterian exegesis of New Testament texts on healing and demon possession? Whether the interpretation in the power-encounter terminology of the School of World Mission, Fuller Theological Seminary in Pasadena, California is a help or a hindrance in this encounter is very difficult to say at this moment. This terminology can be understood as a form of modernization of the pre-Christian worldview. In this respect it fits the dynamics of the encounter. Whether it also fits a deeper reading of the New Testament might be debatable.

At any rate, this is a strange but fascinating story of an unlikely marriage. It poses more questions than it gives answers, for instance: What kind of children will this marriage produce and how will they find their way in the modern world? How will the fact that the marriage has not been officially blessed affect the relationship between the partners? Will the fact that one of the partners, namely the pre-Christian culture, is not officially recognized affect the children? Will they follow the path of Julie Ma, who can fit the pre-Christian culture into her Christian worldview? Or will there appear cracks and tensions in this relationship – as it happened in Europe many centuries ago when the syncretism between Germanic and Celtic religions and Christianity and later between Aristotle and Catholicism (in the work of Thomas of Aquina) was forged – or even more recently in the amalgamation of the Enlightenment with Christian theology or in our time between capitalism and Christianity? What happens if the children of this marriage begin to distance themselves from their parents and what will their parents (for instance the American Assemblies of God) do, if the children begin to formulate their own theology? This conversation between parents and children – of which this book is an important beginning – will inevitably be both painful and exciting. What type of new Asian theology will follow from this?

It is too early to answer these questions but the ecumenical movement and the theological community in the West does well to follow this process with the utmost attention, not the least because it will open our eyes for our own Western marriage with pre-Christian and non-Christian partners.

Walter J. Hollenweger

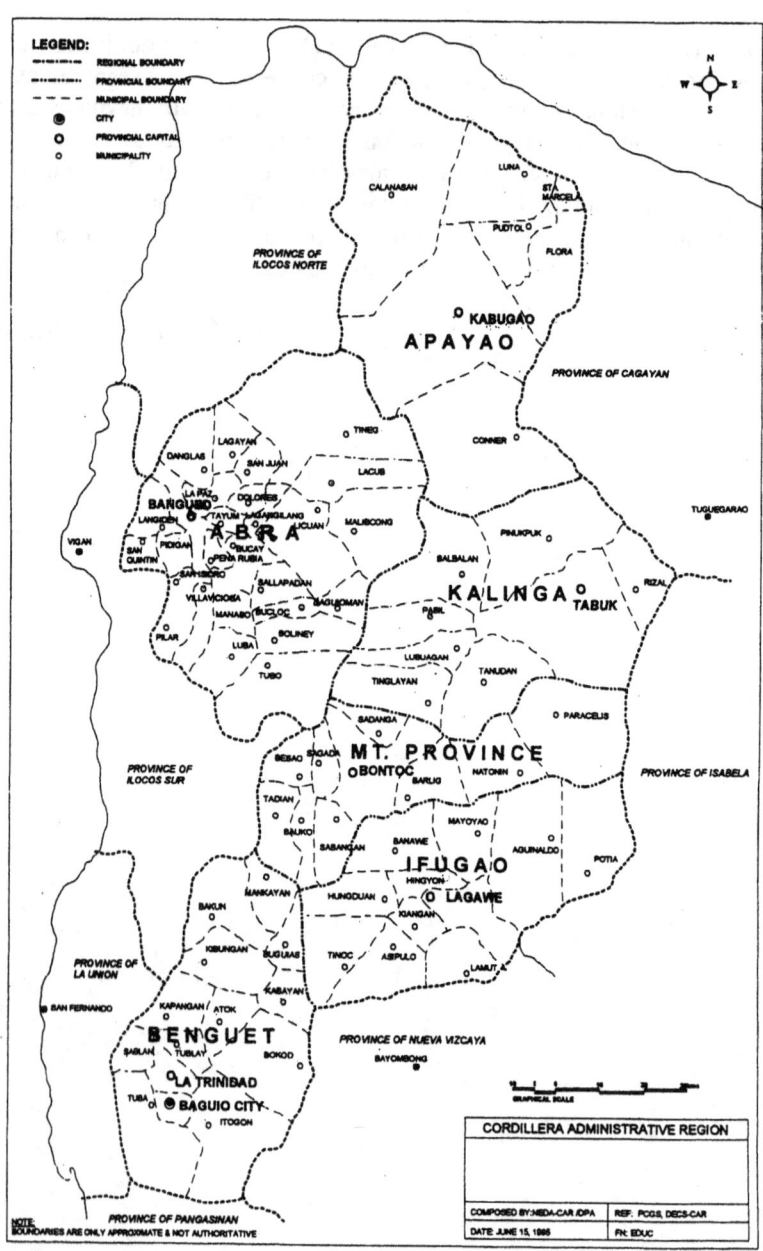

© 1995 by Regional Office of Cordillera Administrative Region, National Economic and Development Authority, and used by permission.

Introduction

1. Geography

1.1 Cordillera

The ministry of the Assemblies of God denomination in northern Luzon of the Philippines began in 1947. Although the Assemblies of God has ministered in all the Cordilleran provinces, the most fruitful and concentrated ministry is found in Benguet Province. The two largest tribes in Benguet are the Kankana-ey and the Ibaloi. The Kankana-ey tribe is concentrated in the northwestern part of Benguet, the largest province in the mountains. The tribe is also found dispersed among other adjacent provinces, rendering the Kankana-ey tribe dominant in the southwest regions of Cordillera (Sacla 1987:4). Almost all the Assemblies of God works have been concentrated among the Kankana-ey tribe, to the neglect of concern for the Ibaloi tribe.

Cordillera Administrative Region (CAR) consists of six provinces: Benguet, Mountain Province, Abra, Ifugao, Kalinga and Apayao with the total population of 187,497 in the 1990 census (National Statistics Office in Baguio). Benguet Province is comprised of thirteen municipalities: Atok, Bakun, Bokod, Baguias, Itogon, Kabayan, Kapangan, Kibungan, La Trinidad, Mankayan, Sablan, Tuba, and Tublay. These lie on the southern part of the mountains, bounded on the north by the Mountain Province, on the south by Pangasinan, on the west by La Union and Ilocos Sur and on the east by Ifugao and Nueva Vizcaya.

Benguet has high and low mountains with rolling hills and occupies an area of 2,556.2 square kilometers. Its population was 187,494 as of March 1, 1990 (National Statistics Office). The Kankana-eys in Benguet are concentrated in the northern part of the province, particularly in the municipalities of Mankayan, Bakun, Kibungan, Buguias, Atok, and Kapangan.

Traditional Kankana-eys work in mining and agriculture. They characteristically are a reserved and peace-loving people. They amicably settle misunderstandings or conflict among themselves, usually employing a mediator. They do not take revenge on enemies. They speak the Kankana-ey dialect, which is similar to the Ilocano dialect used by the Bontoc tribe.

1.2 Assemblies of God in Cordillera

Ministries undertaken by the Assemblies of God have from the beginning been circumscribed by the tasks of evangelism and church planting. In 1947 a single female American missionary and a few national leaders started work among the Kankana-ey tribe. This missionary was commissioned in 1946 by the Foreign Mission Department in Springfield, Missouri (Vanderbout 1946). Thus, neither a body of missionaries nor national workers of the Assemblies of God began this mountain ministry until this individual American woman launched her work. In this area, it was nearly impossible to break through the rigid religious boundaries to introduce Christianity. Such work necessitated that Christian groups bring a distinctive Christian message. The mountain ministry of the Assemblies of God seems to have succeeded in this call and has carried forth the Christian message. They began to evangelize the tribal people through preaching the gospel, teaching the Bible in elementary schools, and conducting revival crusades. A home church was started when a few people came to know Jesus Christ. When the gathering grew large enough, a church building was erected. As work proceeded, more local leaders and missionaries joined the mountain ministry. Thus, the work spread throughout the entire Benguet Province and extended its reach into other provinces. Current reports say that there are about sixty-five Assemblies of God churches in Benguet Province.

2. Background

Before the Assemblies of God began work in the mountain region, other Christian groups – notably the Roman Catholic, the Episcopal, the United Church of Christ in the Philippines, and the Baptist churches – actively pursued ministries in the Philippines. These prominent groups were actively involved in social works such as building hospitals and founding schools and orphanages. In contrast, the Assemblies of God straightforwardly preached the Christian message offering no concomitant social service. Being Pentecostals, Assemblies of God ministers also frequently preached on and prayed for specific healing and supernatural interventions from God.

My personal interest in this movement was heightened over the last seven years, through my participation with the Assemblies of God ministry among the Kankana-eys. After ministering in Manila about eight years, my family and I moved to Baguio City. During the eight years of our stay in Manila, my husband and I were involved in teaching in an Assemblies of God seminary and college, pastoring an international church, and leading a Bible study and preaching in the national prison. The Assemblies of God seminary moved to Baguio City because of its amenities and good weather. We settled in an area on the boundary between Baguio City and Benguet Province, where I would have an opportunity to visit nearby mountain churches. Over weekends we and some seminary students took evangelistic tracts to villages and dispersed them among village people. Often times we gave medical services since the seminary has a ministry team which works with local doctors and missionary nurses. Without such service, people received inadequate medical benefits, for there was not even a single clinic in many villages.

By visiting churches and becoming acquainted with church members, I learned about Kankana-ey culture and customs, and studied native traditional religion. I came into intimate contact with the Kankana-eys' system of deep belief in the existence and power of spirit beings. These people may be classified as animists and ancestral worshippers. They believe that deceased ancestors become spirits and thereby join with existing divinities. Their belief in the supernatural power of spirit beings forms the very basis of everyday life and lies at the heart of everyday experience. They solicit help from spiritual beings to solve daily troubles.

As my husband and I became more involved in work among them, we concluded that sickness was their overriding concern. When a family member became sick, they resorted to ritual sacrifice for healing. They demonstrated belief that, in the ritual, they can appeal to the gods for their need. A priest thus always mediated between divinity and humanity. We likewise frequently saw that manifestations of the supernatural power of God served as catalysts to convert these animists and ancestral worshippers to a knowledge of Christ. My ministry experience among the Kankana-eys has stimulated me not only to collect historical material and to construct a history, but also to identify specific causes for the effectiveness of the Assemblies of God ministry among them.

3. Study

3.1 Purpose

The Kankana-eys are animists who worship their deceased ancestors. They are extensively involved in rituals when there are particular occasions. The Kankana-eys view that spirit beings obtain power to resolve their arising problems, heal and bless. Performing a ritual is a way to meet their needs. Their religiosity is basically power-oriented. The spirit beings are believed to roam around the sphere of the living community and further to associate in the affairs of living kin. Thus, although they are physically departed from the world, their spirits have still remained in the visible world. To this people, the Assemblies of God approached with the message of power as briefly mentioned above. The message and manifestation of God's power penetrated the heart of the people, and they turned to Christ.

The primary purpose of the study is to find reasons why the Assemblies of God has been successful in preaching the gospel among the Kankana-eys. One major reason, as I believe, is the commonalities between the two worldviews: that of the Kankana-eys (animistic) and of the Assemblies of God (Pentecostal). The similarities are evident in many areas. For instance, the Kankana-eys believe that their gods have power to bless and curse while Pentecostals, to which Assemblies of God belongs, also believe that God blesses and provides for the needs of His children. The Kankana-eys also view misfortune as a result of their sin, while Pentecostals, as other Christians, believe that God is a God of love and yet a God of castigation. The Kankana-eys strongly believe that their gods obtain power to heal various sickness. Chapter four will discuss this in detail.

Then, I will study the worldview of converted Kankana-eys. I will probe how far they have changed their worldview after their conversion, and how they understand the Christian God. Their lives have been obviously transformed. They are no longer involved in performing rituals and have followed a traditional belief system. However, the similarities between their former worldview as animists and their new Christian worldview as Pentecostal believers have potential in assisting them to adopt the new belief system. For instance, when they need healing, they seek the work of the Holy Spirit even as they expected the help of the spirit beings in their pre-Christian period. At the same time, one can easily suspect potential syncretism because of the closeness of the two systems.

After discovering how the Kankana-ey believers practice their faith, I will compare the three worldviews of the Kankana-eys, the Pentecostals, and Kankana-ey Pentecostal Christians. In short, it is a comparative worldview study of the animists and the Pentecostals.

3.2 Structure

The following study of this ministry and its theology consists of four parts. The first part examines the sociopolitical context of mountain people and the ministry of non-Pentecostals as well as Pentecostals among the mountain people, from the inception of such works to the present. Each unique approach to the mountain people is viewed historically: non-Pentecostals established the ministry in the mountains with social work, whereas the Pentecostals (Assemblies of God) approached the mountain people with a power emphasis.

The second part deals with an anthropological perspective: the religious practices of the Kankana-eys. A major part of the field research for the study of the religious practice of the Kankana-eys was completed in the years 1988-1992 through interviews and through observing various rituals. A thematic focus was healing and thanksgiving. Through this exposure, I gradually began to understand the Kankana-eys' unique worldview. In participating as an observer of rituals and in interacting with native people, I gained access to their views on gods, healing, power, and the spirit world. The Kankana-eys are power-oriented, believing that spirit beings obtain power to meet various needs. Observing and analyzing the religious practice of the Kankana-eys has improved my understanding of mission approaches appropriate for them.

The third part of the study discusses theological foundations focusing especially on the role of encounters. Since the Assemblies of God approached the Kankana-ey tribal people with a message of power and its manifestations, it is important to examine the impact of the role of such encounters from theological and biblical perspectives.

The fourth part undertakes an ethnotheological analysis of Kankana-ey Christianity. It explores Kankana-ey understanding and practices of the Christian faith and presents a comparative theological analysis of traditional Kankana-ey practice set over against Pentecostal beliefs and practices. Interviews conducted with the Kankana-ey Pentecostal Christians in June and July of 1995 informed my observation of their own ethnic theology.

After conversion, the Kankana-eys learn that the Christians' God is different from the gods in which they formerly believed. For example, God blesses them without demanding sacrifice. There is the promise of salvation and eternal life in God. He is a loving father who provides for their needs and helps solve their problems. God is thus not merely transcendent but is immanent and approachable, allaying fear and hesitation. The people see major differences between their previous religious life and the life afforded by Christianity. What remains for them to do in the course of this Christian life is the task of establishing their own ethnic theology, a distinctively Kankana-ey way of thinking about and learning about God. Accordingly, this study compares worldviews of native Kankana-eys (animism) and that of the Pentecostals, assessing each in terms of a theological analysis. Some identifiable commonalities may point to contact points at which the Kankana-ey tribal people and other animistic people may respond to the gospel.

Part I

History of the Christian Works among the Mountain People

Chapter 1

Sociopolitical Context of the Igorots

The Cordillera, the mountain region in northern Luzon in the Philippines, was discovered by the Spanish. After they had conquered the Philippines, they soon prepared an expedition to northern Luzon. Their greatest interest was to find gold. The term *Igorot* which means "mountaineer," was derived from these Spaniards. After discovering the mountain region, they identified the mountain people with this term. Through such invasions from outsiders, Spaniards and later Americans, the mountain people were able to make political and social contact with the outside world.

1. Discovery of the Cordillera

As stated above, the Cordillera was first reached by the outside world when the Spanish arrived in search of gold mines. Adelantado Miguel de Legazpi learned about the rich mines of the Ilocos only a few months after he planted the Spanish flag on Philippine soil in February 1565, and within six months of his capture of Manila in 1571, his grandson, Juan de Salcedo, prepared an expedition to investigate the west coastal region of northern Luzon for the purpose of obtaining gold (Scott 1987:9).

Salcedo headed north in May 1572, with forty-five Spaniards and nine native Filipinos. Salcedo thus took only fifty-four companions, leaving most of his troops in a fort in Vigan. He and these men sailed around the northern coast and down the whole uninhabited and rugged eastern shore in two boats, entered Manila and brought out fifty pounds of gold. However, he was not able to discover the famous Igorot (Cordilleran) mines but he died in March 1576 (Scott 1987:9).

Why were the Spaniards interested in conquering the Philippines? The primary reason was the hope of locating and controlling rich sources of gold. The main concern for the initial Spanish expeditions to northern Luzon was that gold was being traded all over the area, and it was said to come from "mines" located in the south and south-central sections of the Cordillera. Northern Luzon was geographically in reach of the wealth of gold and mines (Keesing 1962:62). So even during the American colonization (1898), one of the chief interests was gold. As the United States was affirming its status as a new power at the turn of the twentieth century, it found great potential in the Philippines, particularly in northern Luzon, for it promised raw materials which could supply American industries, investment areas for surplus capital and a market for American consumer goods. In this regard, the Cordillera was considered a huge resource where the American vision could be established in the Far East.

The Spaniards likewise reached the inhabitants of northern Luzon because of the attractive draw of gold. As the Spaniards repeatedly raided the Cordillera for gold, they forced the mountaineers to submit to their control. Cordillerans were enslaved to work in mines and other places. Lines of communication were broken from place to place (Scott 1978:14). This same bloody conquest and chaos was dealt by succeeding Spanish administrations (Regpala 1985:5). People who could not sustain great damages abandoned their property to the conquerors and moved to places the Spanish had not yet exploited.

But the Cordilleran did not remain calm nor submit with silence to Spanish exploitation. They defended themselves. Mountain people stood up to fight against the Spaniards and the native lowland Filipinos who were Spanish mercenaries (Keon 1981:1). They fought for their liberty by every means, through the three hundred and twenty years of Spanish control. Their resistance was continuous, self-conscious and sober. They tenaciously persevered to keep their land, which they had inherited from their ancestors. Their tenacity was considered the most significant factor of their strength.

W. Scott (1970:1) has pointed out that "in the face of the uncompromising hostility of the mountaineers and the reluctance of Manila to underwrite the expenses of a prolonged and costly territorial occupation, various military expeditions proved fruitless." According to S. De Mas (1843:9), however, the tribes in northern Luzon were the only independent groups in the Philippines to resist subjugation.

Strangely enough, the ostensible Spanish aim of "Christianization" was not differentiated from the goal of conquering the land of the Philippines, including the northern mountain region. Augustinian and Dominican missionaries were the first apostles to the mountain people, and they arrived on the heels of the Spanish invaders. They were credited with bringing the message of the Roman Catholic faith to the inhabitants of the Cordillera. Their mission work was not immediately successful. Although these missionaries did not lack zeal and generosity, the natives remained hostile to this "imported" Christian religion (Lambrecht 1980-1981:141). Eventually, however, the gospel which Spanish missionaries planted in the hearts of people did sprout and grow, and Roman Catholic churches endeavored to establish work in various regions of the mountains.

2. Origin of the Word "Igorot"

Mountain people are called *Igorot,* the term originally used by the Spaniards. It appeared early in Spanish records (e.g., the *Arte Diccionario de la Lengua Igolota* of Fray Esteban Marin who died in 1601). The term was initially spelled and pronounced *Igorrote* (Infante 1969:5), referring to the mountain tribes of the Cordillera in general. *Igorrote* was a corruption of the word *Igolota.* The corruption was made by the Spanish friars who found it difficult to pronounce certain indigenous words ending in *t* or *k* (Maddela and Tolentino 1972:133).

What sort of meanings does *Igorot* carry? A common linguistic rendering of *Igorot* in English is "mountaineer" (i.e., "one who dwells in the mountain") (Jenks 1905:27). W. Scott (1969:155) further elaborates that from the archaic term *golot* (mountain chain) and the prefix "i" (dweller in or people from), *Igorot* carries the meaning "mountaineer." To the Spaniards, *Igorot* referred to the pagan mountain people whom the lowlanders distinguished from themselves as *Ygolotes,* which means, "infidel." The term, thus, carries negative connotations, such as "uncivilized" and "primitive." "One Spanish historian even derogatorily equated *Igorot* with 'wild beast'" (De Mas 1975:14).

The word "Cordillera" came from the Spanish word *cuerda* which means cord or chain. Cordillera was ascribed to these regions as a description of the continuous chain of mountains which, according to one observation, appeared and reached for the sky thirty-six million years ago, forming the "spinal cord" or backbone of northern Luzon (Reyes 1987:1).

Given the etymology of the above terms, it is understandable that people in these regions would rather be called by their ethnolinguistic group name. They are aware that they are differentiated from lowlanders by the term *Igorot.* Mountain people prefer *Cordilleran* to *Igorot,* because the former has the pure meaning "mountain people."

3. Political Contact

In 1901, civil government in the Cordillera was established by order from General Arthur MacArthur by his military authority. In 1900, military government had been initiated, but ended with this establishment of civil government (Fry 1989:3). However, during the early period of American occupation, northern Luzon, and particularly the city of Baguio, gained popularity among these people. When they discovered the beautiful site of Baguio City and determined that it could be utilized for a summer capital and a hilltop station for the American military, Americans began to develop the relatively primitive northern Luzon area with infrastructure and a constitution of civil government.

3.1 Initial Interest

During the period of American colonial rule (since 1898), northern Luzon was coveted. It was described as "a region of pines and oaks blessed with a perpetually temperate climate and even with occasional frosts." So a commission was sent to this highland region to assess its feasibility for American purposes. The commissioners were Dean C. Worcester and Luke E. Wright (Worcester 1914:449-450).

What was their ultimate plan for Baguio City and Benguet Province? When they arrived in this region, they investigated northern Luzon, and concluded that there was nothing to hinder the making of Baguio into an admirable site for the future summer capital. It would also serve as a health resort. With the help of Charles W. Meade, who was in charge of construction work, the cost of constructing a road up to Baguio was estimated at $ 75,000 (Reed 1976:10).

News about Benguet's potential for future development soon spread. A few American miners, engaged with volunteer military units in the Philippines, were the first to get wind of opportunities. Hearing reports that gold and pure copper were to be had in the northern end of Benguet, these miners, after completing their military service, situated themselves in the vicinity of Baguio, each setting up a hut and digging several prospect holes (Fry 1989:4). People who were skeptical about the scope or the success of this plan were reluctant to invest or participate, whereas others supported it.

During this time, the American-Philippines War continued, and the Cordillera Central was involved in this war. Filipinos fought against Americans by waging a guerrilla campaign, while the United States Army sought to work more systematically by establishing local chains of command. Major-General Loyd Wheaton was the commanding general of the Department of Northern Luzon, with its headquarters in Manila. The first American commanding officer in La Trinidad was Major Evan Johnson (Fry 1989:4-6).

Meanwhile, the American mining prospectors who had settled in the vicinity of Baguio had dug in their heels and established their so-called "self-government." They wanted to take over the political organization for the mountains (Barrows 1873-1954:34). But the Philippine Commission strongly opposed the idea and was determined to prevent its execution. In the end, the miners' attempt would not succeed.

A military government had been set up in La Trinidad in February 1900. The Philippines Commission passed Act No. 48 on November 22, 1900, creating the local and provincial civil governments of Benguet. Civil government in the Philippines was not completely organized, however, until the following Fourth of July (Scott 1975:2).

Benguet Province and Baguio City were found to be adequate places for developing a summer camp for American military people. This led to the establishment of the civil government. It was also a beginning stage of political contact for the Cordillerans.

3.2 The Establishment of Civil Government

In 1901, plans to develop Benguet as the site of a future hill station were launched with the establishment of the country's first civil government. When General MacArthur was appraised of the plan for establishing civil government in Benguet, he agreed. He approved the move and called for the cooperation of all. The provincial governor and provincial secretary were H. Phelps Whitmarsh and Otto Scheerer, respectively. The former had amicable relationships with the mining prospectors, was well educated and had wide hands-on experience (Fry 1989:9).

The establishment of a civil government in Benguet was supported by the governor, Whitmarsh, and people began to settle; some merchants were already interested in trade between one province and another. The authorities began to make a thorough survey of the whole of Cordillera Central, for the purpose of establishing a policy for the whole region.

3.3 Bureau for Non-Christian Tribes

The Philippines Commission attempted to establish a Bureau of Non-Christian Tribes in October 1901. The Bureau would have a twofold task. First, it was to inquire into the current conditions of the pagan and Muslim peoples of the archipelago; second, it was to direct scientific investigations into the ethnology of the Philippines (Fry 1989:15-16). These investigations were intended to help the peoples of the old Mountain Province in the acculturation process, and to enable them to assimilate to modern democratic government, all under the rubric of the Bureau of Non-Christian Tribes.

The task was assigned a chief, David P. Barrows. In 1902, he explored Indian reservations and schools in both the eastern and western parts of the United

States, because the American Indians represented the only direct experience in which the Americans had administrated the affairs of a people whose culture was different from their own (Fry 1989:16).

The president of the United States, William McKinley, gave these specific instructions to the Philippines Commission:

> In dealing with the uncivilized tribes of the Islands, the Commission shall adopt the same course followed by Congress in permitting the tribes of our North American Indians to maintain their tribal organization and government, and under which many of those tribes are now living in peace and contentment, surrounded by a civilization to which they are unable or unwilling to conform... (cited in Fry 1989:16).

However, after his prolonged and careful investigation, Barrows drew his own conclusions. He noted one fundamental difference between the cases of the North American Indians and the Philippines: the North America Indians were hunters, whereas the *Igorots* were primarily rice-farmers. These anthropological and ethnological differences would imply that an alternative administration would be required. In 1903, Barrows therefore initiated his bureau's own program of field research. In order to perform it, he spent six months making thorough reconnaissance of places of the Philippines that had not yet been explored, starting with the Cordillera Central (Fry 1989:17). During his six-month stay in Cordillera Central, Barrows discovered a great deal about diversity in the ways of life and in the ethnicity of these mountain peoples. Notwithstanding the ethnic differences among the people, no single group could properly be called a "tribe," because this term typically denoted some form of political unification; but among these people was nothing of that kind. The later political organization of the Mountain Province would follow Barrows' insights and recommendations (Fry 1989:21). After Barrows was no longer involved in this research, the bureau changed its name to the Ethnological Survey, and a person named M. L. Miller became the new chief of the survey. In November 1904, Miller conducted an expedition through the province of Abra to the territory of the Kalinga people, attempting to discover more about the mountain people and their culture (1989:22). This research contributed to the ethnological demarcations of the different lifestyles of these groups of people.

Later, the entire "tribal" peoples were lumped together in representation by the national legislature – that is, when the Jones Bill became law in 1916. Senators and representatives of the tribes were appointed by the governor general. But this same law required establishment of a bureau charged with special defense of the mountain people. So the old Bureau of Non-Christian Tribes was re-instituted by the Philippines Legislature Act No. 2674, on February 20, 1917 (Scott 1975:2).

In the first decade of American government in the Philippines, the Cordillera Central was formed into a civil government region (1901), for the primary purpose of establishing a military hill station in Baguio. Then later (1917), according to the bureau system, northern Luzon was cultivated as a democratic civil government.

4. Constitution of Mountain Province

The old Mountain Province was created by the Philippines Commission Act No. 1876, dated August 18, 1912. The province was subdivided into seven sub-provinces along generally ethnic lines: Amburayan, Apayao, Benguet, Bontoc, Ifugao, Kalinga and Lepanto (*The Philippines Atlas* 1975:41).

But political gerrymandering in the 1920s gave Amburayan a large portion of Lepanto and Benguet, together with their populations. The domain of the Mountain Province had been governed at the end of the Spanish regime by nine politico-military commanders. But the Spaniards never totally succeeded in pacifying the tribes of what was known as Cordillera Central. Later, the American government set up a separate form of government for the Mountain Province (Scott 1975:1).

Eventually the division of the mountain provinces was again made according to seven areas: Benguet, Mountain Province, Ifugao, Kalinga-Apayao, Abra, and Baguio City. This subdivision delineated what would become the permanent structure.

5. Civil Administration in Mountain Provinces

In 1918, the civil administration was established. In the mountain provinces, the governor served as the executive head. The secretary served as the governor's translator and interpreter; and kept the provincial records. The inspector continually toured the entire province to keep the governor abreast of any developments. At the same time, Benguet Province was subdivided into "townships and wards." In each township, a president, vice-president, and council served as administration. The president and vice-president were elected at large by a vote of residents older than eighteen years of age; the members of the council were to be selected by the residents of the respective barrios which they would represent (Fry 1989:3).

The president of each township integrated his or her position as chief executive with that of treasurer as well; the secretary maintained clerical responsibility. The secretary needed spoken and written proficiency in Ilocano and English or Spanish, so that he could serve as a channel of communication between the people (particularly the non-literate) and the provincial government.

The township president, along with two councilors, handled all civil suits and juridical cases not involving more than $200, and they were to be assisted in the preservation of law and order by police officers. The council was also endowed with considerable power of legislation, though appointment of all its members was subject to approval by the provincial governor. It was expected that by allowing the councilors such powers, and by at once subjecting their appointment to suggestions of the provincial governor, they would progressively learn needed lessons in self-government (Fry 1989:34-35).

These systems were borrowed in part from American structures and followed precedents set by their Spanish predecessors. Did this system work out with mountain people? One may conclude that the system worked out fairly well, especially in the initial period. It needed gradual modification to maintain suitability with the mountain peoples' culture and customs. The systems were in fact altered, as mountain provinces were geographically and ethnographically carved into subdivisions. This organization established by the Philippines Commission brought about a unity of control among the tribes.

6. Social Contacts

As mentioned previously, the earliest (1900) social contact of the Cordilleran was made by Spaniards who established military outposts at Balbalasang on the upper Saltan River and at Balitoken in the region of Guinang on the Pacil River (Dozier 1966:32, 36). They constructed a wide trail which connected this region with the province of Ilocos Sur alleviating the previous isolation of this area. Friendly relations emerged between the Tingians, the Kalingas and the Ilocanos who were newly connected by the trail. Due to this relational opportunity, the people in this region developed their own system of what was known as an interregional peace-pact (Fry 1989:56). Such peace-pacts were thus first brought into these areas at the turn of the twentieth century. Dozier elaborates further:

It is no accident . . . that the peace-pact system arose among the Kalinga who were in an area where Western influences first penetrated the restricted and regionally bounded mountain populations. Peace-pacts are most numerous among the Kalinga of the Chico and Saltan River Valleys, and the peace-pacts between Kalinga and peoples in Abra are more extensive than with any other non-Kalinga people. This is, of course, precisely the area through which ran the newly constituted or vastly improved Spanish trail which opened up travel and trade opportunities into one of the most isolated areas of Northern Luzon (1966:213).

Why was it necessary to make peace-pacts? During this time head-hunting was prevalent in the areas of Kalinga, Gaddang, and Apayao. Taking heads was a way of war. There were such severe attacks that in Amboyan and Talubin, during one fight, one hundred fifty heads were taken away by the invaders. Such heavy loss of life was largely due to the possession of fire-arms introduced by the Americans (Kane 1934:230-231). The risk of rapid annihilation was the primary force urging a system of inter-regional peace-pacts.

In order to enhance construction of the trail, keeping it safe from attack by invaders, marauders and head-hunters, a constabulary was organized. It was comprised of Bontoc mountaineers, Ifugaos and Kalingas. They were deployed as police in their own territories. This system was efficient and satisfactory, because each policing unit knew the topography of the locality, knew its dialects, knew the local personalities and shared local habits of thought. Indigenous service persons were much preferred over American soldiers who would have had to go to great pains to enlist the cooperation and help of the people involved (Worcester 1914:387-388).

The eventual network of trails and the mobility of each local patrol was effective in eradicating the threat of head-hunters. Any head-taker who ignored warnings and rules would be penalized. As constabulary stations increased in that region, the head-hunting and its ever-present peril to the lowland provinces of northern Luzon declined (Early 1918:5).

Initial social progress in the mountains was made by establishing trails to the areas where military outposts stood. This project had two effects: provinces adjoined one another in a system of peace-pacts to end the bloody wars and the Philippine constabulary employed indigenous people.

6.1 Development of Education

The governors in the provincial and subprovincial governments were required to serve as superintendents of the schools in their respective jurisdictions. Jesse George, the first official in charge of the school program in Benguet, once reported that there were only ten people in the whole of Benguet Province who were able to read and write. He soon enlisted the assistance of local leaders to establish schools among these inhabitants. But the one problem which remained was who would teach? The only answer seemed to lie in the recruitment of *Ilocano* teachers. The decision was made to train some to become teachers among their own people. Recruiting local people would also be good for alleviating people's fear and distrust of changes and outside leadership (Fry 1989:64).

Eight schools were started in 1901. However, it was immediately apparent that maintaining local interest in these schools was extremely difficult. Thus, after a one-year trial period, it was determined that these eight schools should be reduced to four (Fry 1989:64).

When the schools were initially established, Barrow, the director of the Bureau of Non-Christian Tribes, suggested that since the preliminary organization of Cordillera Central was completed, it was time to define the principles upon which the education of the mountain people should be based. Two principles were suggested. He first said that the mountain people should be taught English. Secondly, he felt their education should concentrate on industrial training. In contrast, President McKinley stated that ". . .instruction should be given in every part of the Islands in the language of the people; yet, McKinley wanted the use of English to be encouraged as a common medium of communication." Barrow, nevertheless, insisted on compulsory use of English from the beginning (Fry 1989:64).

Barrows argued for English because he desired to see Philippine society liberalized and rendered progressive through education (Report of the Chief of the Bureau of Non-Christian Tribes 1902:685). His ideals were based on his understanding of the Enlightenment and its principles of education employed in the 18th century. He envisioned the Philippines, including the Cordillera, being transformed by the use of English education (Fry 1989:65).

Was Barrows' stress on the adoption of ideological thought from educational models of the 18th century applicable to the mountain people? It was perhaps a noble idea, but it was not feasible to bring such radical transformation among the *Igorot* students' thought patterns and action. They were steeped in the heritage and influence of their parents and elders. Nevertheless, a plan was drafted for setting up industrial boarding schools, starting with one in Baguio, a second in Cervantes, and a third in Bontoc. Industrial schools were modeled according to the following plan:

> Cheap barracks, capable of containing perhaps one hundred and fifty students, will be constructed. . .near the barracks an experimental farm will be laid out. . . . The students will be made familiar with the use of proper tools and implements, new seeds will be tested; improved methods of growing seeds now in use will be taught; irrigation, stock raising, sanitation, construction of houses will all be treated in a simple practical way (Fry 1989:66).

But this first trial met with negative responses from parents. According to the director of education in a 1908 report, "the *Igorots* dislike having their children go away from home. The boys prefer the free life of the village to the discipline of the school and frequently run away..." (Fry 1989:66).

Another problem the public school in Bontoc encountered was stated by Father Clapp of the Episcopal Church mission: "the public schools which are very poorly attended are paid a certain sum by the old men of the town, reckoned to be the equivalent of the work they would otherwise do in the rice paddies" (Clapp 1905:647-650). Funding was not sufficient. According to a former lieutenant-governor of Bontoc, "the Governor in the province of Lepanto Bontoc has...in some cases directed municipal police to assist in getting children out to school." Even though children were not required to be in school, under the education law in the Philippines, they were pushed into it as a local "option," at least to a certain quorum of attendance (Folkmar 1907:119).

Meanwhile, other provinces like Kalinga and Tingian of Apayao could not even start educational work (Worcester 1913:1251). So, to this point in time, Benguet Province had enjoyed the most positive results. In Benguet, people had enjoyed longer contact with the outside world, especially the Spanish. This province was, therefore, more adaptable and better equipped to take advantage of "opportunities from abroad."

They already had secretary-treasurers who had been educated in the schools of the sub-province. These schools thus achieved satisfactory standards.

In order to set up a school for training teachers and equipping students, money had to be invested. Without economic development and progress, it was difficult to build and expand the schools. Thus, in order to improve the educational system, economic development of the Islands, including northern Luzon, was essential.

6.2 Development of Hospital Service

Americans feared the dangers of living in the tropics. Recovery from disease and severe wounds was slow in the Philippines. The American authorities, therefore, began to seek a health-giving hill station in Baguio City. They decided to send the sick or wounded to Baguio instead of sending them to Japan or back to the United States, either of which was costly and resulted in the loss of many lives during the long voyages.

A simple structure with room for eight beds was inaugurated on February 3, 1902 as a branch of the Manila Civil Hospital. This was the very year when cholera afflicted Benguet and other provinces. This dreaded epidemic continued until 1903. Out of the necessity to expand and provide more rooms, a sanitarium with sixty more beds was built. By 1907, it was made available for the use of mountain people. By 1908, the sanitarium was converted into a hospital, and it ultimately became Baguio Hospital. During 1911-1912, the transfer of the seat of government from Manila to Baguio was completed (Fry 1989:70).

The other hospital was established in Bontoc, the new capital of the Mountain Province. On February 2, 1912, a one-story brick building was opened for this public service. The quality of the hospital was initially equivalent with that of Baguio. However, with only thirty beds, it soon proved insufficient to accommodate increasing numbers of patients (Fry 1989:70).

The shortage of physicians was a further problem. There were only two physicians for a total population of more than 300,000 people in the mountain provinces. Thus, young people were encouraged to receive medical training and apprenticeships to serve their people.

6.3 Development of Agriculture

During the American rule, Governor Pack of Benguet stressed the need for agricultural development. He particularly noted the possibilities for the cattle industry. Pack rather ethnocentrically proclaimed that "this is a white man's climate and here may be raised products with which he is familiar. Here he may engage in stock-raising or agriculture" (Fry 1989:76). In response to his influence, people raised livestock such as cows, carabaos, and horses. Trading animals began between highlanders and lowlanders who thereby dealt in large-scale domestication.

In addition to livestock, mountain people began to cultivate wet rice on hillside terraces. The majority of the population adopted this form of agriculture (De Raedt 1964:296). Rice became a means toward social importance. Terraces were so productive that they could be hired for a share in the harvest, thus rendering the farm a direct means of economic control as well as adding prestige to the family (Scott 1988:50). Some fields were tilled twice a year, whereas others were tilled only once a year, depending on the water supply (Reyes and De Los Reyes 1987:72). Modern technology in farming also afforded the introduction of Chinese vegetables, the advent of a cash-economy, and the use of fertilizers (Barnett 1967:299-333).

As a consequence, mountain people developed a new form of livelihood. The basic approach was to cut down the trees and uproot the vegetation, leave it to dry, and then set the area on fire (De Raedt 1964:257). A second, or even a third, season of crops was planted if the soil was fertile enough. Usually, the first crop supplied what was to be the main food supply; after that, the ground lay fallow.

Thus, the majority of the people were farmers; their income came from agriculture rather than mining or other things. Persons who earned money elsewhere, in lumber camps, reforestation stations and government public works projects, usually did so with the ultimate intent of purchasing land and animals or a house to continue their farming.

To summarize, the mountain people, who believed themselves to comprise the backbone of northern Luzon (Reyes and De Los Reyes 1987:1), held fast to the land inherited from their ancestors. Keeping the land was one of their most important responsibilities. They also attempted to keep their identity as mountain people. Although they were persecuted by invaders, they exerted tenacity and persistence to keep the land intact. However, due to the Spanish discovery of mountain ore and American opportunism, political and social systems inevitably were restructured. Through the development of western, political and social systems, the mountain people benefited as the economy and the society developed and stabilized.

Chapter 2

Ministry of Non-Pentecostal Christian Groups among the Mountain People

As discussed in Chapter 1, after being discovered by Spaniards and Americans, the mountain people were able to make social and political contact with the outside world. The intrusion not only assisted social and political development in the mountains but also made an impact for missionaries to share the gospel and to establish works among the mountain people.

Four non-Pentecostal Christian missionary groups were involved in early mountain ministry in the northern Philippines. In 1565, the gospel was first delivered to the Filipinos through one of the Roman Catholic groups, the Augustinians. In 1610 the first Spanish missionary, Father Diego Carlos laid the groundwork for mission labor in the Cordillera (mountain region). Other Christian groups began mission work in the 1900s. The four major non-Pentecostal groups who came here usually launched ministry via social work, establishing schools, hospitals, orphanages and so on. They were of the persuasion that ministry established through these activities would eventuate in people being saved. Of the typical undertakings, they were especially devoted to erecting schools to train young and underprivileged people. Besides social work, the Christian groups did not neglect the task of erecting churches, according to local need.

1. Roman Catholic Church

The Roman Catholics comprised the earliest Christian group involved in the mountain ministry. When the Spaniards conquered the land of the Philippines, Roman Catholic group(s) followed on their heels, launching the Christian mission. These Catholics established missions, not only in cities, but also in remote areas. The ministry of the Roman Catholic Church from the earliest period in the Philippines, and in northern Luzon, to its current works is historically traced below.

1.1 Historical Background of the Roman Catholic Church in the Philippines

The Spanish colonization of the Philippines began in 1565 when Adelantado Miguel de Legazpi raised the Spanish flag on the land of the Philippines. The Augustinians shortly thereafter came to this land as the earliest missionaries, beginning work in evangelism and preaching the gospel (Henry 1986:10). In 1577, the Franciscans arrived in the Islands. The Jesuits came in 1581. The primary purpose of their ministry was to help the needy and protect the innocent (Anderson 1969:13). The Dominicans came in 1587, and finally the Recollects arrived in 1606. By these five religious orders, Christianity saturated Philippine soil (Phelan 1959:32).

Within a month of the arrival of the Dominicans, 400 Filipinos had been to confession, and some had received communion (Cushner 1971:88). The initial conversions were not many; the effectiveness of work, however, increased as missionaries continued to understand Filipinos and learn their dialects (Deats 1967:15). The Jesuits skillfully used their order as an instrument to consolidate Christianization. The members implemented two areas of ministry. The first was to visit the sick and the dying to urge them to receive the sacraments. The second was to persuade the "infidels" to request baptism. Why did the Jesuits demonstrate such concerns for the sick? The purpose of visiting was to discourage the sick from appealing to pagan priests for consolation. The Jesuits attempted to help the sick find consolation in the Church.

Spanish Catholics made their aim to create a Catholic community consciousness in which the teachings and the spirit of the church would penetrate the daily lives of the converts. The church reached out more to unreached people and converts increased.

1.2 Historical Background of the Mountain Ministry

The Spanish Roman Catholic missionaries started their mission work among the Isnegs (the tribal group in this region was called los mandaya, which meant people who lived "upstream") of Kalinga-Apayao Province (Reynolds and Grant 1973:12).

In 1595, Fray Miguel de Benavides became the first bishop, and the Dominican priests set up the first mission work in Cagayan, Benguet (Catholic Directory of the Philippines 1976:215). In 1610, the Spanish missionary named Father Diego Carlos set up a mission work in Futtul (Pudtol) of Apayao. In 1612, two Dominican missionaries established a ministry in Capinatan, but it was discontinued due to persecution by the Mandayas tribe; two missionaries were martyred. In 1684, Father Petro Ximenez, was sent to Futtul to reestablish the work there in the midst of the Mandayan persecution. Father Ximenez opened a mission work in Nuestra Senora de la Pena Francia. In 1688, other works were accomplished, including three stone churches which were built then (Scott 1978:1128). These works resulted from Christianization of some Isnegs in Apayao Province. In 1688, the work of San Jose de Taga was founded by Father Juan Yniguez. In 1718, the believers were threatened by non-believers who burned the church. In 1821, the Dominicans activated their mission work among the tribal people in Magaogao, but once again the church was destroyed by non-believers. A few years before the end of the Spanish regime, the Augustinian Fathers penetrated into southern Apayao and attempted to establish a church at Basco (Lambrecht 1980-1981:142-143).

In 1849, two Dominican Fathers, Ruperto Alarcon and Jose Tomas Villanoza, founded two churches among the Mayaoyaos in Bunglan and in Balambang of Ifugao Province. In 1855, Father Alarcon started a mission work in San Joaguin of Lagawe. In 1864, Father Jose Lorenzo, and Juan Villaverde, the most enthusiastic Spanish missionaries among the southwestern Ifugao were sent to the region of Kiangan. They established their work near Ibay Village (Lambrecht 1980-1981:145).

In 1668, two Augustinian Fathers established a church at Kayan, at the site of Asdan. The church was demolished by non-Christians five years later. In 1881, the Augustinians established a mission work in Kayan, at Bontoc. In 1887, Father Julian Malumbres was sent to Kiangan to establish a church. In 1890, the mission work in Santa Cruz de Gumpat was developed by Father Joseph Galfarosa. In 1891, the Augustinians founded a church among the Ibalois in Benguet, under the patronage of San Jose in La Trinidad. Around that time, two other churches were established in Kopangan and Dakian. In 1893, Father Iglesias constructed a church in Bontoc but it was ruined. The work was thereafter bolstered and spread to other principal settlements, including Banaao, Sabangan, Sacasacan and Basco. During the period 1907-1917, Father Contan Jurgens and Jules Sepulchre were involved in mission work in Bontoc. Their efforts were, in fact, exerted to reestablish works that were dwindling, and were considered by many hopeless. In 1911, chapels were built in Tabulin, Bayyo and Canew by the direction of Father Francisco Belliet (Lamburecht 1980-1981:144-146).

Although the Augustinians and Dominicans endeavored to establish churches in various mountain regions, missions failed due to severe persecution from native people. The mountain people who kept their own religion did not allow other religions to invade their territory. However, humble works which were successfully established became a seedbed to expand the mission work among these people.

1.3 Current Ministry in the Mountain Provinces

At the present, there are forty-four Catholic mission stations, some of which also serve as churches: six in Baguio; eleven in Benguet; six in Ifugao; eight in Mountain Province and thirteen in Kalinga-Apayao. There are thirty-two native priests and twenty-two foreign missionaries who currently are working in the mountain regions. The majority of the latter are Belgians, one is from Zaire, the others from Holland. Most of these missionaries are stationed in Kalinga-Apayao and serve as priests. Their main responsibility is to conduct mass, visit the people, and build stations. Some of these priests are also directors of the schools.

1.4 Contextualization Methodology

Catholic missionaries first of all attempted to learn the culture of the tribal people. They respected and appreciated the culture. The gospel was not directly preached to the people; rather, it was indirectly administered to them. However, the Catholics did not seem to devise any particular method to contextualize the word of God. It appears that the Catholics contextualized the gospel mainly through social work. One way of reaching out with the gospel was through teaching religion in the mission-founded, mission-directed schools. Religious subjects were in every curriculum.

What results might such contextualization have expected? One may surmise that this process of contextualizing the gospel through means of social ministry would take a long period of time, because social work carries little overt conviction about or message of the gospel. To contextualize the gospel in this way also seems destined to suffer converts' participation in or complete reversion to pagan practices along the way, for no clear knowledge or discernment about boundaries of the gospel faith was demarcated in this process. In fact, some of the missionaries themselves even joined in pagan practices, considering it a gesture of respect for, involvement in, and preservation of native culture. Other missionaries objected and attempted to convince their fellow workers to refrain from participating in pagan practices, but such persuasion was futile unless conviction was clear, strong, and persistent.

1.5 Leadership Training Program

The basic foundational training for Catholic leaders is done through the yearly Catechetical Summer Institute (CSI). This is a program that is offered over the course of four summers in Baguio City. The staffs from the Catechetical Formation Center supply most of the people in charge of training enrolled students. When the students graduate, they are assigned work in local areas. The Catechetical Formation Center is responsible for the formation of all catechists of the vicar of the mountain provinces. It is thus also responsible for training in evangelism methods (Sabay, Lee and Tan 1991:7). Why is the focus on training directed toward evangelism? The probable reason is that the catechists tend to penetrate the more remote provinces which priests and sisters can seldom reach. People of these remote provinces have not yet heard the gospel. Priests are involved in teaching religious courses in schools and in conducting prayer meetings on Sundays in communities where no priest is available to lead.

1.6 Social Works

The Roman Catholics emphasize religious education, for such is the primary function of the Catholic school. The most important agencies of religious education are the church, the home, and the school. The Catholics believe that their teachings offer the only viable approach to salvation, both for the individual and for society. Why do the Catholics regard education as so important? The Catholics understand that through teaching, human lives will wholeheartedly become devoted and be enlightened. Therefore, education is a notable part of the Catholic missionary work.

The Roman Catholics in the mid-1950s were maintaining about 12 high schools and one junior college with a total enrollment of 2,247 students (in the mountain regions). A recent report says that they are running about 36 high schools in places like Baguio, Ifugao and Kalinga. In Baguio district, nursery, kindergarten, primary, elementary and high school levels are intact in each mission station. However, in some other mission stations – namely: Kabayan in Benguet district; Barlig in Bontoc district; Potia in Ifugao; and Conner, Luna, and Naneng in Kalinga-Apayao – there are no mission schools (Sabay, Lee and Tan 1991:8).

In the mission schools, teachers teach religion, beginning at the primary level. Reading, writing, music and Christian doctrine are taught in local dialects. This education has brought about remarkable transitions in economic, social and cultural development. Early on, the Roman Catholics were concerned about building dormitories in the mountain provinces for the purpose of accommodating students who were in need of dwelling places. Students served, both boys and girls, were from the remote mountain provinces and the surrounding towns of the lowlands. Provision of a dwelling place invited more mountain young people to come and demonstrate eligibility for receiving education and other training. Around 1950, dormitories were built in provincial communities like Kalinga, Tabot, and Kapangan. Most of the students in the dormitories were given free lodging and boarding. If the students' parents were able to donate some rice, their contributions were accepted (Sabay, Lee and Tan 1991:9).

The Roman Catholics also built clinics in the mountain provinces. They found it incumbent upon themselves to provide such facilities. Why was it important to establish clinics? There were no hospitals or clinics for the sick in the mountain regions. The sick had to be cared for by religious groups, like the Roman Catholics. If, therefore, the Roman Catholics were to establish a mission station in a region, they felt compelled to offer sufficient ministry to meet urgent needs. Secondly, mission clinics served any people, regardless of their religious affiliation. Through this ministry, there was a spirit of ecumenism and contact extended to various religious people. Since one of the reasons for building a clinic was to help poor mountain people who were not able to afford necessary medication, needy people were given medicine at a minimal price. The clinic also served as a means of bringing people to church.

The Roman Catholics have specific ways of raising mission funds. They approach a community, asking it to donate funds if such are within the community's capability. This means of gathering an offering is intended to develop in communities themselves a sense of participation in what the Catholics do in the mission work. In other instances, if the Catholics build a church, they join with believers around them in the building process as a way of jointly doing mission work. Meanwhile the Catholic missions also expect and depend on donations from their home countries.

In order to consolidate and extend their work, the Catholics publish and distribute two mission magazines, *The Little Apostle of the Mountain Province* and *El Missionero*. This is also one way of raising funds. Besides these magazines, they also regularly publish parish newsletters for the purpose of maintaining open communication (Sabay, Lee and Tan 1991:9).

Other social work in which the Roman Catholics are involved are: prison ministry, social/civil affairs, credit unions, cooperative stores, family life, vocation promotion groups, social action groups, community improvement projects, maternal health programs, emergency relief services, used clothing projects, recreational facilities, and socioeconomic projects. The Roman Catholics believe that humans should base their spiritual lives on the conviction that religion is not entirely personal, but also social; that the faith should eventuate not only in providing for the individual's need but also in serving and changing the world, rather than escaping from the world. Based on this principle, the Roman Catholics strive to promote social work and economic welfare wherever they serve in mission.

2. The Episcopal Church

The Episcopal Church was one of the four active Christian groups in the early ministry among the mountain people. The following section overviews the wide-reaching ministry of the Episcopal Church in the mountain provinces from its inception to its current functioning.

2.1 Historical Background of the Church

In 1899, the Episcopalians became interested in missions in the Philippines, when the Reverend F. R. Graves, Bishop of Shanghai, was given oversight of the Episcopalian Missions for the Philippines. He recommended a permanent appointment be made and a bishopric be established. As a result, in 1901 the Reverend Charles H. Brent was elected the Episcopal Church's new bishop of the Philippines by the authority of the General Convention (Fry 1989:140). In April 1901, representatives from Protestant missionary agencies met in the YMCA building in Manila. The Evangelical Union was organized with the participation of Methodists, Presbyterians, American Baptists and United Brethren (Gowing 1967:126). They cultivated a Protestant "spiritual geography" in which most Protestant denominations that later began work in the Philippines joined. But the Episcopal Church conspicuously did not join in the "spiritual geography" (Neil 1964:93). Brent, the first bishop sided with the Roman Catholics in their approach to reaching unevangelized folk in the mountains rather than in the cities. So, the Episcopal Church attempted to settle its mission work independently, not with a group. Bishop Brent strategized his own mission idea for ministry in northern Luzon. He was concerned with reaching unreached people in the mountains rather than in the cities.

2.2 Historical Background of the Mountain Ministry

Brent planned to establish a lasting Episcopal Church work of missions. He was especially concerned for work among the Cordilleran peoples. He also gave his attention to missions among the Chinese Muslims. Brent wanted to minister among the Chinese in Manila. However, Bishop Brent by and large focused

Episcopalian work on pagan tribes of the Philippine mountain provinces (Sato, Choi and Setiawan 1991:2).

Bishop Brent stressed three kinds of Episcopalian social programs: hospitals as ministry for the sick, schools for teaching and training capable young people, and churches for spiritual nurture. This tripartite structure became characteristic of Episcopalian ministry throughout the Philippines.

After deciding to set up ministry in the Benguet area, Bishop Brent sent the Reverend John A. Staunton to canvass the province and report upon the prospects of working among the people. Around 1902, Bishop Brent, together with Father Staunton, began traveling through the Cordillera (Fry 1989:143). A mission station was instituted by Father Staunton in 1904 at Sagada (1989:153). Sagada was chosen for this assignment because the location was at the crossroads of the horse trails between Bontoc, Baguio and the coast. In 1906, Brent opened a school in Baguio, which was intended for those children in the city and surrounding provinces who showed leadership potential and superior intelligence. This school later became known as the Easter School and was one of the earliest educational institutions ever established in the city of Baguio.

In 1908-1909, the mission sawmill in Sagada was demolished by a strong typhoon which also tore the roof from the church. In 1930, the rundown Sagada Station was reconstructed. The Sagada mission struggled with a deep economic depression, and Father Staunton had to lead the rebuilding of it without the help of Bishop Brent. Due to the withdrawal of the American Army after World War I, and for various other reasons, the economic situation here was at its worst. It was in these circumstances that Bishop Brent decided to quit his ministerial career in the Philippines (Fry 1989:153).

During the early stages of the Episcopal mission on the Cordillera, a rapid shake-up of personnel made it clear that training native people for the priesthood would be necessary to ensure existence and stamina of future leaders. Later, three Cordilleran priests were ordained in Manila. These three provided valuable leadership during the Japanese occupation, when all foreign clergy were imprisoned (Fry 1989:163). The church in Baguio during the wartime internment proved to be an important and respected influence in the community.

In 1917, when Bishop Brent left the Philippines, he went to France to serve as a chaplain. After the departure of Brent, Father Staunton and his colleagues grew closer to the Belgian Fathers (Sato, Choi and Setiawan 1991:3). They came to a joint agreement that the church should aim at drawing the population of a large area into nominal adherence to the Christian faith. They were convinced of the impossibility of imposing on the people a deeper level of Christian instruction. They thought that a few generations must pass for people to become rooted in doctrines and practices of the Christian faith. This had been Bishop Brent's view as well.

2.3 Current Situation of the Church

As has been stated, the Episcopal principle was that outreach and church should be established through education. In terms of this principle, three major schools – Brent and Easter School, both in Baguio, and St. Mary's in Sagada – played significant roles. There were twenty-three more schools throughout the Cordillera (Filson and Santonia 1991:5). The schools were the churches' bridge to the unchurched. They provided contact with parents and extended contact with the students. Brent School, in particular, was instrumental in providing leadership for government and Filipino clergy as well (Helsema 1988:225). In the long term, it was thought, the schools would provide the society's future leadership.

The Episcopalians have established forty-one churches in this area. A further twenty-five outreaches called "missions" are endeavoring to reach out to the unreached communities in the mountains. The church also has access to seventy-six "preaching stations." These are locations where there is neither church nor mission (Sato, Choi and Setiawan 1991:5).

The Episcopal Church in the Philippines became independent on May 1, 1990. This official status implied that the church had self-government, with only advice and supportive direction, not authority, from foreign sources. However, the church still receives subsidies from the Episcopal Church in the United States. The church has chosen the theme, "Decade of Evangelism" to observe the close of the twentieth century (Filson and Santonia 1991:2-3). This is a costly ministry and undertaking. It takes 1.5 million pesos to support the present active clergy and the bishop's office for one year. One-half million pesos annually come from Brent School. One-third of all it takes to run the diocese is thus provided by this one institution.

The Episcopalians still regard education as a means of reaching out to unreached people, particularly young people. A further intention for education is to train leadership in the future for church and government. The education thus seems to play an important role in establishing churches in the mountains.

2.4 Leadership Training

The Episcopalian Church provides training places and means for educating potential leaders, including lay people in the church. However, Saint Andrew's Theological Seminary in Quezon City, Manila is the only Episcopal theological seminary for the training of leaders in the Philippines. Courses offered include Pastoral Education, Christian Education, Liturgical Education, Moral Theology, Canonical Education and others. The seminary was founded in 1938 in Sagada of Mountain Province and transferred to its present site in 1947, for the improvement of the school services and for the convenience of the students. In 1948, the first fruits of the school were produced.

The school offers two programs: Bachelor of Theology and Master of Divinity. An applicant for the B.Th. program should: 1) have at least two years of college work; 2) be approved by a priest with a specific ministry within the church where he/she will serve on a regular basis; and 3) commit to receive seminary training for the next four yours. For the Master of Divinity program, an applicant must have a four-year college degree. This applicant must also be prepared to invest three years of study in the seminary. As further criteria for admission into the M. Div. program, substantial evidence of parish involvement and prominent parish work are to be part of any application (Yacuan 1991).

Every summer, or sometimes twice a year (April-May, September-December), practical training is offered under the auspices of the church's urban exposure program. Young students are assigned to work in a local church so that they will be exposed to diverse settings, including hospitals, squatter settlements, other urban areas and some rural areas (Yacuan 1991).

There are a few Episcopal hospitals in Manila in which students can minister freely and gain experience. Other hospitals may open up to such programs when granted permission from appropriate authorities. It is the school that makes the assignments, together with a few parish priests. The primary objective of these ministries is to give students opportunity to gain working skills and to enrich students' ministerial experiences. Usually within a few months, students find themselves literally living in the places where they also minister among numerous people (Yacuan 1991).

This program structure also serves an evangelistic purpose. Some non-hospital assignments, for example, include practical hands-on experiences, like raising chickens on farms, planting trees, and harvesting vegetables. All of these are supervised by priests already experienced in these areas. Results are in turn reported to the seminary. The school thus uses a variety of adaptable teaching methods to ensure optimal learning on location of student service sites. Methods for both learning from and evaluating programs also include group buzz sessions, face-to-face lecturing, giving of research papers and guest lectures (Yacuan 1991).

In order to be ordained, candidates are required, as a first step, to apply for postulancy. Postulancy normally takes about eighteen months, but in some circumstances can be shortened to seven months. After this period, eighteen months are required to prepare for holy orders. Following a year of deaconship, the candidate is eligible for full ordination into the priesthood. For this ordination for priesthood, the same steps are to be followed once again. Only the bishop has the authority to ordain candidates.

In order to apply for deacon and priesthood ordination, candidates are to be recommended by the vestry or the mission council. Following this, they will be endorsed by a commission for ministry. The commission is composed of three lay people and three members of the clergy. There is, furthermore, a standing committee which consists of four lay people and four clerics. The responsibility of the standing committee is to check all documents and to ensure that all paper work is in order, then to extend permission and proclaim permission for ordination (Yacuan 1991).

In each diocese, the bishop is the head. The bishop has the authority to appoint a priest to a certain church. The churches also follow a whole yearly plan set by the diocese. Individual churches set their own agendas, but they must be aligned with the guidelines set by the diocese.

The priests in the various churches are responsible for training lay people. There is a pre-set curriculum determined by the diocese to aid the priests in their training. This study consists of five main courses which are listed below:
1. Scripture: Historical background of the books of the Old and New Testaments and each chapter of these books is studied.
2. Doctrine: Creation, covenant, resurrection, redemption, second coming, and Christology and so on are studied.
3. Liturgical training deals with definitions and forms of worship and ways to set up programs for service on Sunday. The Book of Common Prayer is also studied.
4. Church History covers the founding of the Episcopal Church and its development. Contemporary study involves present issues; for instance, ecological problems, moral issues, problems in church and society, war and various other matters. Particularly at issue here are Christians' responses to current issues.
5. Homiletics is the study of how to prepare and preach sermons.
6. Canonical Study is that which deals with the laws of the church. One law applies for all Episcopal Churches in the entire Philippines (Yacuan 1991).

There are subjects that are not core requirements, but can be included at the discretion of the instructors. If any lay student wishes to have more formal training, the theological seminary is the place for such enrichment. There are about fifty to sixty Episcopal lay ministers in the Cordillera. They work in Benguet, La Union, Pangasinan, Tarlac, Nueva Ecija and Zambales. After their training, a license will be given them from the bishop. They can then assist in church worship by reading Scripture during the Sunday service; sometimes, given permission of the priest, they may also preach.

The Episcopal Church thus provides leadership training for church leaders and lay people through Seminary education. The leaders receive training from both formal and informal education to enrich their leadership. The school facilitates various programs to produce qualified leaders. At the same time, the school assists them to obtain tangible and practical experience in the field. These programs represent the church's unique way of training leaders for effective ministry.

2.5 Ways of Contextualization

The Episcopal Church in the Cordillera does not generally use liturgical forms and rituals, because they are too closely and misleadingly associated with pagan deities. When liturgy has been applied in the past, the tribal people have been sensitive and make various reactions. The use of the gong, for example, is associated with the pagan spirit *Anito*.

Music among tribal people is chiefly associated with paganism. This association has, in fact, retarded efforts to contextualize Christian forms in indigenous music. It is, therefore, a complex and sensitive matter to incorporate native music into worship. A current project within the Episcopal Church over all Asia is in operation to collect native music. An *Institute of Liturgy and Music* has been formed at Cathedral Heights, St. Luke Compound, Espana, Manila. This religious school is specifically focused on developing indigenous music in Asian churches. It is intriguing to note that it has been found that the native music from Malaysia and Thailand was very similar to the native music of the Cordilleran in Bontoc. Perhaps there is some common anthropological significance of music among tribal groups, regardless of its role in different countries (Filson and Santonia 1991:7).

Seeing the universal power of music, the Episcopal Church believes that native music can be used in worship, but they have yet to resolve how to sensibly, doxologically, and orthodoxically contextualize it for Christian worship.

What is the central problem in contextualizing native music? The Episcopal Church is very traditional. The Episcopalians tend to share the gospel message only occasionally in the church. There is, furthermore, no frequent service wherein people have an opportunity to sing the gospel songs. The church needs to press hard in coming to terms with the contextualization at Christian music for ministering among natives. They may then attempt to translate gospel songs and use them with native tunes. This may be an attractive element to bring people to Christ.

2.6 General Social Works

The Episcopal Church emphasizes education more than church planting or any other mission work. Brent and Easter Schools are described below as typical of these works.

2.6.1 Brent School

Upon arriving in Baguio, Bishop Brent realized that the place was blessed with an excellent climate. In 1902, Brent decided to build a school, on the premise that "what is most needed is medical and educational work, after which everything else will follow naturally" (Helsema 1988:28). Brent saw the need to establish a boarding school for American children whose parents were either residents in Manila or the provinces. Brent knew that some day-schools were built in Manila, but they lacked a vital element. The existing institution offered education that did not set Christian discipleship "as its dominant motive," and its "ultimate aim" was not Christian Education" (1988:29). For Brent, education was the business of the church and was integral to evangelism, the church's most important business. Why did Brent think of education as a core part of church ministry? He believed that, through education, the Episcopal Church would also provide for and enrich various church activities such as evangelism, training future leaders, and so on. In this way Brent School set the mold for Episcopal endeavors to establish mother schools in the Philippines.

Brent School, originally called Baguio School, officially began classes with ten students on January 5, 1910, in Baguio. However, classes had previously commenced in Manila on November 1, 1909. A typhoon had rendered the road impassable, so the official opening had been delayed and the temporary abode was sought in Manila. In the early years, Baguio was a tiny city built by Americans as a resort area for summer vacationing. It was run by Americans and for Americans (and for some upper class Filipinos) who could afford summer houses there. Fresh mountain air and temperatures twenty degrees lower than the lowlands had attracted Americans to develop such a city. It was thought that cultivating a portion of the mountain would be worthwhile for maintaining and improving the health of American children in the tropics. At one time, when fatal diseases were still ravaging the families of the lowlands, at the end of the school year, there had been no such cases of sickness in Brent. In 1912-1913, a new dormitory, dining room and kitchen were added. The school, as of 1988, had more than fifty boys as boarders (Helsema 1988:90).

In 1913, a girl's school was opened in Baguio. However, it closed in June 1918, due to finances and the World War I depression. After Bishop Brent resigned as headmaster in 1917, the school was unable to open for two more years. In 1921, the school reopened and admitted its first female student. It was at this time that the school was also renamed. Instead of being called Baguio School, the name was changed to Brent School, thus named after its founder. In 1925, a girl's dormitory was built (Helsema 1988:91).

The school constantly struggled with financial problems. In 1924, rumors began to surface that the school was going to close. The teachers took a twenty-five percent cut in pay, but by 1933 the accumulated debt led to even more radical measures, and the teaching staff was cut in half.

Bishop Mosher of Baguio played a vital role in the determination to rescue the school from its inevitable collapse. One factor affecting the bishop's resolve was that President Franklin D. Roosevelt ordered the U.S. Treasury on October 31, 1933, to buy gold at the new world market price of $ 35.00 per ounce, (instead of the previous $20.67). This started what was called the gold boom, and, in its wake, people began to flock to Baguio (Helsema 1988:106).

On Monday December 8, 1941, Japanese bombers invaded Baguio, bombing Camp John Hay (Reyes 1986:63). The classes at Brent were stopped, and the boarding students looked for other places of refuge. Brent did not open its doors again for six years. All non-Filipinos of Brent, including the teachers and students, were taken captive to Camp John Hay. Children of all ages constituted over a quarter of the internment camp's population. Parents grew concerned about their children's education as the imprisonment was extended. Brent's principal was, in response, able to organize camp classes within two weeks (Fry 1989:191).

During the war period, the school was continually troubled with financial problem. Even so, the school kept growing. In 1948, enrollment registered forty-four students. The following year the school had ninety-two students enrolled which was more than double. By 1952, an average of one hundred students were attending (Filson and Santonia 1991:4).

Brent School in 1990-1991 proudly came to recognize itself as an international school. The students and faculty came from twenty-seven nations. This diversity enhanced the school with a new multicultural dimension. Enrollment of the boys and girls has, since 1909, grown to three hundred and five students. Eighty boarders currently occupy four dormitories.

The school's primary aim also seems to have been realized. Bishop Brent intended to provide Christian education for children who had potential to become leaders of nations, in the Philippines and beyond. The school offers Bible classes to teach the word of God to children on a weekly basis. The students today are no longer merely the children of American civilian and military officials, as was the case in the colonial 1909. They are children of both expatriates and Filipinos; hence the realization of the goal to educate children for leadership of various nations.

2.6.2 Easter School

Bishop Brent, who has been well recognized as a committed educator, opened another school besides Brent. This school was to serve mountain young people who were underprivileged. He named the school Easter School. It is also located in Baguio City.

Why did Bishop Brent establish such a school for mountain young people? He detected among mountain youth some intelligent youngsters who had no opportunity to study. This school was also intended to offer leadership training. In 1903, Bishop Brent purchased the lot, eight hectares, upon which the school would be reconstructed. Construction of the school demanded physical cooperation of the teaching staff and all people who worked for the school. There were both American and Filipino teachers. American teachers taught English and Filipino teachers taught other subjects in the national language (Tagalog) (Sato, Choi and Setiawan 1991:12-13). However, students were to speak only English, to improve their English ability. Another reason for requiring that everyone speak in English was that the student body was comprised of different tribal young people representative of various dialects (Ilocano, Ibaloi and Tagalog). To allow all dialects to be spoken in dormitories and classes would create confusion, misunderstanding and inconvenience. The school was so firm on this rule that punitive measures were taken when the students spoke in their own dialects.

In 1906, Easter School began with eight boys who had been brought from Bontoc by Reverend Walter Clapp. The separation of the boys (and later, girls) from their families was considered by Brent to provide the best means of identifying those who demonstrated superior intelligence or capacity for leadership. Easter School later became co-educational, with emphasis on vocational skills.

Easter School was operated as an elementary school until 1963 when it annexed a high school. The administration was led largely by Filipinos. In 1988, further expansion made available a new laboratory, library, practical arts rooms and additional classrooms. The school received accreditation of the Association of Christian Schools in May, 1989. Easter School draws eighty percent of its students from the Cordillera, and another twenty percent from surrounding provinces. Overseas students form only a small proportion of the student body. Fifty-four percent of the students are Episcopalian; thirty-four percent are Roman Catholic; twelve percent are from other Protestant denominations (Filson and Santonia 1991:2).

At the start of the school, financial support came from the United States, through Episcopal bishops and priests. Overall, the school has run smoothly, except for during the two wars. The school became independent in 1946, which meant Americans were no longer involved in any school policy. Furthermore, American teachers no longer taught at the school. After the school was proclaimed independent, hence, it received no further subsidy from the Episcopalians in the United States, but, rather, depended on self support. Part of its income was earned by the school of weaving, a vocational art which girls performed in the classroom. Weaving, for the girls, started in the second decade of the 1900s. Later, this class work expanded to the point that it virtually constituted a small industry from which bountiful income was made available for the other school operations (Sato, Choi and Setiawan 1991:13).

Currently, the school, for its costs, largely depends on student tuition fees. The implication is that tuition fees are increased each year. However, the school has increased the tuition in direct proportion to its increasing costs, and not beyond that. Furthermore, it bears remarking that, compared with other schools, the tuition fee is still low.

In the school's vocational education program, students learn and do manual labor. The school has offered vocational education to the degree that industrial work has formed an integral part of school life. In vocational education, the students also learn honesty, good work habits, and right attitudes towards completing assigned work. This program has, thus, not only taught them proper and skillful use of tools, but has also provided them with a balanced and work-ethic-oriented education. It is holistic and prepares them for productive and vigorous engagement in the working world, with trained bodies, minds, and spirits.

The school has also facilitated training programs in community living, so that the students learn to make themselves employable in trade and in home industries and occupations. The boys have traditionally been taught the arts of agriculture, carpentry and masonry. The girls are conventionally placed in programs for learning to sew, embroider and (in a select few cases) native weaving with the use of looms.

2.6.3 Other Works

The Episcopal Church has a sizable and reputable hospital in Sagada, and the hospital maintains international medical standards. This hospital, called St. Theodore's, was established early in the church's mission in the Cordillera. The church also runs a few small health clinics in various mountain areas. Why is it that the church is so concerned with opening hospitals and clinics? Brent's rationale was that erecting a hospital in a community lacking such a facility is a foundational church goal and ranks in importance with building schools. In this same view, it is believed that people who come to a hospital or clinic will hear the gospel. So the hospital serves an evangelistic purpose. It is a significant point of socializing and community contact as well. However, for many mountain people today, hospital facilities are too far away. In other cases, patients do not consider themselves sick enough to warrant the trip. Other clinics have, therefore, been set up to meet these more local, outpatient needs, and they appear in places which are remote and rural, in factories and in schools. In Kalinga, as mentioned previously, the clinic has become so substantial as to now constitute a mini-hospital (Yacuan 1991).

Another institution run by the Episcopal Church is known as St. Elizabeth's Dormitory. Recognizing the acute shortage of accommodations in post-war years, the Church of the Resurrection constructed this dormitory alongside its parish hall in 1952 in Kalinga. This was to provide a safe shelter for girls. Originally, it was designed for thirty residents, but in 1971 it was rebuilt to house 150 girls. St. Elizabeth's Dormitory has been successful and well occupied, in comparison with the Episcopalians' other dorm, St. Ursula's, which closed its doors in 1982 (Yacuan 1991).

The Episcopal Church is also concerned for the human rights of the mountain people – that is human rights violations, conflicts and community social issues faced by the mountain people, which cannot be resolved without some external source of support. The affairs of the Cordillerans, in this regard, benefit from the church's aid. For this reason committees have been formed in the various dioceses in order to address such problems. Committees designed to be limited to specific spheres of activity, such as offering consultation, often find themselves investigating human rights violations, mediating tribal conflicts, and making intermediatory trips to military bases.

The Episcopal Church facilities have been also designed and equipped to meet emergency needs of the people. During times of disaster, such as earthquakes and typhoons, the churches' doors are open. They serve as relief centers, offering shelter, food, ministry and communication. Often, in outlying villages, the church is the sturdiest building, so an entire village gathers under its roof during a severe typoon.

While the church maintains an interest in political and ethical problems, it attempts to make that interest "observatory," rather than "participatory." However, there are exceptions. During recent elections that resulted in the late President Marcos' downfall, all the churches added their voices in protest of corrupt government. This united voice proved to be very powerful and eventually brought liberation to an oppressed people. The Episcopalians, of course, also, with their wealth of knowledge and experience in the Philippines, contribute scholarly perspective, ideas, and practical suggestions with respect to these political and ethical problems. Thus, despite its official stance on limiting itself to offering consultative services, the church often finds itself the vocal representative of the community in the organization of meetings calling for action (Yacuan 1991).

The Episcopal Church also runs a few kindergartens throughout the Cordillera. These facilities provide for the children's early contact with the church. There is an orphanage in Sagada that, until 1970, focused on "in house" children. Following international trends, it now attempts to find suitable homes for orphans and sees its role as supporting them rather then bringing the children up in an institution.

A further institution of the church is the Episcopal Renewal Center. It was established in 1987 by a missionary from Singapore. His vision was to contact lay people, particularly youth, and to train them in renewal and evangelism. This center is still functioning and provides a basis for significant Episcopal Youth Ministry. Another couple of schools are St. James High School in Kineway and St. Paul's High School in Kalinga (Yacuan 1991).

The Episcopal Church has been greatly concerned with social work. According to the Episcopal Church's principle, a church must be established only on the basis of institutions of education and medical work. The church thus identifies itself through intimate connection with social ministry.

3. The United Church of Christ in the Philippines (UCCP)

The ministry of the United Church of Christ in the Philippines, which has been established in the mountain provinces, is overviewed below through an historical sketch. Its involvement in and methods of ministry are also analyzed.

3.1 Historical Background of the UCCP

In 1901, the Protestants established the Evangelical Union, and this resulted in the opening of Protestant work in the islands, with careful preparations for a united approach. Such Union was a remarkable achievement. Mission boards sought in this union to avoid duplicating denominational work accomplished by Methodists, Baptists, Presbyterians, United Brethren, Congregationalists, Disciples of Christ, and Christian Missionary Alliance; so each was allotted specific regions. This meant that only one evangelical church would be started in each area; the system would also possibly guard against schisms that can be created by denominational alliances (Deats 1967:95).

In 1929, the United Evangelical Church was founded. It consisted of persons desiring a single church; they together represented four different denominations: Congregationalists, United Brethren, Presbyterians, and United Church of Manila. This formation resulted in a provision of cooperative programs, which would gradually lay the foundation for a united and indigenous church (Deats 1967:97-98).

During World War II, the union was dissolved. However, after the war, in 1948, a resurgent hope for a more inclusive church was again realized with the formation of the United Church of Christ in the Philippines (UCCP). There was continued strong belief among members that true Christian unity and the existence of a truly indigenous church were closely linked. The merger in 1948 involved the United Evangelical Church, the Evangelical Church, and the Philippine Methodist Church (Deats 1967:108).

The United Church of Christ in the Philippines had its official beginning in May 1948. Representatives of the uniting churches held the first meeting at Elinwoor-Malate Church in Manila. The delegates present from diverse backgrounds, adopted as a simple basis of union their shared belief that all Christians "acknowledge Jesus Christ as the Son of God and as the Savior and Lord of life, and enter the church by the sacrament of baptism as Jesus Christ himself exemplified and commanded" (Deats 1967:110).

When the Protestants came to the Philippine Islands, they saw a need for reformation. They thus desired to show the relevance of Christianity for daily life. Their effort was exerted through a ministry emphasizing preaching, teaching, and serving. Although the various Protestant missions coming to the Philippines did not have identical policies among themselves, they demonstrated a remarkable capacity for unity from the outset of their labors.

3.2 Historical Background of the Mountain Ministry

In 1950, the United Church of Christ in the Philippines (UCCP) launched its work in the mountain provinces. The UCCP carried the gospel into provinces of Kabayan, Ifugao, and Kalinga, but no church was erected. Around 1951, the UCCP established one church in Baguio City. The church began with 25 people. But as of 1991, the church had grown in number so that it included 1,300 people (Lee, Ponce and Yoon 1991:1).

In the history of the UCCP, foreign missionary work was seldom involved. Generally, native pastors and members endeavored to establish work in the provinces. There was only one foreign missionary involved in the mountain work, in La Union, Benguet (Dalnnan 1991). Why did native workers gear up to establish work in the Cordillera, rather than solicit the guidance or attendance of missionaries? The UCCP's overriding aim was to see the development of ministry that was indigenous, and for that purpose nationals were trained for leadership. This structure, method and strategy was probably adapted from an earlier stage when the Evangelical Union was formed in 1901. The philosophical undergirding of the organization was oriented toward, and indeed emphasized, the great need both for training leadership and for indigenization. However, missionaries' involvement was crucial when ministry first began in the Cordilleran, because missionaries' cooperation and fortitude was a great encouragement for national leaders in their initial efforts to extend ministry to the mountain reaches.

3.3 Current Status of Ministry

Churches which are now part of the United Church of Christ in the Philippines are chiefly located in Kalinga and Benguet. The pioneering work of the UCCP in these two provinces was initiated by Filipino national workers, at first through organizing Bible study. In 1964, a church was planted in Loakan, Benguet. At present, membership is between seventy-five and one hundred. In 1980, a church was established in La Trinidad, Benguet. This church was formed of persons from Ibaloi, Ifugao, Kalinga, and Baguio. Though they use four different dialects, the communication problem does not interfere with unity in Christ, because most of them speak and understand English, Ilocano, Kankana-ey, and Ibaloi (Ilocano is a major language among the dialects) (Lee, Ponce and Yoon 1991:1-2).

Public crusades are seldom practiced for the purpose of UCCP church growth. Pastors of the UCCP prefer to contact people individually to evangelize them. Why is the church hesitant to employ methods of a crusade for evangelism? They assume that a crusade is not an effective way to reach non-believers. So, home visitation and Bible studies are the principle ways of outreach when a new church is formed and a church edifice is built. Nevertheless, crusades occasionally are seen as one effective way of evangelism if specific and vital elements are involved. These crusades are not intended simply to draw large crowds. Their essential purpose is to reach out and bring souls to a saving knowledge of the core message of the gospel.

UCCP churches are self-supported by tithes and offerings of church members. Members are mainly farmers, planting flowers and vegetables, and derive their sole income from this business. Thus, church pastors are proud of being self-supported.

There are 82 churches and 13,000 members that comprise the UCCP in the Cordillera. The UCCP has adopted a grand plan that by the year 2000, about 2,000 new local churches will be planted throughout the entire Philippines. The UCCP will attempt to expand this ministry by church planting and the methods detailed in the foregoing.

3.4 Leadership Training

Training involves practical church training conducted by the church pastors, occasional seminars and conferences, and trainee participation in exchange programs. These methods are designed to help the trainees benefit from hands-on experience in actual ministry. Other specific areas of training include missions training in church programs and seminars under the rubrics of Christian education, counseling, and even hospital chaplaincy (Lee, Ponce and Yoon 1991:2).

There are a few Bible schools in the Philippines at which potential national leaders may receive academic biblical training. These are located in Laoag City, Alisha, Kalahan and Cabite. These schools first require applicants to obtain one year of practical work experience in a local church. This experience is expected to enhance understanding in the course of learning the Scriptures. But of utmost importance in determining a student's acceptance to a school is his or her own personal conviction of the call of God into ministry. It is believed that this conviction of God's call upon students' lives will help them look to God in all areas of their future ministry as they apply and adapt what they learn in the academic setting.

3.5 Typical Ways of Contextualization

The UCCP has from its inception been aware of the cultural values held by tribal people. The UCCP work accordingly, has adopted tribal people's eating habits, (e.g., using hands) and life style. The language barrier in communicating the gospel is minimized because a common dialect (Ilocano) is spoken among the tribes, in addition to their own dialects. Some simple gospel songs for worship have been translated into the Ilocano dialect; other songs have been composed and popularized by native converts. Some improvisation and native musical instruments (e.g., bamboo drums) have been used in worship and praise. The church attempts to utilize native musical instruments as much as possible in order to enable villagers to easily join in with the service (Lee, Ponce and Yoon 1991:4).

The UCCP instructs church members with respect to avoidance of pagan practices; and it also warns against a modified form of *cañao* (ritual). Why does the church attempt such control or restriction in teaching worship? The church first of all, teaches Christians that certain ritual practices are unbiblical; no opportunity should be given to conduct *cañao,* nor to participate in it. Prior to such instruction, the church explains to church members reasons why Christians must forbid such religious practice. The church alternatively suggests modified notions of *cañao.* For example, it may propose that the service be used for invoking hope for a good harvest, and for a call of victory in war, for healing, for expressing joy and thanksgiving in social gatherings and for wedding occasions.

It is never easy to rid a tribal culture of deeply ingrained anti-Christian notions regarding the significance of a customary ritual practice. Not only have people participated in such a system from birth, but the system has been passed down from generation to generation. Its power has been imbedded in people's minds. Unclear notions about modifications can send mixed messages and may result in syncretism.

3.6 Social Works through Various Institutions

The UCCP was geared to establish kindergartens ever since it started its ministry among the Cordillerans. At the present there are twelve kindergartens in Baguio City and other mountain provinces (Lee, Ponce and Yoon 1991:3).

No orphanages have thus far been built. One may think that there must be many orphans in the mountain provinces, so why has the church not been concerned about founding orphanages? The church's official "philosophy" is that people have to take care of their own relatives. This, according to the pastors, is also a part of the Asian culture, which should be encouraged. Asian families are close-knit in contrast to western families, and it is the conviction of the church that these close family ties should be maintained.

The church tries to give the community financial assistance. The church operates so-called mini banks to which people contribute to a common fund. The purpose of this common fund is to lend money to members at minimal interest rates. This enhances cooperative living. This system also well serves particular needs of the people.

Another type of social work involves the church promotion of inter-church activities. The UCCP works together with churches of other denominations to counter drug abuse and environmental degradation. The church has also been at work in relief ministry in the aftermath of earthquakes and volcanic eruptions. In these cases, funds are set up to provide for basic needs.

Besides church planting, the UCCP cultivates various social works to help people. The UCCP is aware that the mountain people lack social care. The church attempts to meet people's various needs. Through such ministries, their intention to share the gospel is also fulfilled to some extent.

4. Southern Baptist

The ministry of the Baptists among the mountain people is discussed in this section. It provides historical background on the Baptists in the Philippines, on their mountain mission work, and on their various other involvements.

4.1 Historical Background

There are seven Baptist sub-denominations in the Philippines: American Baptist Mission, Association Baptist, Southern Baptist, Bible Baptist, Conference Baptist, Conservative Baptist and General Baptist. Out of these, the Southern Baptists are the ones who established a ministry in Cordillera. There are four groups of Southern Baptists in the Philippines: Philippines Baptist Mission, Luzon Convention, Mindanao Convention and Chinese Convention. Each is operated independently of the others in terms of leadership, but they work hand-in-hand in propagating the gospel in the Philippines.

The beginning of the Philippines Baptist Mission occurred after Admiral Dewey defeated the Spanish fleet in Manila Harbour in May 1898; then, several Protestant mission boards gathered in New York to direct plans for entering the Philippines. Among these was the American Baptist Missionary Union, which sent Eric Lund and Braulio Manikan as their first missionaries to the Philippine Islands. Lund and Manikan landed in Manila on April 26, 1900 and launched their mission in the Philippines (Munger 1967:17).

The ministerial strategy they adopted in spreading the gospel in the Philippines, particularly on Panay Island, involved the following (Braver 1988:27):
1. Distribution of evangelical tracts and the gospel in Filipino dialects,
2. Utilization of central towns to locate base operations such as Jaro and Bacolod, and
3. Reaching both the rich and the poor through home Bible study.

The Mindanao Convention was formed around 1950. In Mindanao Island in the south, two churches have since then been established, specifically in Cotabato and Davao Provinces. This latter island has been the most fruitful for Southern Baptist ministry. When Southern Baptists began evangelism on Mindanao Island, they found numerous Baptist migrants from the Visayan Islands. These Baptists were welcomed to assist in starting new Baptist churches (Posey 1968: 146).

The Chinese Convention was created for the Baptist mission in 1957. Churches for Chinese were established in Davao City, Dagupan and Manila. The Chinese Baptist Convention was organized with four congregations who, as of 1970, maintained active Christian testimony among their own people (Skivington 1970:119).

The Southern Baptists would be considered a relatively new denomination among all the missions which have come into the Philippines. With regards to the Cordillera, the Baptists have mainly focused their activities on Benguet Province. For this reason, and because of my own limited access to historical information, most of the information for presentation to follow is confined to Benguet Province. The Southern Baptists have not been involved in other provinces of the Cordillera.

4.2 Mountain Ministry

The Luzon Convention is one of the four groups that comprise the Southern Baptist operation in the Philippines. It started in 1948 when China closed its doors to foreign missionaries. A group of Southern Baptist missionaries from China were, at that time, temporarily moved to the Philippines to continue language study and wait for China to reopen. The evangelistic witness of missionaries located in Baguio City soon resulted in the organization of a Chinese Baptist Church (Skivington 1970:119). Missionaries began to evangelize the Chinese in the Cordillera. They chose Baguio City as their home base of mission, since it was the central town of Cordillera. In the initial ministry, they were involved in gathering Chinese children in every neighborhood, teaching them about Jesus Christ. They held Vacation Bible School, which also functioned as a bridge to reach the parents of these children. For two years, these American missionaries focused their ministry on the Chinese, until gradually they developed interest in the need to reach Filipinos with the gospel (Filson and Santonia 1991:2).

Their ministry to the Filipino community thus started in 1950 at Aurora Hill in Baguio City. The ministry of the Southern Baptists grew and spread to other provinces in the vicinity. Such growth inspired them to establish a training school for future leaders so the mantle of leadership would be passed on from American missionaries to natives. The Philippine Baptist Theological Seminary was founded in Baguio City in 1952, and the Baptist Bible School was started in 1955. By 1965, the seminary had an enrollment of forty-two students (Jowers 1965:52). From its inception in the church in Baguio City, the work of the Southern Baptists was soon to spread throughout all Luzon.

4.3 Present Situation

The current strategy of the Baptists is planting churches in mountain provinces and districts. Within the last five years, they have planted about ten churches in the Benguet region. Their system of church planting happens through invitation, identifying Christians in a community, establishing Bible study groups or through crusades. These new churches are to be supported and assisted by already established local churches as they sponsor or give financial assistance to the pastor. For obtaining church sites, they largely depend upon donations of land and funds for church buildings. The Baptist community numbers approximately 2,000 in the mountain areas (Firmantes 1991).

The Baptists use the BABBCA (Baguio and Benguet Baptist Churches Association) as a body to coordinate their efforts to evangelize tribal people. This organization was established in the late 1970s, but it was banished to play a background role when the Baguio Baptist Missions Society was actively reaching tribal people. However, the Missions Society was dissolved in 1989, and the BABBCA reactivated. It stretches its reach to those communities farther away from local churches. Within the last three years, the BABBCA has successfully planted four churches; and, in response to its stress on the involvement of youth in missions, many young people have gone into seminary training. The BABBCA has yet to establish long-term goals, but recognizing the affairs of communication between Baguio (lowlanders) and Benguet (highlanders) people, the executive committee is considering dividing BABBCA into two chapters, a plan which was to be in effect in 1993. This division may facilitate further development of training methods (Firmantes 1991).

Each of the churches planted by BABBCA is involved in a program called "Cooperative Missions Program" (1991). The agenda or design of this program is to require that each pioneering Southern Baptist Church has three sponsors. The pioneer church should be supported by the local church or association, the Convention, and possibly by foreign aid. Each of these three groups, ideally, would contribute a third of the expenses.

In review, the Baptist Church utilizes the BABBCA to plant churches and reach out to tribal people. Trained leaders are able to participate in mission work and evangelism via this association. It has been an effective method to establish ministry in the mountains.

4.4 Leadership Training

The Baptist Church uses the model of retreat for leadership training. This occurs once a year in a leadership training center in Baguio City. Ilocano is employed as the medium of verbal communication. The primary purpose of this leaders' retreat is to help develop self-image among the trainees. Trainees have the opportunity to affirm and be affirmed in their image as God's servants and as God's creatures. The aim is to set goals and strategies for outreach, and to encourage work in establishing churches.

The next training method is holding summer camp. Every summer, the Baguio and Benguet Baptist Church Association organizes this program. Lizette Firmantes is the coordinator. A regular group of four to five college students, who can speak Ilocano and are over eighteen years of age, stay for one month in a designated place. Preparations such as orientation, training the locals, and cultural aspects are attended beforehand. People who are in charge of this program have to raise 1,000 pesos for personal expenditures. People who come to the summer camp are awakened to the needs. It is the purpose of summer camp to imbue participants with mission-mindedness; it is hoped that as they experience the field work, they will want to go back to the field in the future (Firmates 1991).

The third type of leadership training is directly offered by the BABBCA. This caters to key leaders of churches and occurs every Saturday for a period of six months. It is intended to prepare key leaders for summer missions. Each of the six months covers a different discipline. These include worldview, hermeneutics and interpretation of the Bible, preaching and teaching, administration, missions, evangelism, pastoral care and workshops (Firmates 1991).

The last training to be mentioned here is training specifically for church planting. This training is extended to missionaries, pastors and church leaders for fostering among them the vision of planting churches. The strategy for church planting is set forth as follows: start with a Vacation Bible School for children, and then hold a Bible study with the children's parents. This is their strategy for the inception of a church.

4.5 Ways of Contextualization

The Baptists are known for holding a strict position on biblical standards and biblical life style. The Baptists, nevertheless, do attempt to exercise cultural sensitivity in relation to the people to whom they introduce the Christ of the Scriptures. They, for example, evaluate ritual practices of mountain pagan people on a case-by-case basis. During *cañao* which is reputed as both a pagan festival and a religious practice, the Baptists join in, regarding it as social festival rather than a patently spiritual activity. For funerals, the Baptists do not try to prohibit all traditional practices, such as burying in the evening, the people's building their own coffins, or giving eulogies.

The Baptists do not "Christianize" such activity, but rather they seek to find functional alternatives, like Christian gatherings or camps, which may meet deep social needs of fellowship. The overall initial approach of the Baptists may be summarized as follows: they teach their members to make their own decisions concerning their participation in "pagan festivals" (1991).

Why do the Baptists not take a firmer stand on guiding funerals in Christian ways? A pagan priest or elder in a village is vested with leadership in conducting funerals. This involves *cañao,* which is a religious practice. Funerals are also part of the cultural glue bonding tribal people. The Baptists probably take the philosophic stance of refraining from trying to "reform" funerals to render them "Christian," for that would do more harm than good by trouncing on highly sensitive culture and custom (*cañao*). So the Baptists try to respect the cultural values.

4.6 Social Works

Social work comprises one of eight spheres of church functioning. The other organized efforts include: Missions and Evangelism, Instruction and Training, Worship Committee, Prayer Committee, and Stewardship Committee (Firmantes 1991).

Relief Operation falls within the sphere of the social work. It endeavors to address emergency needs, such as those presented by the earthquake in July 1990 and the volcanic eruption of Mountain Pinatubo in June 1991. Relief operations provide physical commodities, such as sugar, salt, milk, rice, clothing and blankets. Important aspects of spiritual needs are also addressed. Relief Operation is, however, activated only when exigencies arise.

The Baptists are also involved with medical and dental service. A medical and dental mobile team works for the spiritual and physical well being of the people. But, the work is usually in process only during the summer months. The team includes three doctors, one dentist and one driver, supervisor and administrator. Consultation and treatment in health care provides a vital evangelistic dimension in the church's mission (Firmantes 1991).

The Baptists have also expanded their ministry into the counseling realm. Both spiritual and physical needs are shared during counseling time, which may be either formal or informal. Formal counseling, such as legal counseling, is also available through people competent in this field. Informal counseling may take place as Christians share in friendship evangelism or in the context of the medical team. The Baptists have endeavored in a commendable way to establish social work. It seems that in the process of social ministry, evangelism is also at work.

In summary, each Christian body reviewed in this chapter, has endeavored to establish mission work among mountain provinces in its own distinctive way. These Christian groups commonly have concentrated on meeting dire needs and on social work. They comprehend that social work serves as a catalyst to bring non-believers to church. Besides, the Christian groups have firmly understood that establishing social work in the mountain province is critical for the survival and security of tribal people who, otherwise, have no means of receiving such aid. Through provision in this way, many dying souls may also be added to the church.

Chapter 3

History of the Assemblies of God among the Kankana-eys

In the previous chapter, I delineated the ministry of non-Pentecostal groups and their approaches among the mountain people. These Christian groups commonly shared the gospel through social ministries such as building schools, hospitals, and offering various social services. The present chapter will describe the ministry of the Assemblies of God among the Kankana-eys in the northern Philippines from the beginning to the present. Through this survey, I hope that its unique approach and emphasis emerge as effective in bringing people to Christ.

1. Historical Survey of the Assemblies of God in the Philippines

The Assemblies of God ministry in the Philippines began in 1926 by an American missionary couple, Benjamin H. Caudle and his wife. Their initial work was evangelism, distributing large numbers of tracts and Assemblies of God literature on the streets. The Caudles preached in the markets and parks in Manila. They started a home church in their residence and conducted a Bible study once a week with young people. However, due to the wife's health problem, their work did not last long (Esperanza 1965:17-18).

Around the 1930s, a few Filipino-Americans who became Christian returned back to their home provinces and started a ministry for their own people. They were full of a burning desire to preach the gospel to their fellow native people. They received their training in Assemblies of God Bible schools in the States. They were: Cris Garsulao, native of Antique Province in the island of Panay; Benito Acean of Vigan, Ilocos Sur; Rosendo Alcantara from Aringay, La Union; and Rudy Esperanza of Rosario, Pozorrubio, Pangasinan (Esperanza 1965:17-22).

The first convention was held in San Nicolas Villasis, Pangasinan in March, 1940. An American missionary named L. E. Johnson, the superintendent, appointed by the General Council of the Assemblies of God in Springfield, Missori, presided over the meetings. A constitution was ratified. The elected officers were: R. C. Esperanza, secretary; Pedro Castro, treasurer; H. P. Abrenica, and R. Alcantara, presbyters. The newly organized Philippines District Council of the Assemblies of God was incorporated and registered with the Securities and Exchange Commission of the Department of Justice of the Philippines on July 11, 1940 (Esperanza 1965:32).

2. The Ministry in the Northern Philippines

The Assemblies of God started its ministry among the Kankana-ey tribal people in 1947. The ministry was initiated by a single missionary from America together with a few local leaders. The missionary, Elva Vanderbout, was commissioned by the Foreign Mission Department in Springfield, Missouri in 1946 (Vanderbout 1946). Until she launched her work in the mountains, no missionaries nor national workers of the Assemblies of God had attempted mountain ministry.

The Assemblies of God approached this tribal people with a unique Christian message, God's power. Through the message of divine power and its manifestation, churches were established and the mountain ministry of the Assemblies of God was successfully carried on. There are now about sixty-five Assemblies of God churches in Benguet Province. Pastors and lay leaders have also attempted to open work in other villages where no churches exist.

2.1 Elva Vanderbout

2.1.1 The Call of God

In 1944, a missions convention was held in Bethel Temple Church in Los Angeles, where Vanderbout was attending. A speaker was Howard Osgood, a missionary to China (Sturgeon 1960:28). The second morning of the convention, Vanderbout took a seat in the very front of the church auditorium. The song service immediately started and, during this time, she felt a great sense of brooding of the Holy Spirit in her heart. Mission songs seemed to speak to her more personally and directly than she had ever experienced. When the speaker was sharing a message on the millions of people who were lost, idol worshippers and those people who were in darkness and paganism, the message pointedly reached her. The speaker invited church members who wanted to give their lives for the lost. Her heart was broken as she sensed the presence of God. Vanderbout was one of the first to answer. She almost ran to the altar, put her hands up in a gesture of total surrender and prayed, "I give myself to You! I will do what You ask me to do! I will go where You ask me to go! Oh God." Then she heard the voice of God, "Whom shall I send, and who will go for me?" From the depths of her heart, she was answering, "Here am I. Send me. . ." (Sturgeon 1960:30).

In the mean time, Vanderbout's husband was terribly ill, due to a cerebral hemorrhage. The disease paralyzed the left side of his body, rendering him bedridden and in need of full attention. When her husband died, Vanderbout's heart was indeed broken (Sturgeon 1960:36-47). A few months after the funeral, Vanderbout turned her thoughts to where she should go. One day, the pastor's wife asked her if she had decided which country she wanted to go to for mission work. Mrs. Turnbull, the pastor's wife, mentioned the Philippines. Upon hearing the name of the country, she loved thinking of going to the Philippines.

Some time later, a chance came to Vanderbout to make contact with a missionary couple from the Philippines. Vanderbout learned necessary information about the country from them. She was then all the more excited about thinking of going to the Philippines as a missionary (Sturgeon 1960:54). She was officially ordained to be a missionary in the year 1946, by the Foreign Missions Department in Springfield (Vanderbout 1946).

December 15, 1946, Vanderbout left her own land to take up residence in the Philippines. She traveled by a ship which went to the Philippines via different countries. The ship was jammed with adults and children, so that she could hardly find a space to lean her body. Vanderbout felt unutterable weariness with the situation. She managed to find a tiny space on the third deck, which was the worst place (Sturgeon 1960:69-75). However, she attempted to get through long days and nights with prayer. After twenty-three days of a long and tedious journey, the Islands of the Philippines began to loom near. Vanderbout sparkled with joy to reach the destination that she was longing for.

On January 7, 1947, Vanderbout finally trod the soil of the Philippine Islands to begin mission work. After a twelve-day stay in Manila, she left for Baguio City where she would eventually start her ministry among these people (Sturgeon 1960:76-80). The road was extremely rough. Most of the bridges had been bombed during the war and had not yet been rebuilt, so the bus had to ford streams and gullies.

At that time the population in Baguio City was 30,000. Much of the city had been demolished during the war (Vanderbout 1962:1). However, Vanderbout was gladly welcomed by members of the Assemblies of God church.

Vanderbout's clear call of God eventually directed her to the Philippines. It was apparent that God's hand was upon the specific path of decision. The burden that Vanderbout had for the mountain people was endowed by God. God's divine intervention in her life was vivid and vital. Her desire to reach out to the mountain people was, thus, slowly coming to realization.

2.1.2 Vanderbout's Initial Ministry

In 1947, Vanderbout began her ministry in Tuding, Itogon, which was notorious as a nest of criminal elements and the most wicked and sinful place in the mountain province after World War II: there were robberies, assaults, knifings, and police raids. About 2,000 people lived in Tuding and 21,000 inhabitants lived in surrounding areas (Vanderbout 1962:1).

Vanderbout visited Tuding one night, wanting to know what sort of place it was. When she returned home that night, she could not erase from her mind the picture of the Tuding barrio. She became so deeply burdened for the people. National leaders advised her not to begin the ministry in such an evil place; it might endanger her life. But Vanderbout persisted and started her ministry in Tuding. In spite of the peril she would encounter, she was assured that God had called her to these people (Caput 1993). Vanderbout thus sincerely responded to the call of God and her commitment paralleled the call.

For a few months Vanderbout wrestled with how to begin her ministry among these people. She, of course, spoke in the Baguio church, started Bible study classes and conducted prayer meetings; but she wanted a stable ministry to win souls in darkness. With much prayer, and understanding that a woman would find it difficult to approach pagan people with a new religion, Vanderbout thought of children in a public elementary school in Tuding as a population among whom she could begin her ministry. That ministry became, for Vanderbout, a stepping stone to spread the gospel among the mountain people.

She visited Tuding Elementary School to meet the principal and suggest her idea. To her amazement, the principal granted her permission to open a Bible class (Caput 1993). It was marvelous for a single woman to get permission to do ministry in any local public school in the male-dominated mountain world. It was another apparent work of the Holy Spirit.

July 26, 1947 was her first day at the Tuding school. Vanderbout presented the gospel through the interpretation of local workers. She supplemented her words with interesting materials which fascinated the children; they had never seen such objects. The visual aids drew their rapt attention to the message of the gospel (Sturgeon 1960:87).

Vanderbout continued her ministry among the children. Distinctively, the fifth and sixth grades were the most interested in the gospel. The children comprehended the gospel quite well and responded heart-warmingly (Sturgeon 1960:87). Vanderbout's initial ministry among children was thus successful. The ministry became a foundation to spread the gospel further to the children's parents.

As Vanderbout continued her ministry among these school children, some girls and boys wanted Vanderbout to visit their parents. Vanderbout prayed earnestly about visiting the homes of these girls and boys. The Holy Spirit spoke to her that this was the very door that God had opened for her to reach these people. She made up her mind to accept invitations and visit the homes. She and her local workers who assisted her in interpretation hiked twelve miles to visit the children's homes. The parents, indeed, positively responded to the gospel message; and this was the first time for them to hear the Word of God (Caput 1993).

One of Vanderbout's experiences with a sick person who was the father of one of her "students" resulted in bringing a whole family to God. When the missionary visited the girl's home, her father was paralyzed on his whole left side and had been on the floor for six months. Their living condition was so poor that there was not even a blanket or pillow needed for the patient. This scene broke Vanderbout's heart, especially in retrospect of her husband's death. A burden to share the gospel welled up in Vanderbout's heart. Vanderbout regularly, faithfully visited the paralyzed man and shared the living Word of God. Through her ministry to the sick man and earnest sharing of the message, the whole family found the Lord as their Savior (Sturgeon 1960:88, 89, 92). After many such conversions, many of these parents became the pillars of what was to later comprise the Tuding church (Caput 1993).

Vanderbout, even though she was a female, single missionary, was well accepted by native Kankana-ey people because of her passion and love for these people. One advantage for Vanderbout, in spite of being a female, was that she was a white woman and the mountain people tended to respect white woman. Above of all, the Holy Spirit intervened in her ministry to bring effectiveness.

2.1.3 Pentecost in Tuding

Vanderbout did not confine herself to children's ministry. She wanted to expand her work in Tuding, Itogon. She and her ministry team thus started evangelism in Tuding. Vanderbout soon found that each time they preached the gospel, more and more people were coming to hear the message of God. Vanderbout eventually decided to hold open-air services to accommodate the crowds. As she frequently met these people, she noticed many attenders were afflicted by disease. She learned that during the war most of the mountain people lost all of their possessions, and this left them poverty stricken and devastated. Poor living conditions caused them to lose bodily resistance to disease (Sturgeon 1960:93).

The earliest converts among the Codilleran were Paran Bukayan and a few of his relatives. Bukayan opened his house for Sunday morning and evening services (Soriano 1948:1). Bukayan had heard about the ministry and compassion of

Vanderbout among the mountain people and had invited Vanderbout to a service to speak. At this point, Vanderbout was well known among the village people in Tuding. News of Vanderbout's preaching in this service spread among the village people through Bukayan's relatives. Pagan people came to the service, with interest in what a white woman would attempt to speak (Caput 1993). The message was powerfully delivered to people gathered, and many newcomers turned to Christ. The power of the Holy Spirit empowered people attending. The good news of Christ began to work to change people's hearts. The congregation of the house church grew larger.

In 1948, Vanderbout and local ministers held revival meetings in Tuding week after week, besides having regular services on Sunday nights. The Holy Spirit moved among gathered people. Many non-believers were saved, and more than 150 were baptized in water. The old, the young adults and the children shared wonderful testimonies of the power of God, which saved their lives from darkness and the bondage of sin. They rejoiced with salvation and became new creatures (Soriano 1948:1).

Every Sunday night service, a lot of people were also baptized with the Holy Ghost and fire, as in Acts 2:4. It was like old time Pentecost. As the place for service was packed full every Sunday night, Vanderbout came to see the urgent need for building a church. What attracted the animists? Why were they so receptive to the message of Christ? It was apparently God's power, revealed so vividly through the message and prayer. The power they experienced was something different from the power of ancestor spirits mediated by a pagan priest. Many received visions from the Lord and many were called into God's service.

A remarkable Pentecost was indicated in Vanderbout's newsletter sent to the Department Foreign Missions of the Assemblies of God. It said:

> Two weeks ago, after a wonderful time of prayer, we were about to dismiss and go home, when the power began to fall again, and a message in tongues came forth and the Lord gave the interpretation. Everybody fell to their knees again and began to cry out to God. There were many sinners present who had just come in to see what was going on, and they too began to call on the Lord. Praise God for His mighty convicting power! (Soriano 1948:2).

2.1.4 Building Tuding Church

As more and more people came to God, Vanderbout felt the need of having a church building where all of the people might comfortably worship God. She began to pray with strong faith to be able to build a church within Tuding. But, it was not an easy job to do, because the first materials purchased cost $2,000. After several months, Vanderbout wrote to her former pastor, Turnbull, regarding this project and her needs. To her surprise, Pastor Turnbull sent a check for $2,000. Later the Foreign Missions Department sent a sizable amount to be used on building the church. Vanderbout set about purchasing property to build a new church right away (Sturgeon 1960:111).

At last, the building was sufficiently finished for dedication, even though the ceiling and the interior were not complete. The dedication service was held December 9, 1949. Vanderbout invited Reverend Howard Osgood, the former missionary to China and the speaker at the missionary convention in Bethel Temple Church where Vanderbout had received her call. A mass of people flooded into the service (Vanderbout 1961).

Juan Soriano, a mountain ministry team member, was chosen to pastor this church (Vanderbout 1958a:1). Why was Soriano selected as the pastor for Tuding church? Was Vanderbout not qualified to be the pastor herself? First of all, Soriano was enthusiastic and dedicated for evangelism ministry. He was, thus, well suited to pastor this newly erected church. In Kankana-ey culture, men are dominant in every part of social activities. That probably influenced the selection of this leader over Vanderbout, although it was a female missionary who had endeavored to erect the church building. A native pastor was also preferred to a foreigner to effectively lead the congregation. Later, the Tuding church became a place for conducting seminars, short training of church leaders, revival meetings and various other agendas.

2.1.5 Evangelism and Power Encounter in Tuding

Vanderbout once a week preached the gospel in an open-air services in Tuding during the year 1954. She proclaimed the healing power of God during the service, based on Scripture from Mark 16:15-18: "They shall lay hands on the sick and they shall recover." She saw the need of these people, and with simple faith in the Word of God, called on her ministry team members to pray for the sick (Sturgeon 1960:95).

A young boy who was fourteen years of age had ulcers on his leg. The boy was somewhat treated by witchdoctors, but he could not be cured. When this boy was seven years old, he had fallen down and his leg was broken right at the knee. The next five years of his life were very difficult years, because as the leg was healed the bones grew together bent. His leg was stiff and he could not straighten it. He could not touch the ground, which meant he could not walk. He struggled to walk, hopping along with the help of a stick or by just crawling along on the ground, and he certainly lived a miserable life (Vanderbout 1954a:3).

The boy's mother became a Christian because of the sickness of her son and because she believed in God. The boy's parents gave up their pagan worship, determined to follow Christ. Vanderbout and her ministry team came to the boy's home to visit. Vanderbout laid her hand upon him and prayed, believing in Christ to heal. This boy threw away his stick, believing in the healing of God (Vanderbout 1954b:3). From that time on he did not use his stick any more, and little by little his leg straightened out. The ulcers disappeared by God's power.

Many souls were saved by healing experience through God's power manifested in the ministry of Vanderbout and her team members. There was a little girl who had not been able to walk for a couple of years. She began to walk by a miracle of God. Her parents turned to Christ through their daughter's healing, and they attended the services regularly (Vanderbout 1957). Such testimonies of healing caused revival to grow and added to the number of believers. The crowds attending normally comprised the whole barrio population. The revival in Tuding was to shake the whole of Benguet Province, and this news was spread far and wide to sow the seed for the work to be done throughout the mountains.

2.1.6 Salvation-Healing Ministry in Baguio City

Baguio City is an access point to different provinces. In fact, within a thirty minute drive, people can even reach places where tribal people dwell near by Baguio City. In 1955, Vanderbout had a plan of revival for salvation and healing in Baguio City, located 6,000 feet above sea level.

Vanderbout probably knew the strategy of holding a revival meeting in this city. She went to the mayor to request a permit for the most eminent spot in the largest place, Burnham Park, for her revival meeting. The mayor's response was somewhat negative due to time conflicts. A carnival planned to use this particular place. Vanderbout again asked the mayor to consider her request. The mayor checked with his clerk to confirm the dates, the clerk told him that the carnival was scheduled for a later date. Vanderbout thus got permission from Mayor to use that place. She almost shrieked for joy because it was the first time that this place was ever given for a religious aggregation (Vanderbout 1955:2).

Vanderbout finally set the date, March 1, 1955, for the revival meeting. The speaker was Mrs. Ralph Byrd from America. About 1,500 came to the morning meetings. Through those services hundreds of newcomers accepted Christ as their personal Savior.

God performed miracles of healing in different services. One girl, eighteen years of age, who suffered as a deaf-mute for twelve years, was instantly healed. During each morning and night service, the sick lined up for healing (Vanderbout 1955:4). God healed deaf-mutes by the scores. The blind became able to see. Paralytics were healed. People suffering with tuberculosis and many other sicknesses were healed. One famous woman in the city was healed of a very large goiter. It partly diminished when she was prayed for on Saturday night, and when she came to the services Sunday morning it had disappeared. A man twenty-eight years of age, who had been a deaf-mute all his life, was cured instantly one morning (Vanderbout 1955:2).

The eight days of the salvation and healing revival was marvelous that countless people came to the Lord and myriad sick people were healed. These phenomena were recognized as the work of the Holy Spirit.

2.1.7 Salvation-Healing Ministry in Mountain Province

Vanderbout wanted to hold consecutive salvation and healing meetings in Mountain Province. Since the missionary had met with empirical experience of the power of healing in previous meetings, she attempted to repeat the effect in Mountain Province, not fully anticipating the true empowerment of the Holy Spirit (Vanderbout 1958a:2). During eight days of meetings in Baguio City, there was a mighty outpouring of the Holy Spirit in the midst of services. Nearly forty were baptized in the Holy Spirit. There were several outstanding conversions of distinguished government officials, including the deputy-governor of the sub-province, his wife and daughter. The mayor of a nearby town was saved and healed from sickness. He gave a resounding testimony.

After this meeting, Vanderbout decided to evangelize further in the mountains. She loaded into her car camping equipment, a public address system, and an electric light system. The missionary and national workers drove nearly all day over rugged, mountain roads into head-hunter territory. Almost the whole village came out to the meetings (1958b:3). In the village where they held a service, the hearts of people were stirred by God's power. The Holy Spirit moved among people and many miracles of healing were performed. Many of the new converts took a clear stand for Christ, even against persecution and the raving of the heathen priests and witchdoctors.

In another large village with many surrounding villages, God gave Vanderbout and local workers a marvelous meeting of six days. Hundreds came from all different directions and filled the town market place to hear the gospel. For most of them it was the first time in their lives that they had heard the gospel. As Vanderbout recognized, this was exactly what Christ came to the world to do; to minister with power, to save the lost and to heal the sick (Vanderbout 1958c:2).

Miracles continually took place. An old man was carried by his friends from another village to attend the meeting. He was all bent over, and could walk only on his hands and feet, like an animal. The man instantly stood up and walked. He gave his life to Christ, and began to preach to the people with excitement. He did not go back to his home, but stayed at the meeting place, telling everybody what

God had done for him. He almost joined the evangelistic team to share his testimony (Vanderbout 1958c:3).

Many sick people experienced the healing power of God. An old man who had been deaf in both ears since he was a young man was instantly healed in the service. There was an old woman who had been blind in both eyes since 1942; she was also healed and could see with both eyes. One paralyzed woman spent most of Sunday morning crawling to attend the service. God instantly healed her, and she stood and walked across the ground to the platform to testify of God's healing power. A blind old woman attended one meeting by her granddaughter's encouragement. God instantly opened both of her eyes, and she pointed out the lights and different objects. People in the meeting were amazed by such incidents and glorified the name of Jesus Christ (Vanderbout 1958c:3).

As a result of these meetings, believers in a village inhabited by 12,000 people wanted to build a church. In another village, known as head-hunters, men had already started to build their church. Vanderbout planned to begin a short-term Bible school as well as to have special classes for the new converts. God indeed had done a great miracle in opening up these villages.

2.1.8 Establishment of an Orphanage

In the course of ministry, Vanderbout noticed that there were many babies suffering with sickness. Erecting an orphanage was not quite her intention; she did it but more or less out of necessity. As Vanderbout became known as a white missionary who had a loving and caring heart for the mountain people, believers and even non-believers sought her help for their needs, including problems with their children's sicknesses (Sturgeon 1960:121-122).

There was a baby who was badly crippled and needed an operation almost immediately; otherwise, he would die. The mother of this baby desperately searched for a way to save her baby's life. The only person in whom the mother put her trust was the missionary. The mother pleaded with Vanderbout for help. The next morning Vanderbout took the baby into Baguio City to her doctor. The doctor carefully examined the baby. He said, after five weeks of treatment, the baby's foot would be all right. As the doctor had said, the baby's foot indeed recovered in exactly five weeks of treatment. Even though he had slight limp, it was hardly noticed (Sturgeon 1960:121-122). Vanderbout's sacrificial love for a little soul touched the hearts of many people who then turned to the Lord.

The news spread through the villages that such miracles frequently took place. Vanderbout tended to meet more sick children. Children who did not have places to live were also brought to Vanderbout. Many orphans were crying for help. A number of children, who would certainly have died, were kept alive because the missionary took them in and nursed them back to health.

Vanderbout still felt the pressing need of erecting a building to accommodate the children continually coming to her, and she began to pray. Vanderbout's prayer for this need was answered through the Rotary Club of Baguio City. They donated a generous offering for building the orphanage. The new building for the orphanage was quickly finished enough to allow children to live in it in 1953. They named it Bethesda Children's Home (Sturgeon 1960:130-131).

Undoubtedly, more children were added after the founding of the orphanage. While operating the orphanage, Vanderbout had an exotic experience. An unwanted child was put in a cage in the village of Bua; the child was put there by the father and stepmother. The child was in a cage for many days – no one could tell how long. The child's body was deformed and her hair covered her face, like a jungle creature. The child also had an oversized chest, a clubfoot, a paralyzed right hand, and very big eyes. The child was brought to Vanderbout. The missionary's compassion and love saved the life of this little child.

Another of Vanderbout's testimonies was about twin boys who were abandoned by their parents. People in the mountain believed that twins were bad luck, so these were left on the floor of a hut with a thin blanket. Two of Vanderbout's workers found the twin boys and brought them in. When they got to Tuding, the children were already blue near death. However, the twin boys' lives were saved. Vanderbout then had twenty-two children in her orphanage (Vanderbout 1954b:3).

A significant story that Vanderbout left was about how a twelve-year-old boy from the jail in Baguio became a family member of the Bethesda Children's Home. After a short while because of outside influences, he went astray. He was repeatedly in and out of the city jail several times. At one time, he spent five years in Muntinlupa National Prison, a maximum security facility in Manila. While this boy was there he indeed met the Lord and was transformed. This boy was probably touched by a meaningful message of someone there. When he came back to Bethesda Children's Home, he was a new person and even sought to go to Luzon Bible Institute out of his own desire. This boy grew to become a wonderful minister for God's Kingdom (Vanderbout 1961).

The first child who entered the Bethesda Children's Home, named Gervacio Tavera, Jr., later became an ordained minister and one of the ablest interpreters in the Philippines. Many of the children in the orphanage became marvelous Christians and Christian workers (Vanderbout 1954a:1).

What result did Vanderbout expect through her care for children? For Vanderbout, erecting Bethesda Children's Home was not just to establish an institution for social work as other people did. Nor was it merely a place for homeless, sick, and poor children to live together. Vanderbout's intention for the Children's Home was to make children grow in the living Word of God so that they would become messengers of Christ.

2.1.9 Development of Children's Ministry

Vanderbout continued to develop ministry for children. She envisioned children as future workers for the mountain ministry. Vanderbout had the particular intention to organize activity with this aim. Thus, in 1961 the first kid's camp in the Philippines was held. At this time the concept of kid's camp was unfamiliar to local churches in the Philippines. In this initial kid's camp, about seventy children came, and thirty-five of them received Christ as their personal Savior. About ten were baptized in the Holy Spirit. Unusual experiences that children had included having visions of the Lord, feeling the sweet presence of God during the time of prayer, and so on. God mightily poured out His Spirit upon these precious boys and girls. The Kid's camp was then to serve as an avenue to others meeting the Lord (Vanderbout 1961).

Vanderbout organized the first Missionette Club in the Philippines, at the Tuding church. Why did Vanderbout constitute a Missionette Club with children and teenagers? Its purpose was to train children and teenagers to be missionaries in the future. Vanderbout initiated these programs for all children. Children were intensively trained to memorize Bible verses to prepare themselves to be soldiers of Christ. In the opening ceremony, an impressive candlelight and pledge signing service was conducted for twenty-two Missionettes and thirteen Junior Missionettes. District officers and a number of sectional presbyters attended the service (Schumitsch 1962:1). Each girl proudly wore her Missionette uniform, consisting of a navy blue skirt, white blouse, and light blue vest. The Missionette emblem was embroidered on the left side of the vest.

Occasionally, Vanderbout had special prayer meetings in which children and teenagers were spiritually saturated or bathed in prayer. A number of children were baptized with the Holy Spirit. Later, many children became beautiful Christian ministers.

2.1.10 Training Young People

In the year 1962, Vanderbout began to train young people who had burdens for serving the Lord. They were recruited and sent to a Bible school. As Vanderbout continued the mountain ministry, she came to feel the need for more hands to reach out to more unreached non-believers. She also felt the need of training native young people to reach their own people. What was the result of her work among the young people? Four of them from mountain provinces graduated from a Bible school and were involved in pioneering works. Others graduated and became evangelists in areas deep in the mountains where no Assemblies of God workers had ever penetrated. These young people were enthusiastic to hike through dense forests to preach the gospel, in spite of difficulties and danger (Vanderbout 1957).

When Vanderbout started the mountain work, there were only two national ministers for the mountain ministry. But, ten years later, twenty-two full-time national workers were involved in the mountain ministry and fifteen young people were ready to go to a Bible school for preparing future work. The mountain ministry through the young, ministers continued with vitality and abundant fruits.

2.1.11 Conclusion of Vanderbout's Ministry

Many villages were entirely transformed because Vanderbout was willing to lay down her life. Foxes had holes and birds had nests but she, like the Son of Man, had no place to settle. She fearlessly entered pagan villages and head-hunters' country. She spread the vital and precious message of Christ. Vanderbout trusted that God would protect her from harm (Vanderbout 1962:3). Her ministry among the Kankana-ey tribe and other tribes seems to have been inexhaustible and is not recounted in one paper.

The desire of her heart to live and minister in the mountains was fulfilled and with it came satisfaction in knowing that her work was not in vain. Surely, she would receive her crown in heaven and her work would not go unnoticed by the Lord. This was her own reflection in 1962.

From the initial time of Vanderbout's ministry in 1947 until the year 1959, eight churches were constructed under her direction. There were over one hundred preaching points throughout various mountain areas. She reached more than one hundred villages with the gospel. In the year 1955, Vanderbout had started to work in villages of the head-hunting mountain people, a singular accomplishment of the thirteen years of her service in the mountains (Vanderbout 1959). Besides the ministry of evangelism and church planting, Vanderbout did not neglect training devoted young people. As a result of her labor, approximately one hundred young people from the mountains went to Bible school, and a majority of them became ministers to reach their own people. Vanderbout, out of necessity, erected an orphanage to care for poor, neglected and abandoned children. She took care of fifteen of the original children of the orphanage (Vanderbout 1959).

However, after nineteen years of mountain ministry as an Assemblies of God missionary, she departed the denomination, following in a new direction. She married the local pastor, Juan Soriano, who had accompanied her to assist her ministry. That arrangement was not permissible according to the Assemblies of God Foreign Missions Department in Springfield, Missouri. The policy held for all female missionaries. So in 1966, Vanderbout resigned her missionary position under the auspices of the Foreign Missions Department and the Philippines General Council of the Assemblies of God (Vanderbout 1966).

It is impossible to present a complete picture of Vanderbout's life among the people she loved. From the day of her arrival in the Philippines the Lord directed her life and she ceaselessly labored to do His will. I suppose that besides what has been recorded in written records of Vanderbout's mountain ministry, there was much more accomplished by Vanderbout prior to her leaving the Assemblies of God. The ministry that Vanderbout had established among the mountain people was continued through young people who were trained by her and in whom was planted the seed of the fruit-bearing gospel. She died on October 16, 1990.

2.2 Ministry of Mountain Workers

The Assemblies of God Church in the Philippines provides training institutions for those people who have a definite call and are committed to the mountain ministry. Bible schools offer training programs for pastoral work for local congregations. Besides formal training institutions, the church facilitates informal apprenticeship and short-term training programs. Trained leaders have opened churches, and they have grown. Through the continuing work of local leaders and involvement of missionaries, churches are planted and expanded.

2.2.1 The Recruitment of Leaders

In the earliest stage (1950-1969), some people felt the call to the ministry on an individual basis. This was often evidenced by a sudden conversion, strong conviction to serve the Lord, and a great desire to save the souls of neighbors and relatives. These individuals normally volunteered themselves to accompany or assist established pastors and workers, especially when they were not busy farming. This often served as a time to observe the genuineness of the call and to train them for ministry. The concept of call is not unusual in the pagan environment. A god or spirit can call an individual into divine mission and grant capability to function as religious personnel. As the genuineness of their call is often tested by the effectiveness of their religious practices, so is the evidence of the call of Christian workers. Often the effect of their prayer becomes a criterion by which to judge their divine call. They also often visit neighboring communities to introduce Christ to pagan relatives. As the seriousness and genuineness of their call is proven, they are assigned to regularly minister to specific communities under the supervision of a pastor.

Within this system, early on, young people began to emerge to join the leadership. More educated and promising young people were sent to Bible schools for formal education. The recruitment was headed basically by local pastors. Often missionaries assisted local churches to help the students. The non-formal type of leadership still continues to emerge among more mature members. New pastors for Bagu and Bolibo are two recent additions belonging to the formal type of leadership.

In observing some characteristics of leaders, the divine call is the most prominent element, although it is quite subjective. Then their age, marital status, and moral standing are considered. The current rule for a leader's age says that he or she should be above twenty-two. But in the earliest period, workers were selected without consideration of age because of the great need for workers. In terms of marital status, earlier leaders were both male and female, and married. Their married life was expected to be exemplary. They needed to earn their respect from the community. In later periods as more younger leaders emerged, some single workers joined. If a married leader divorced, however, he or she was denied leadership position.

2.2.2 Leadership Training Program

Mountain pastors and workers received training basically through three avenues: 1) informal apprenticeship under an established pastor or worker; 2) basic biblical and theological orientations through occasional short-term training programs instituted by the district council; and 3) formal Bible school training through Luzon Bible Institute (later Assemblies of God Bible College) or Bethel Bible Institute (later Bethel Bible College).

Through the informal apprenticeship, they learned how to counter various difficult ministry situations. They developed counseling techniques, evangelism approaches, and ability in sharing the word. They also built their confidence in exercising ministerial authority and spiritual gifts to counter pagan spiritual manifestations.

The short-term training has produced many excellent leaders in the mountains. Many "elders" in villages had inherent respect from people. As they became Christian, they also inherited leadership expectations. They were in their forties at least and were influential. They had families and farms. It was impossible for them to go to a regular Bible school. The short-term training duration ranged between two weeks to one month. Leaders and would-be leaders gathered in one church and spent the entire period for learning, fellowship, sharing, prayer, and discussion. Bugtong and Organo are two excellent examples of products of this program. One problem with the program, however, has been lack of consistency. There were years in which no training took place. Sometimes a missionary initiated a more systematic program, but the program stopped when the missionary left the field.

Luzon Bible Institute in Rosario, Pozorrubio, Pangasinan, was initially started in Tuding Church, Itogon, Benguent. In 1953, the district council approved a resolution that led to the establishment of Luzon Bible Institute. The Bible school began by offering a short-term program for mountain leaders, teaching biblical courses. The founding president was Benigno Maningan. At the initial stage, the institute encountered many difficulties, and they forced the school to close temporarily. In 1955, the institute reopened with an enrollment of thirty-six students. The following year, the seven first fruits of the school graduated with the name "Fishers of Men." The curriculum for short-term training was modified and converted into a three year course. The school mainly offered biblical courses. It was also agreed that the school would be moved to Rosario, Pozorrubio, Pangasinan (Horn 1994:1).

In 1958, Rudy C. Esperanza, the general superintendent of the Philippines General Council of the Assemblies of God, presented a need for a school to the American brethren who graciously gave funds for the construction of school buildings. Girls' and boys' dormitories were erected by the financial assistance of Rena Baldwin, a former missionary, and by offerings from the American churches (1994:1).

During the years 1966-1975, various people assumed the position of presidency: Celedonia Gagno in 1966, Constantino Lagmay in 1969 and Leonardo Caput in 1975. On May 23-24, 1989, a faculty and board meeting was held to make a decision as to how to revise the internship program. Instead of the seniors going out for their internship after completing their third year, the juniors were to be interned after the second year. As a result, only the freshmen and sophomores were left on the campus during the school year 1990-1991 (Horn 1994:2).

From the beginning of the school in 1953 until 1993, the institute has graduated five hundred twenty students. The teaching staff is comprised of ten people at the present (Horn 1994:2). From the 1970s, Bible school graduates have taken leadership in the mountain ministry. Among them are Antonio Caput, John Vicente, and Alex Simeon, all of whom pastor key churches in mountain towns.

Others are ministering in remote mountains and they are mostly female pastors, such as Pynie Bacasen in Bugias and the Ifugao area, and Tita Cayso in the Bakun area.

Bethel Bible Institute was founded in Baguio City in 1940, and the founding president was Leland Johnson. Bethel Bible Institute had gone through difficulties in its initial operation during World War II, and due to the war the school closed during 1941-1946. The school reopened in 1946 in Pangasinan, and the new president was Rodrigo Esperanza. When the school was located in Baguio City, early mountain church leaders had biblical training in this institute. The school faced an ongoing difficulty in operation because of financial problems. However, in 1949, the institute was relocated to Bulacan, near Manila, and a new president, Glenn Dunn, was installed. The school then produced its first fourteen graduates. During the years of 1956-1977, seven different people took the position of presidency. The student body grew rapidly and the physical structure of the school took shape. The school's curriculum was designed to offer a three-year program. The institute intensively offered biblical courses at the initial stage. In 1986, it began to offer programs in Christian Education and Music, in addition to Theology (Kalawili 1991:1). These programs attracted people, and the student body grew as a result. A few years later the school received accreditation from Asia Theological Association, and it became a four-year Bible College. The school graduated one thousand sixty-nine students between 1949 and 1991. There are about twelve people on the teaching staff in three different programs.

The Assemblies of God has thus provided an avenue for training leaders. Through these institutions and other training programs many young people have received leadership training and prepared themselves for future ministry. They have been able to be effectively involved in pastoral ministry in the mountain. At the present, Northern Luzon Bible College likewise offers a special training program for those students who plan to be involved in pastoral ministry in the mountains.

2.3 Works Established by Ministers, 1950-1969

Mountain pastors during the 1950-1969 era were immensely challenged by Vanderbout for the mountain work. Several ministers had worked closely together with her until she departed. Many mountain pastors in this time period generally concentrated their pastoral effort in the eastern and northwestern parts of Bakun, Abatan, Mankayan and Buguias municipalities in Benguet Province. Some of the trained pastors took care of more than one church.

2.3.1 Basic Assembly of God Church

In 1950 Mary Mapanao was involved in pastoral work in Basig Assembly of God Church in Basig. Mary Mapanao had been a key church member of Tuding Church. Mapanao also used to assist the mountain ministry of Elva Vanderbout. Having gained hands-on experience in the mountain ministry, she was appointed to be the pastor in Basig Assembly of God Church.

The church started with converts from a spiritistic group. Some active believers in this group were persuaded by the Word of God shared by Vanderbout, and they accepted the Lord.

Converted people from the spiritistic group invited Vanderbout, Pastor Soriano, Mapanao and some elders from Tuding Church to hold an evangelistic meeting in Basig. This meeting even reached a neighboring place, Guinaoang. Church members invited Mary Mapanao to their church as the pastor. The earliest converts were: Solomon Cawa and his family, Pablo Continguey and his family, Ramon Bugtong and his family, and Bayani. The first church structure was made of bamboo (Caput 1994).

In April, 1954, after two years of pastoring, Mapanao returned to Tuding church. Mapanao did not continue her pastoral work for a long period. A pastor, Leonardo Caput, was then asked to take over the pastoral position in Basig Church. After a few years of pastoring, Caput resigned the position and was involved in ministry in the Tuding Church to help in the preparation for the opening of Luzon Bible Institute the following year (Caput 1994).

The church in Basig could not grow as fast as other Assemblies of God churches due to the continuing change of pastors. However, in 1966 the church was renovated, expanded, and put into better shape. Later, the church was again restructured by the financial assistance of a Finnish missionary, Walter Erola.

It is not clear why Mapanao discontinued her pastorate. I conjecture that, at the early stage, for women, ministry involvement was not quite recognized, even though she was called into it. Men were dominant in every aspect of social life in the mountains. That culture probably affected church people's acceptance of female leadership.

2.3.2 Poblacion Assembly of God Church

Ciriaco Dalino opened Poblacion Assembly of God Church in Mankayan in 1951. The church was started in response to the healing experience of a man. Its story is as follows: Vanderbout, with some church workers, actively held an evangelism crusade in different mountain villages during these years. She and her team had a chance to preach the gospel in a village called Sapid in Mankayan. They stopped at the house of an old man named Pablo Lagman. Lagman had suffered from an ear problem for a long time. Lagman complained of an irritating ringing in his ear. He concluded that this was probably the work of a devil. Vanderbout and her company prayed for his healing. Lagman, after their prayer, was bothered less by the ringing sound. His family was converted because of this incident. He became a bold witness, persuading his clan and neighbors (Bangsaliw 1994). One on-going problem that the pastor and the church members encountered was having a place for Sunday services. Since there was no adequate place to hold the Sunday services, the pastor rented a room of one church member's house. After struggling long with finding a place for the Sunday meetings, the congregation then fortunately rented a larger place, the village hall, for the Sunday gatherings. On April 26, 1976, a church lot was purchased with the help of the Finnish missionary, Walter Erola. In 1982, the construction of the church building began. Erola and American missionary Wesley Weekley, both through finance and labor, immensely helped to complete the church building. At present, about forty families attend the Sunday service.

2.3.3 Tabuk Assembly of God Church

In 1951, Mariano Tinong started his pastoral work in Tabuk Assembly of God Church in Tabuk. The church began to grow upon the healing experience of a woman. This woman was so critically ill that her family had tried to bring her to a hospital. Tinong, out of his compassion and expectation of God's power to be manifest among the sick, offered prayer for the woman. The family members accepted the offering of Tinong's prayer. Remarkably, the sick woman was instantly healed after the prayer. This incident provided an opening for the ministry of the Assemblies of God among the Kankana-ey tribe in Tabuk (Caput 1993). In 1951, Tinong started his pastoral ministry through leading a house church. Those people who knew what had happened to the sick woman gave their hearts to the Lord, and more people in the village were added to the congregation. Within a few years, the Tabuk Assembly of God Church rapidly grew in number and even opened several daughter congregations. Between 1951-1954, Tinong, besides pioneering Tabuk church, further pioneered churches in Pudtol, Kalinga-Apayao.

2.3.4 Takadang Assembly of God Church

Daniel Cogoy established Takadang Assembly of God Church in Takadang in 1951, starting with a few members. The church did not grow until an unusual occurrence. A pagan woman in the village, led by her Christian friend, attended

Sunday service. Pastor Daniel Cogoy preached in the Sunday service. The woman, named Tepan Ngiacan, was touched by the message of the pastor. She immediately gave her heart to Jesus Christ at this service. In the course of her Christian life, she met with unfortunate circumstances. She became pregnant, but in the process of delivery she lost her life due to lack of physical strength. The pastor conducted her burial according to the Christian tradition. Of course, her whole family was non-believing. Hence, the pastor had mounting anxiety in his heart for the family, for what they might say against the church. However, after the burial the pastor invited all in attendance to partake of the food which was prepared by the church. Pagan people tended to forbid eating the food served by the church for such an occasion. They were afraid that if they joined the meal, their gods and ancestors would inflict on them sickness and disasters. They held onto the notion that a priest in the village rather than any other person should bless food. Nevertheless, some of them partook of the meal, while others refrained. Strangely, after the funeral the family decided to attend the church instead of blaming the pastor for the loss of the mother's life after she had become a Christian (Cayso 1993).

Why is the funeral so important to them? In their belief, the supreme deity does not have much effect on human life. It is ancestral spirits which, they believe, can bring blessings as well as misfortune. When a family does not conduct the funeral in the right pagan way, their gods or ancestors will be angry and punish the family, even to the point of death. So, the entire village, who were practically all relatives, closely watched to see if anything would occur after the funeral recounted above. But days went by and even years passed and nothing happened to the family. The family looked rather healthy. The village people began to analyze why nothing had happened against what they expected. They gradually began to realize that there was something in believing in Jesus. They, in fact, became convinced of their need to become Christians. The testimony of this family served powerfully to turn many pagan people to the Lord. The church grew and was revived by this occurrence. The name of Jesus Christ prevailed more and more within the village and even beyond the village. A decent church building was built and dedicated in 1991.

2.3.5 Taneg Assembly of God Church

J. Soriano, after established Tuding Assembly of God Church in Tuding (the first Assembly of God church), began to open a daughter church, Taneg Assembly of God Church. He opened this daughter church in Taneg, Cabitan, around 1952. Before starting this church, J. Soriano and another couple of national workers had frequently come to Taneg to conduct open-air service. They worked tirelessly to preach the gospel. Many pagan people turned to God, as usually happened in any evangelism connected with Vanderbout and national workers (Continguey 1994:2). Once established, Taneg Assembly of God Church also continued to grow in number. In the year 1976, its first church building was demolished and it was reconstructed by the sacrificial work of dedicated church members. Soriano left the Taneg Assembly of God later to join Vanderbout's ministry.

2.3.6 *Papasok Assembly of God Church*

After stabilizing Takadang Church, D. Cogoy opened a church in Papasok in 1953. During the early days of his ministry here, an incident persuaded the whole village of Papasok to turn to Christ. It was a case of demon-possession. A woman of the village suffered the effects on a daily basis. The members of the family attempted to cast out the demon by performing *cañao* (pagan ritual), and in fact, they tried numerous times. They went to the *manbunong* (priest) to consult him regarding this problem, but the priestly effort was made in vain. Thus, the family and relatives almost lost their hope for rescuing this woman from the demon. They were despondent. One day a member of Papasok Church, out of concern for this woman, came to her house. The visiting woman carefully began to mention Jesus and encouraged the troubled woman to go to church. The church had just been pioneered by a dedicated young man of God. Thus, the church had very few in attendance. However, when the members of the family heard the story of the Bible they became interested, and their hearts began to be drawn into it. In human sight, there was no hope for the woman to be healed. Going to the church would, in fact, be a last resort. Yet, the next Sunday the woman and her husband went to the church for the Sunday service. They were accompanied by the church member who had introduced Jesus to them. The demon-possessed woman was brought to the pastor after the service (Cayso 1993). The pastor invited the members to join him in prayer. As expected, the woman who had been demonized writhed and screamed. But the pastor continued to pray, holding to an adamant position against the evil. The prayer lasted as long as an hour. All of a sudden the woman cried out loudly and became calm. The pastor and the rest of the people immediately noticed that the demon was cast out and the woman became well. This amazing news spread, the whole village heard and people came to the church. The church grew in number. In 1994, they built a new church building through the support of a Korean church in California.

2.3.7 Longboy Assembly of God Church

In 1953, Wisitor Bugtong pioneered Longboy Assembly of God Church. The church grew after a revival meeting. The revival meeting lasted for a week. The Holy Spirit moved mightily among the people gathered. Sick people were healed by the power of the Holy Spirit. Pagan people heard this amazing news and attended services in curiosity. The attendees were baptized in the Holy Spirit and were converted. After the revival meeting many village people regularly came to the church and the church grew in number.

As Bugtong went on with pastoral work, he added other congregations. Villages where he started church work were: Bolibo (1983), Kayan (1988), Madoto (1988), Bagoyos (1989), Liwang (1988), and others (Sasaki 1990).

2.3.8 Beto Assembly of God Church

Around the year 1955, when D. Cogoy was taking care of a congregation in Beto village, Bakun, an incident caused a new congregation to emerge in this village. There was a man who was conducting *cañao* (native ritual) according a priest's prescription. He was stricken insane in the middle of it. This man was crazy for several months. But there was no one who could do anything for the man. The final option was to invite a few church pastors to pray for him. The pastors nearby came and laid their hands upon him and prayed. Through prayer, the man became a normal person. Many pagan people who conducted *cañao* turned to Christ through this incident. This event served as a seed to plant a congregation. The church continued to grow in number.

2.3.9 Abatan Assembly of God Church

In 1956, Abatan Assembly of God Church was opened through the healing experience of a boy, Juanito Ricardo. The boy was not able to walk but for no apparent reason. This pagan family kept their customary beliefs and performed all pagan rituals for the healing of their son's leg. But nothing happened. The family was brought to the church. The pastor and church members in other village laid their hands upon the son. Fervent prayer was offered for the son to make progress and to walk. In less than a month the child had immensely improved (Ricardo 1994).

The church building was erected in 1965. The church was rebuilt in 1966 through the financial assistance from the Finnish missionary Erola (Continguey, Saliw-an and Bugtong 1994). In 1968, Jones Ciriaco became the pastor. But after a few years of pastoring he left due to a serious illness. In 1973, Mario

Dayaoen took over the pastoral position. In 1975, John Vicente became the pastor. He continues pastoring until now.

2.3.10 Kaang Assembly of God Church

In 1957, Liwayan Organo pioneered Kaang Assembly of God Church in Bakun. A congregation in Kaang village in Bakun was initiated through the healing experience of a priest. A pagan high priest named Kuba was critically ill. Cognizant of this fact, Organo and the pastor Cogoy, who came from the neighboring church, approached the priest to try to persuade him of Christ, but they did not expect to be receptive. The priest had held a high position of prestige with the respect of the people for a long period of time (Cabatan 1994).

However, the pagan high priest asked Cogoy two questions. The first question was, "What if my cow fell from the cliff the moment that I believed in God?" The second question was "What if I believe in God? Then will Satan, my master, take away my breath so that I will die?" Cogoy responded to his questions with two answers. The first answer Cogoy made was, "If you will believe in God, He will bless your cow as well as your other animals because He not Satan is the Creator of them." The second answer Cogoy offered was, "If you believe, you will not die but live, because He is the giver of the breath of life." The priest was not assured by the answers Cogoy gave, but he allowed Cogoy to visit him to share the gospel. During a one-month period Cogoy convinced the priest to believe in Christ. The priest was gradually healed. Cogoy told the priest not to consult with, not even to eat any food which was offered to a spirit and not to drink *tapey* (wine) which was devil's wine made of fermented rice. The priest strictly followed this instruction until his death in 1976 (Cabatan 1994).

L. Organo had eight congregations under his wing in the Bakun municipality. These were: Kaang (1957), Bagu (1973), Lamew (1975), Beyeng (1979), Igigang (1977), Tagpew (1979), Yugoc (1979), and Banga-an (1980) (Cabatan 1994). These churches were started and grew through people's healing experiences of God and revival meetings.

In summary, during the years 1950-1969, the Assemblies of God churches in the mountains were pioneered and established as a result of healing experiences of people. As described in preceding pages, various sick people were cured by the touch of the Holy Spirit. Pastoral prayer was powerful, and divine power was manifested upon the sick. Revival meetings were effective to bring non-believers to the Lord and to spur churches toward growth. It should be acknowledged that the Holy Spirit moved mightily among people in services, and they were baptized in the Holy Spirit. From the beginning of the Assemblies of God ministry among these people while establishing churches in the mountains, God's power continued to be manifested.

2.4 Works Established by National Ministers, 1970-1990

Pastors during the period 1970-1990 were of a young generation and were more or less challenged by aged mountain church pastors who had sincerely been pastoring in the mountains for a long time. However, the degrees of passion and enthusiasm of young pastors were as strong as those of the mountain workers in the earliest stage. Total submission of young pastors to the call of God for the mountain church ministry was clearly demonstrated. During this period of time a few missionaries, such as Masaaki Sasaki, a Japanese missionary, and Korean missionaries, were actively involved in evangelism and church planting.

2.4.1 Tinek Assembly of God Church

In 1970, Tinek Assembly of God Church was established by the pastor Daniel Vicente. Vicente was led by the Holy Spirit to those people who were hungering after the Word of God in Tinek. Vicente was himself devoted to these people and strove to bring church members to Christian maturity while also exerting great effort to add numerical growth to the church. While pastoring in Buguias, Vicente opened an outreach in Dontogdo, Ifugao in 1973. This was the first Assemblies of God congregation in Dondogdo Village (Ma 1994). Vicente continued pastoring in Tinek Church and provides members with pastoral care and still does so at present.

2.4.2 Binabulayan Assembly of God Church

Binabulayan Assembly of God Church was established by Alex Simeon in 1970. The Binabulayan congregation was small with only a handful members when Simeon began his pastoral work. However, Simeon endeavored to bring non-believers into the congregation. He carried on pastoral work with solid Bible study. The members, who learned Scriptures in Bible study, were stimulated to share the good news of Jesus Christ. They began to approach their relatives with the gospel. Response from them was rather poor at first. But as years went by, the relatives and people around the village became inquisitive about what was going on in the church. One by one they came to join the church activities.

On December 8, 1971, the construction of the building was started, and it was completed in March 1972. But two years later, the church was rebuilt on another lot donated by Cotilla Calubandi, one of the church members. The church building was mainly built by pledges and free labor of church members of Balili Assembly of God and Buguias Central Assembly of God Church. The church was also renovated as a two-story building.

2.4.3 Ambiong Assembly of God Church

A congregation in Ambiong Village in La Trinidard was started in 1977 by a Bible school student named by Edilyn Lizardo. She invited various church people of the nearby Assembly of God Church to evangelize and to have Bible study. Some young people who heard the gospel wanted to grow in the knowledge of Christ. The church kept growing through the influence of Bible study.

In the year 1990, through the help of a Korean missionary, Wonsuk Ma, the church building was erected. But in an earthquake, the church building collapsed. The following year it was re-erected. After the church was built Sunday service attendance increased. Currently there are about fifty children and sixty adults in attendance at Sunday services. George Padsing is pastoring at the present.

2.4.4 La Trinidad Assembly of God Church

There was no existent Assemblies of God Church in La Trinidad until the year 1979. Walter Caput began a church with the support and help of young people from Tuding Church. They helped in leading services and attending regular prayer meetings. It was apparently a challenge for him to pioneer this church. However, Caput's pastoral work was so successful that the church grew rapidly. Caput exercised his pastoral gift in his desire to build a solid congregation. He was not only concerned for his church to grow, but also opened outreaches in other mountain villages. Outreaches that Caput opened were in villages of Beckel (1985), Sablan (1984), Acop (1991) and Lamut (1985) (Verana 1991:1).

2.4.5 Sebang Assembly of God Church

Preaching the gospel was started in 1984 for a few villages (Cayapas, Lubban and Sebang) by Samuel Dayaoen and elders of Palili Assembly of God Church. As usual, Dayaoen started Bible studies at the houses of some converts. Vacation Bible School was held in Sebang Elementary school in May 1984 and was conducted by female teachers Pynie Bacasen and Mila Balagnot. It was successful, and many children turned to God. As Dayaoen continued to attend the church, many young people joined Bible studies. The Sebang Assembly of God Church mainly consisted of young people and newly married young couples (Dayaoen 1977).

As the congregation grew in number, church people set their desire on building a church structure. In 1990, through financial support from a Korean missionary, the church building was completed with church people's labor. At present, the church is independent and under the leadership of Nelio Balagnot.

2.4.6 Palali Assembly of God Church

Actually, in 1984, Palali Assembly of God Church was started by Josephine Bilanggo, a native of Palali in Sablan. However, with her lack of theological training, she could not be considered for ministry. Joven Encarnacion took over a pastoral leadership. The first meeting was held in the house of Bilanggo's relative. About ten people attended the Bible study (Catipon 1991:5).

A small weekly Bible study group has been holding meetings since then. The meeting place for the Bible study moved from one house to another. This was certainly inconvenient for the members. A Canadian missionary named Ozmo donated money to buy a piece of land and materials for a church building. A building was built in 1988 and it serves as a permanent gathering place.

2.4.7 Lamut Assembly of God Church

A congregation with a few converts was started in Lamut by the outreach of La Trinidad Assembly of God Church in 1985. Young people from La Trinidad Assembly of God Church held regular Bible study. The Bible study interested young people in the village. Many people came to the meeting. A few years later a member of the congregation surprisingly donated a lot of money for a church building. He also cared for church members while there was no pastor in the church.

Pastor Walter Caput assigned Marcelo Vicente to be a pastor in Lamut Church in 1986, through the permission of the district superintendent. Vicente dedicated himself for church growth and spiritual nurture of church members. After the church building was constructed (1989), the membership increased to sixty, including children. Vicente also attempted to open outreaches in villages where no churches existed.

2.4.8 Goldfield Assembly of God Church

In 1987, Goldfield Assembly of God Church was started by Tito Inio. The church began to grow in response to the manifestation of God's power upon a sick village woman. In desperation, the family of the sick person invited Pastor Inio to their home to pray for her. In a conversation she mentioned a terrible dream that she had had, after which she became fearful and got sick. The pastor led a devotion and prayed for her. He sensed the power of the Holy Spirit moving among them while prayer was offered. At this moment she felt the touch of God and was instantly healed (Inio 1993). A few months later, coincidentally a granddaughter, Antonio, was ill with the same symptoms the grandmother had had; it began with a fearful dream. Inio was again asked to pray for the granddaughter, and she too was healed. In 1991, the church was built through the support of a Korean missionary and it has continued to grow in number.

2.4.9 Pudong Assembly of God Church

The community of Pudong in Kapangan was steeped in paganism. People in this village frequently conducted *cañao*, the pagan feast of appeasing the dead spirits. People were fearful of the spirit world. The departed ones were believed to have taken on spiritual being and ability to cause capricious harm among the people. When there was unexplained sickness in the community the people ascribed it to disturbances of the spirit world (Phoon 1991:6).

However, R. Rimendo, prior to starting a church in Kapangan, offered extensive tract distribution. She was thus well accepted into the community and was invited to their festivals as a special guest. In January 1991, Rimendo began to do house-to-house Bible studies. She was able to begin a church service in March 1991. Since the group was small and the school hall was made available for services, there were no plans to buy any property or to build a church building. Due to continuing Bible study and evangelism, the church congregation grew and members were actively involved in church ministry.

In summary, during the years 1970-1990, more mountain churches were opened in unreached villages, according to various causes and needs. Young pastors were whole-heartedly involved in pastoral work. During this period, some churches were still opened through individual's experiences of healing power of God, in the same pattern of the early spread of Christianity. But a significant number of churches were distinctively started through Bible study. Bible study played a vital role in bringing young and old people to church and helping the church grow. The pastors trained lay leaders in order to delegate part of their pastoral responsibilities.

Evangelism and church planting have continued to be carried out since 1990, by both mountain pastors and missionaries. During this time, Korean missionaries have become actively involved in church planting, supporting church finances, and participating in church activities.

Part II

An Anthropological Perspective

Chapter 4

Religous Practices of the Kankana-eys

In Part I, I surveyed a brief history of several Christian groups that have ministered among the mountain people. In Part II, I will examine Kankana-eys' belief system based on the role of the spirit beings, priests, and various rituals. As briefly mentioned above, they are animists and ancestral worshipers. They are deeply involved in ritual practices. Through my personal experiences and interviews, I also discovered that the Kankana-eys faithfully preserve their traditional religion. Hence, they believe not only in the existence of spirit beings but also in their involvement in human life. They perceive that the spirit beings obtain power to do both ill and good for living kin. They frequently resort to ritual practices to have their various needs met – needs for healing, blessing, and preventing misfortune.

1. Spirit Beings

The Kankana-eys believe that there are many spirits in the skyworld and underworld. They believe that all creatures have spirits, and their spirits join other spirits after death. These spirits intimately interact with people, associating with their lives as if they were living, local resident creatures. Norma Lua states:

> The human reality is intertwined not only with the creatures of the natural-environment but also with the beings of the superhuman realm. This intertwining makes interaction with these beings inevitable and weaves mystery into the human life as made evident in the incomprehensible experiences of mysterious pregnancy, illness and death (1984:15).

The Kankana-eys maintain the belief that these spirits communicate with humans through dreams and mediums. Thus, they seek communication with the spirits by performing rites and rituals. Through the centuries, the Kankana-eys have developed this system as part of their life and thought.

1.1 Adika-ila

W. D. Sacla, a native man (1987:10-11), describes spirit beings as follows: *Adika-ila* is the highest spirit, the one who has created the sun, stars, moon, earth, and creatures. This spirit is the supreme maker of the universe. The Kankana-eys believe that all other spirits, including the human spirit, are under the sway of this highest spirit.

A priest invokes the name of *Adika-ila* for wisdom and knowledge, for fairness, and for justice in making decisions for the public affairs in the interest of the tribe. The priest asks disputing parties to look up to the sky in order to seek justice and fairness from this spirit. This spirit can help people in cases of determining who is a thief, for example, when a farmer has lost his or her cow, who is guilty in cases of fraud, or who is to be held accountable in land disputes (Sacla 1987:11, 15). When people are in trouble, or experiencing bereavement and sorrow, they look up to the sky for help from this highest spirit, believing in this spirit as protector.

1.2 Kabunyan (gods/goddesses)

The *Kabunyan* are spirits who have supernatural powers and are next in rank to *Adika-ila*. The Kankana-eys believe that *Kabunyan* dwell in the skyworld, and have limited powers in creating the universe. There are twenty-four such gods/godesses in the spirit group of *Kabunyan* (twelve gods and twelve goddesses). The names of the twelve gods are: *Bal-litoc, Kabigat, Lumawig, Gatan, Pati, Suyan, Amduyan, Kalan, Wigan, Lopis, Bentawan,* and *Maudi.* The names of the twelve goddesses are: *Bangan, Bugan, Ub-bang, Pe-ey, Angban, Yapeng, Lingan, Angtan, Apinan, Daungen, Tengnan,* and *Ibagan.* According to legend, the gods are handsome, and the goddesses are beautiful. If humans were to see them, they would not even be able to close their eyes and might even forget their spouses. The most familiar gods among all these deities are *Lumawig* and *Pati,* They are the gods of war and of hunting. They are also involved in the general activities and occupations of the people. *Bal-litoc* is known as the god of gold, as the god who controls and distributes gold among those with whom he finds a favor. *Kabigat* and others are known as the gods of silver and money (Sacla 1987:16-17).

Despite these generalizations, it should be noted that among the tribal groups in Luzon, understandings of *Kabunyan* differ. For instance, the Ifugao tribe believes that only one *Kabunyan* exists and is merely the nature/sky god, whereas the Ibalois and Kankana-ey tribes recognize *Kabunyan's* existence as important and believe these deities function in plurality of forms (Scott 1988:151) as indicated above. The Bontoc tribe has its own deity called *Lumawig* (different from the *Lumawig* noted above) who can never be identified as *Kabunyan* (De Raedt 1964:309). In thanksgiving rituals, the names of the above deities are always pronounced in chants, prayers and songs of the priest.

1.3 Ap-apo

The spirits of people who have long been dead are collectively called *Ap-apo*. The Kankana-eys believe that these spirits live with the deities. These spirits travel from the skyworld to the earth, to the underworld and back. *Ap-apo*, while up in the sky, are easily awakened by the inviting sweet flavor of *tapey* and the sound of gongs. In ritual, a celebrating family invites or calls upon these dead ancestors. During such rituals, *Ap-apo* come down to the earth bringing good luck to the family (Sacla 1987:18). The good luck is evinced by way of omens and signs. For such detection of luck, the priest carefully observes intestines of pigs. An example of a good omen is the well-filled bile of a ritual pig offered, signifying that the celebrating family will have long life, will make lots of money and will have herds of animals. *Ap-apo* can also cure family members afflicted with sickness caused by other spirits of the underworld.

1.4 Kak-kading

Spirits of humans who have recently died are called *Kak-kading*. They remain on the earth. During rituals a host family offers and pours several drops of wine to signify acknowledgment of their presence in the ritual. People believe that when a jar or bottle of wine is opened, the wine's flavor invites the spirits to come to partake. The offering of the wine to the spirits is necessary at initial stages of the ritual to bring the spirits (Sacla 1987:18). The spirits, in turn, bring good luck on the host family.

If a host family omits this procedure, the spirits will be offended and may find recourse in violence. The fury of such spirits can render offenders mentally abnormal. However, if victims offer wine, the spirits will be appeased and their anger will be allayed.

1.5 Anito

The spirits of the underworld collectively are called *Anito*. The *Anito* involve several groups: *Pinad-eng, L'ebek, Tonoton/Debek, Ampasit, Tayab-ban, Mandoweng, Nante-es, Bilig, Liblibayan, Amlag, Tinmongao, Penten, Butat-tew, Banig,* and *Pamakan*. Priests and Kankana-eys think that these beings dwell everywhere in the earth. The particular dwelling places of some of these groups of the spirits are detailed below (Bagamasped and Hamada-Pawid 1985:103):

Pinad-eng stay in the forest and, as owners of wild pigs and chickens, are spirits to whom hunters offer sacrifices to ensure successful hunting. *Tinmongao* dwell in the mountains and are called mountain spirits. They cruelly inflict sickness and injury on people who walk on their dwelling places. Victims are required to offer sacrifice to mollify them. *Penten* dwell in water and are called "water spirits." They are believed to be spirits of those people who have died violently by accident or by drowning. They cause rivers to rise when people cross during rainy days. *Butat-tew* live in caves and group themselves at night to misguide humans from their path. They appear and disappear unexpectedly. *Ampasit* also live in caves. They are generally malevolent spirits and have power to steal the souls of people. They also mislead people traveling at night.

The rest of the spirits dwell in big rocks, cliffs, ravines, caves, abandoned tunnels, abandoned buildings, bushy trees, bushes, water falls, creeks, springs, lakes, rivers, oceans, in the ground and various other places (Sacla 1987:19). These spirits are easily offended when people trespass, forget to open wine, neglect sacrificial offerings, and commit other acts of negligence. Offended spirits may cause illness, death and misfortune. Sick people are required to offer a ritual to appease the anger of spirits and thereby to be cured.

1.6 Makedse

Makedse are malevolent dwelling in the underworld. They are known to be both sensitive and selfish. Due to sensitivities, these spirits are easily hurt by human beings who neglect their duty to them. The spirits quickly lose their tempers when they are offended (Sacla 1987:18). Their anger brings wrath leading to bad luck.

1.7 Maeya

Maeya are known as benevolent. The spirits stay in the underworld somewhere in the forest, as do some other spirits. They are believed to own animals such as boars, deer, cats, chickens and birds. Because so many animals need to be overseen the spirits reside in the forest (Sacla 1987:19). Farmers offer animal sacrifice to them so their animals will grow healthy and have long life.

In summary, the Kankana-eys believe in various kinds of spirits, including ancestral spirits to whom they can bring their needs through ritual forms. The people are thus closely bound to the expectations, demands and sensibilities of the gods, and especially to the ancestors who are interested in the day-to-day life of human beings (Lower-Palmer 1980:63). The Kankana-eys take comfort in the belief that they have such spirits through which they may endure the hardships of their lives.

2. Data Analysis: Spirit Beings

James Spradley (1980:87, 89) has identified four categories for analysis of themes and cultural meaning to be discovered in the field. Domain analysis is the first type of ethnographic analysis. It involves the use of language: cover terms, included terms, and semantic relationships. Second, taxonomic analysis involves a search for the way cultural domains are organized. Third, componential analysis involves a search for the attributes of terms in each domain. Finally, theme analysis is intended to search for relationships among domains, and it is directed at showing how they are linked to the cultural scene as a whole. This section, accordingly, summarizes data analysis of the particular terms (indicated in the previous section) in relation to spiritual beings. Each of Spradley's four different types of analysis – domain, taxonomic, componential, and theme – are employed.

2.1 Domain Analysis

Through the study of spiritual beings, I have found a number of cover terms. I had a chance to investigate the various names of spiritual beings and their characteristics. This investigation was done through reading published material and interviews with native people. The gods are absolute beings for the Kankana-eys. They relate spiritual beings to power. The Kankana-eys believe that spirit beings have ability to resolve human problems and to meet their needs with power.

Spirit beings are also capable of healing and causing sickness, injury, and death. They have various capabilities among the Kankana-eys and are deeply involved in their lives and activities.

I have observed that, for the Kankana-eys, knowing the functions of spiritual beings is crucial for their welfare. It is equally essential to be able to establish proper contact with and perform appropriate rituals for securing various needs through alliance with spirit beings. For instance, calling upon different names of some spirit beings, and thus inviting them to come to communicate with people, is part of the priestly procedure in several rituals. This is often accompanied by priestly chanting and/or prayer.[1] Table 1 lists the names of the spirit beings or groups of beings which are significant to domain analysis

Included Terms	Semantic Relationship	Cover Term
Adika-ila		
Kabunyan		
Ap-apo		
Kak-kading	is a kind of	spirit being
Anito		
Makedse		
Maeya		

Table 1: Domains of Spirit Beings

Through interviewing Kankana-ey people, I discovered that understanding how spirit beings interact with human beings, especially through the beings' respective powers, is significant in determining what kind of ritual is to be performed. My informants were consistent in their representations that performing a ritual is a way of meeting with spirit beings and experiencing their power. By such means, people's problems were resolved and their needs were met. Table 2 lists the power capabilities of the spirit beings in terms of powers exerted upon Kankana-ey life.

---

[1] For detail, see Chapter 5.

Included Terms	Semantic Relationship	Cover Term
Protecting	is a kind of	power of spirit being
Healing		
Bringing good luck		
Bringing bad luck		
Health and long life of animals		
Blessing with gold and silver		
Causing illness		
Misguiding		
Misleading		
Inflicting		
Guiding animals and plants		
Guiding war and hunting		

Table 2: Domains of Power of Spirit Beings

Table 3 contains findings on manifestations of the powers of the spirit beings. Through interviewing Kankana-ey people, I found that knowing how the power of spirit beings is manifested is crucial to interaction with spiritual beings. Spirit beings manifest their power in various ways. Interviews revealed that, on occasion, the community priest would summon the victim and a suspect to determine a thief. The two would be called, and spirits would be invited by slaughtering a chicken. Then both would dip their hand into boiling water. The spirits were believed to protect the innocent while bringing harm to any offender. In observing such a case, it becomes important to understand which spirits are to be invited, how they can be summoned, and what is to be expected from them. Related knowledge of this spirit world applies to other areas listed under "Included Terms" in Table 3.

Included Term	Semantic Relationship	Cover Term
Long life		
Money		
Blessing with animals		
Good harvest		
Good health		
Quick recovery		
Sleepiness		
Strength	is a kind of	manifestation of power of spirit being
Dizziness		
Headache		
Finding a thief		
Discerning right and wrong		
Causing death		
Causing sickness		
Causing injury		
Wrong direction		

Table 3: Domains of Manifestation of Power of Spirit Beings

2.2 Taxonomic Analysis

I examined the relationship between the two domains: beings and power. Then I constructed taxonomies based on my personal understanding of spirit beings' categories. Accurate analysis of these domains was, of course, foundational for validating the present research process.

Figure 1 displays the taxonomy constructed based on the domains of the spirit beings. It seems that a discussion of these spirit beings is extremely pertinent to my research concern. Why is discussion of the powers of spirit beings so significant? Because they are viewed and experienced as primary sources of spirit power. I was first informed of this significance through interviews and study of spirit beings. I then noted that the Kankana-eys recognize different characteristics of diverse spiritual beings. According to these characteristics, various spirit beings are vested with different areas of concern to the Kankana-eys. For instance, some gods bless with gold and silver, whereas others bring long life and good luck or bad luck. Certain other gods protect, comfort, and heal. Some cruel gods cause misfortune and sickness. Knowing what sorts of spirit beings bear which characteristics determines for the Kankana-eys both knowledge of spirit beings and deep-level relationship to these beings. The Kankana-eys perform ritual based on such experiential knowledge and relationship.

Through taxonomic analysis (see Figure 1), I have characterized and positioned spirit beings according to their ranks, their functions or character, and their names.

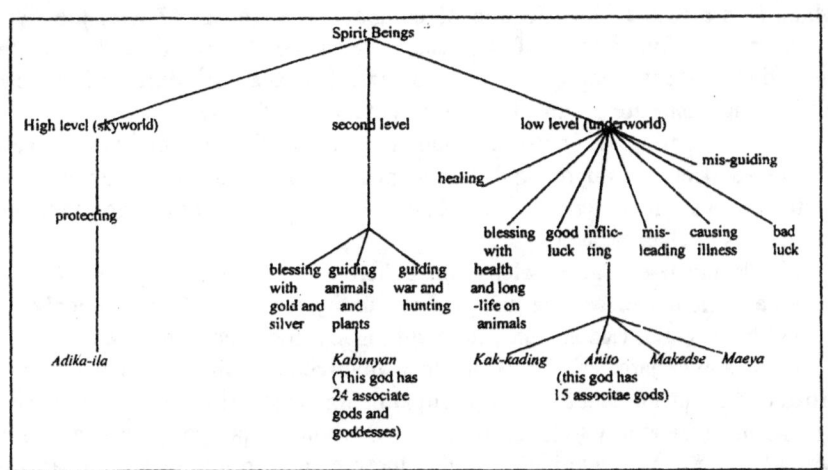

Figure 1: Taxonomy of Spirit Beings

A second taxonomy summarizes the powers of spirit beings (Figure 2). I found that it is significant to develop this taxonomy. Spirit beings are associated with specific powers. I have thus describes powers of the spirit beings and various manifestations of power. This taxonomy reinforces the above suggestion that the Kankana-eys believe that the spirit beings have power to cause and resolve problems.

Figure 2: Taxonomy of Powers of Spirit Beings

2.3 Componential Analysis

The next stage of analysis involves contrast. My guiding question at this stage was: Within given domains, what characteristics distinguish one item from another? For this analysis of the domains of spirit beings and powers, I took data which informed the identification of components of meaning with their contrasts. In composing a chart of contrasts, I was helped to investigate both different and similar characteristics of spirit beings. This analysis confirmed that each spirit being (some are groups) has a different source of power.

In the dimensions of contrast, I found three dimensions of contrast (see Table 4). The Kankana-eys approach different spirit beings according to their different characteristics. The function of each spirit being differs according to the beings' unique sets of characteristics.

The Kankana-eys acknowledge that there is one supreme god (*Adika-ila*) who made the universe. This god also has ability to protect. They recognize the second highest god (*Kabunyan*), involving many gods and goddesses who have many different characteristics. Thus, their involvement with the Kankana-eys is broad and frequent. Other sets of spiritual beings who are lower in rank such as *Ap-apo* have the ability to heal. *Anito* includes some small gods who vary in nature. My informants have indicated that these beings are the most popular; they are invited to ritual more frequently than are any other spirit beings. Their popularity seems to stem from their characteristics and functions' having direct bearing on human life. They are also mischievous, so that, for example, at certain times they cause sickness, injury, or inflict illness. Their names are often cited during prayer and chants. Of course, the names of other spirit beings are also mentioned in ritual.

Based on my own personal contact with the Kankana-eys, I have determined that they frequently receive from spirit beings revelations regarding causes of sickness. They experience such revelation through both direct and indirect contact with the spirit beings. When I interviewed one native woman, she testified that her mother became gravely ill after having a dream one night. The dream was so fearful that her body was soaked with perspiration, and she was completely captive to the fear.

This evidence would point to *Anito* (associated gods) as causes of sickness. The family normally takes the sick person to the priest for consultation in order to determine the cause of the sickness. The priest prescribes an appropriate ritual to appeal to the spirit beings. Similarly, when animals suddenly die, or when plants in flower gardens or farms are destroyed by typhoons or other natural disasters, the Kankana-eys immediately attempt to determine which spirit being(s) caused the misfortune. Then the people search for the next step to take.

The characteristics of spirit beings described in the taxonomy of Table 4 summarizes the componential analysis conducted for this study.

Means End (X is a way to Y)	Dimension of Contrast		
Domain	High level	Second level	Low level
Healing			Ap-apo
Protecting	Adika-ila		
Good luck			Kak-kading
Blessing with gold and silver		Kabunyan	
Guiding animals and plants		Kabunyan	
Guiding war and hunting		Kabunyan	
Causing illness			Anito
Misleading			Anito
Inflicting			Anito
Bad luck			Makedse
Blessing with health and long life on animals			Maeya
Misguiding			Anito

Table 4: Componential Analysis: Characteristics of Spirit Beings

2.4 Theme Analysis

The final stage of Spradley's (1980:140) model analysis is that of theme analysis. For this stage I asked the following question: Does a theme emerge as one of the primary issues of study or analysis?

Based on the foregoing discussion and tables, I have contrasted elements within the inventory of cover terms from the domains obtained through domain analysis, with an eye to detecting one theme. I attempted to discern a theme that is relevant to as many cover terms as possible. In analysis of the various cover terms of the domains, the following major theme has emerged: "To experience the power of spirit beings, knowing about them and their characteristics is required." I found that knowing spirit beings and their respective characteristics is important to determining what ritual is appropriate in a given situation. It is then through ritual performance that the Kankana-eys experience the power of these spirit beings.

3. Roles of the Priests

Fuer-Haimendorf (1989:94) says that a priest is normally a descendant of the village-founder, and member of the lineage of the first man who settled in a locality: The priest thereby gains power from a close connection with spirit beings. He is regarded as the head of the village and the mediator between persons and deities who dwell in various parts of the world. Paul Hiebert and Daniel Shaw (1993:227, 228) offer further perspective noting that the priest's role in complex social and religious contexts is to meet human needs, often handling critical situations and providing care for people by acquiring wisdom from spirit beings.

The priests in the Kankana-ey tribe enact the roles of the spirits in matters of people. They act individually and collectively as ritual advisors and administer rituals. Their role of mediums between spirits and people is regarded as critical. They are known as the ones who have power to address and to gain a hearing with the deities, the spirits of ancestors. Demonstrable powers that the priests exercise include interpreting signs and omens, ritual counseling, giving authoritative words, maintaining keen memory of ritual procedures and orally chanting genealogies.

Other Philippine tribal groups, like the Sagada, have no such notion of a professional priesthood. Ceremonies are conducted by the heads of families, old men who have memorized traditional prayers, and individuals in the community with inherited rites over specific ceremonies (Scott 1969:143). However, ritual and festival life are highly elaborate among the tribal groups of Northern Luzon, and both female and male shamans, or mediums, exercise responsibility in religious affairs (Keesing 1962:121).

This section discusses specific roles of different priests in the Kankana-ey animistic context.

3.1 Manbunong

The *manbunong* (shaman) can be either male or female. He or she is called by the *Kabunyan*; thus, the function as priest is legitimated. The *Manbunong* is not required to have had formal theological training; a *manbuong* typically comes from a poorer class (Moss 1920:284). He or she obtains power through experiences with spirit beings or through the spirits of dead *manbunong*, via dreams or visions (Beals and Hoijer 1971:456). When a person is sick, a *manbunong* is invited to perform ritual for healing. Prior to conducting ritual, a sick person consults with the priest about the symptoms of the sickness. The priest then communicates with spirits to relieve the afflicted person of his or her suffering.

Upon completion of the ritual, the priest comforts the afflicted person, assuring him or her of the cure from the gods as long as the ritual has been done according to the wishes of the spirits (Sacla 1987:25).

The *manbunong* also has authority to conduct thanksgiving rituals both for reversing the sorrows of the aggrieved and to comfort victims of misfortunes in order for them to receive fortune and blessing. The *manbunong*'s duty during ritual is to offer animals, wine and other food. Before butchering, cooking, eating, drinking, or playing instruments, the *manbunong* offers prayer for each prescribed ritual. After the ritual, the *manbunong* is given one of the forelegs of a pig as a gratuity for his or her service. Sometimes money is given in addition to meat.

3.2 Mansib-ok

When people get ill or experience misfortune, they seek the *mansib-ok* to consult for discernment of the cause(s) and to prescribe a ritual cure. The *mansib-ok* has the ability to interpret the cause of illness, as the *manbunong* does also. In many aspects, in fact, the role of *manbunong* and *mansip-ok* overlaps. In some cases the *mansip-ok* may be a *manbunong*. But the *mansib-ok*'s role is more or less to find out the causes of illness and causes of other problems. In order to precisely detect the cause of a sickness, the *mansib-ok* thoroughly interviews the patient to extract all pertinent information. Then the *mansib-ok* employs other methods for determining the cause of sickness (Sacla 1987:23).

One of the many methods is to use a short iron bar or a piece of stone tied to a string and held by both hands with the iron bar or stone hanging. When the iron bar, or stone moves, the *mansib-ok* detects what kind of ritual is fitting for curing a person of his or her specific sickness (Igualdo 1989:242). A *mansib-ok* not only has ability to discern the cause of the sickness and to prescribe ritual but also can determine the cause of a death or misfortune.

3.3 Mankotom

The *mankotom* is known as a wise man and advocate of peace in the community. He or she is an elder who exerts influence to preserve customs and conserve traditions, holding them in high regard according to strict taboos and rituals. They interpret omens, signs, and dreams that other priests may not be able to interpret.

The *mankotom*'s particular role in the community among the people involves such work as helping to settle disputes or misunderstandings over divorce or property ownership, and other civil cases arising among the people; assisting in counseling people disturbed from bad omens arising out of breaking taboo; counseling persons disturbed by bad dreams; counseling families afraid of the appearance of strange birds and animals in their homes (bad omens); helping people who suddenly lose their possessions; and helping families who are grieved by death of a family member (Sacla 1987:28). The *mankotom* interprets all signs to foretell if good or bad luck will come in the future. The *mankotom* also interprets omens by observing the bile and liver of animals and informing a host family if omens are good or bad.

Each priest has some involvement in one of the roles discussed above. Priests exercise their skills and abilities to fulfill their roles and function as mediators between gods and people. Because of the employment of human insight, the role of the priests is somewhat ambiguous because this role involves the appeal to spiritual powers to discern, to interpret, to foretell, to proceed with ritual, to gain wisdom, and to be endowed with powers from gods and ancestral spirits. A priest's role is highly significant among people of the Kankana-ey tribe, because priests closely associate so many events of daily life with the activity of spirit beings.

4. Data Analysis: Roles of the Priests

This section will analyze the discussion of the role of priests according to four different categories: domain, taxonomic, componential, and theme.

4.1 Domain Analysis

I have analyzed domains based on descriptive study of the priestly role. For research of this study, I was able to contact priests while I was in the mission field. The three types of priests are: *manbunong, mansib-ok,* and *mankotom.* I attended several ritual performances administered by the priests. I was thus informed about their significant roles and contributions in performing rituals.

The priests have diverse roles with varying functions. These roles are individual as well as collective. Their roles and functions include administering rituals, prescribing appropriate rituals, counseling, and finding causes of maladies. When the Kankana-eys encounter daily problems or disasters, they first of all need to decide which priest they should consult. Without a priest's presence and advice, the Kankana-eys cannot communicate with spirit beings, perform rituals or have power experience.

Table 5 summarizes the domains by priestly names, and Table 6 deals with priestly roles and occasions (see also Figure 3). I have drawn cover terms from descriptive data on priestly roles.

Included Terms	Semantic Relationship	Cover Term
Manbunong		
Mansib-ok	is a kind of	priest
Mankotom		

Table 5: Domains of the Priests

Included Terms	Semantic Relationship	Cover Term
Consulting about cause of sickness		
Performing healing ritual		
Performing thanksgiving ritual		
Prescribing ritual		
Serving as wise man		
Relieving affliction		
Healing sickness		
Bringing fortune	is a kind of	role of the priest and occasion
Bringing blessing		
Discerning cause of misfortune		
Discerning cause of illness		
Treating misunderstanding		
Handling divorce		
Finding property of ownership		
Counseling for bad omen and dream		
Interpreting omen, sign and dream		
Interpreting liver and bile of animal		

Table 6: Domains of the Roles of Priests and Occasions

4.2 Taxonomic Analysis

The analysis of domain is basic for taxonomic analysis of the roles of priests. At this stage I asked: What are the roles of the priests? and Why are their roles significant? I found that each priest has a different role and function. One of the *manbunong*'s roles is consultation for causes of sickness. However, his or her major role is to perform healing and thanksgiving rituals. The role of a *mansib-ok* is to discern the causes of sickness or misfortune and prescribe a ritual. A *mankotom*'s role is counseling, serving as a wise man, and interpreting signs and omens revealed in the entrails of sacrificial animals.

According to my interviews and observations on the roles of the priests (Figure 3), the priestly role is significant in meeting various felt needs of people. Their roles in fact are crucial in ritual performance. The priest's role is critical as he or she serves as a legitimate mediator between spirits and members of the Kankana-ey tribe. Because of their cultural significance, I expected the analysis on the domains of their roles to turn up significant findings. The analysis is summarized in the taxonomic chart, Figure 3.

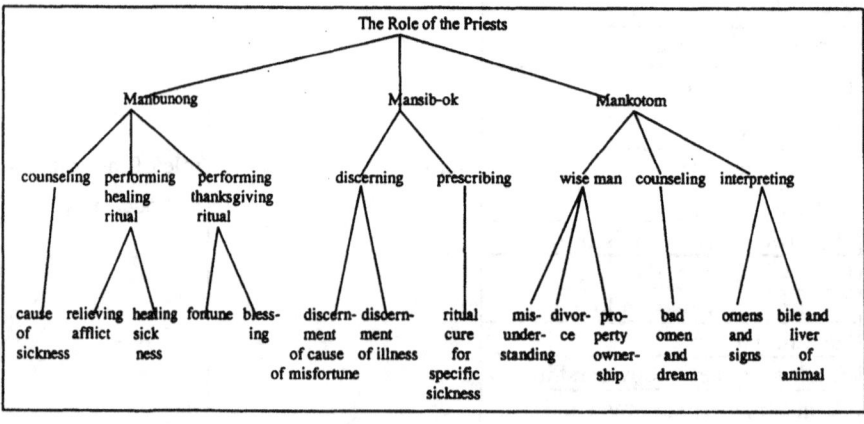

Figure 3: Taxonomy of the Roles of the Priests

4.3 Componential Analysis

The next step is contrast. The guiding question is: In a given domain, what are the characteristics that differentiate one item from another? The domains of the roles of priests provides significant data to identify components of meaning. I have used the relation of means-ends (x is a way to y) as the dimension of contrast.

I discovered when I arrived at this point of the study that a chart helps to organize and to contrast different roles of the priests. The componential analysis in Table 7 is based on differing priestly roles in terms of their related components of meaning. As explained previously, when someone in a family becomes sick, the family members seek *mansib-ok* to discern the cause. The *mansib-ok*'s role is to discern the cause of misfortune and illness, or even the cause of death. After the priest hears the sick person's testimony, he or she determines and prescribes the appropriate ritual. The *manbunong* by contrast, is more popular, because he or she may be consulted for a broader variety of sickness. However, both the *manbunong* and the *mansib-ok* have the gift of finding causes of illness. The *manbunong*, furthermore, is also capable of performing both healing and thanksgiving rituals. The *manbunong*'s role is thus seen as more effective than the others in terms of performing rituals. The *mansib-ok* as well as the *mankotom*, is not officially qualified to perform rituals. However, in urgent circumstances, especially when a *manbunong* is not available, the *mankotom* or the *mansib-ok* may assume further duties in ritual performance. The *mankotom's* role is interpreting omens, signs and dreams, and interpreting bile and liver of an animal's entrails. The *mankotom* perceives, through interpretation, if good or bad luck will come in the future. Further, when there is a controversial issue in the community, people seek the *mankotom*'s advice. Other domestic matters are also normally brought to the attention of the *mankotom*. (Once, while I was there, someone in a village had his animal stolen and the victim sought the advice of the *mankotom*). Thus, the *mankotom* is also a family counselor. For example, when people are disturbed by the appearance of strange animals or birds in their homes (bad omen), they seek the *mankotom* for counseling.

In the componential analysis of Table 7, I have noted the different roles of the priests.

4.4 Theme Analysis

The final stage in study of the priests' roles was theme analysis. Out of the generalized relationships noted in the study of various domains, a specific theme did emerge. The theme that surfaced through the componential analysis is as follows: "To adequately solve problems and perform appropriate rituals, knowing the roles of the priests is required."

Means End (X is a way to Y)	Dimension of Contrast									
Domain	Property ownership	Misfortune	Thanksgiving	Sign and omen of animals' entrails	Bad sign and omen, dream	Divorce	Healing	Cause of sickness	Misunderstanding	Specific sickness
Counseling					Manko-tom					
Discerning		Mansibok						Mansibok		
Performing ritual			Manbu-nong				Manbu-nong			
Interpreting				Manko-tom						
Consulting						Manko-tom		Manbu-nong		
Serving (as wiseman)	Manko-tom								Manko-tom	
Prescribing ritual										Mansibok

Table 7: Componenential Analysis: The Roles of the Priests

By mediating, priests function to satisfy the needs of the people and assist in resolving problems, through accessing power and obtaining the help of spirit beings. As the theme implies, the roles and functions of the priests among the Kankana-eys are critical for the stability of the whole community.

5. Ritual Practices

Kankana-ey ritual practices, specifically thanksgiving and healing, are addressed in this section. Both thanksgiving and healing rituals are commonly practiced. Thanksgiving is practiced on various occasions of gratitude, and healing rituals are performed for people who are sick and who seek healing from spirits. For the Kankana-ey tribe, practicing ritual is a deeply meaningful activity. In fact, ritual performance plays the role of legitimating institutions, such as community leadership, agricultural rites, marriage, and so on (Tabora 1978:494-515). Ritual, in a sense, is perceived as a total world (Shaw 1990:132) in terms of significance of meaning it holds in Kankana-ey life. Rituals which provide a sense of order and access to supernatural powers (Hiebert 1974:146), thus merit careful delineation and explication.

5.1 Thanksgiving Rituals

Thanksgiving rituals are practiced for diverse events. This subsection focuses on occasions celebrating new marriage. A newly married couple is encouraged to perform a ritual two or more days following their wedding festivities. The specifically prescribed ritual is called *pedit* and involves several stages of performance.

Pedit starts with *teteg* (one pig), then *tolo* (three pigs), followed by *lima* (five pigs), *pito* (seven pigs), *siyam* (nine pigs), *sinbaked ya esa* (eleven pigs), *symbaked ya tolo* (thirteen), *sinbaked ya lima* (fifteen), *sinbaked ya pito* (seventeen), *doway baked ya esa* (twenty-one), and *bengngey* (twenty-five). The numerical figures indicating the stages of *pedit* are all odd numbers, because the Kankana-ey believe them to be lucky. As the numbers increase at each successive stage of ritual, more pigs are sacrificed. The ritual procedures in the higher stages of *pedit* are similar to those practiced in *tolo*. Other animals, such as carabaos, cows, horses, and chickens, can be used for the ritual, but the pig is preferred (Sacla 1987:39).

The procedure of the first two stages of ritual, *teteg* and *tolo,* and a couple of other rituals in the overall category of thanksgiving are described in the following pages.

5.1.1 Teteg

In the first stage of the wedding ritual, *teteg,* a newly married couple, who are wed according to divine original will (Bolislis 1967:24), is required to offer one pig to the *Kabunyan* and dead ancestors in order to ensure a propitious start of a pleasant and prosperous married life. The two wish for the gods and their ancestors to bless and bring good luck upon them. The priest, *manbunong,* advises them to observe any strange or unusual events, like the laying of eggs by a hen inside their house near their fireplace or in a corner. Any such event is to be reported immediately to the *mankotom* or elders for interpretation. If the *mankotom* says that it is a good omen and thus favorable to the couple, then they are advised to go on with the ritual (Sacla 1987:39).

In the procedure of *teteg,* the *manbunong,* first of all with a prayer, offers a cup of *tapey* (rice wine) to the spirits. The purpose of the prayer is to invite the *Kabunyan* and dead ancestors to come down to earth to bestow blessings upon the couple. Then, the *manbunong* passes the cup of offered *tapey* to the couple, and they share in drinking it as a symbol of their oneness. The flavor of the *tapey* symbolizes perseverance: the more years the couple lives together, the tighter and sweeter will grow their love. During or after the ritual, relatives, friends, visitors, and invited guests are invited to the couple's house to drink *tapey*. It is believed that the more people are drunk and fully fed, the more blessings will be brought.

After this event, a full-grown male pig is offered as a sacrificial animal. The *manbunong* sits by the pig covering its head with a blanket. Then, he begins to chant and pray, as a way of offering the pig to the *Kabunyan,* to the celestial bodies and to the spirits of ancestors (Sacla 1987: 41).

After the prayer the pig is pierced by a sharpened wood stick directly impaling the heart. It is singed on a pile of burning firewood. Now, the people wash and put the singed pig on a bed of reeds on the floor of the house. Then the four legs are cut from hind legs to forelegs, and an incision is made across the center. From the center, the participants cut downward to expose the internal organs. Intestines are removed for closer observation. The *manbunong* inspects the bile and liver as to size and position. If the bile is normal, it is a good omen, and the couple will have a blessed married life, good health, and prosperity. If the liver or bile are abnormal, or the sizes are smaller or bigger than ordinary ones, the *manbunong* interprets the meaning or discusses with the *mankotom* for further recommendations. The *manbunong* predicts the future life of the couple on the basis of this interpretation.

After the *manbunong*'s words to the couple, the host family slices meat from the pig and boils it in plain water. When the meat is cooked, it is placed in a basin for the offering of more prayer. The host family brings items, such as native blankets and clothing which their ancestors have used, coins, and *tapey*, and places the objects beside the offered meats. They also bring entrails of the animal and place them by the *manbunong*. This gesture is intended to invite the spirits to eat with them (Chidoro 1989).

The couple is told to remain at home for one or two days without doing any work outside. The new husband and wife are also advised to keep the embers in the fire burning throughout the second night of the *teteg*. It is believed that keeping the fire alive demonstrates respect in the solemnity of the ritual at the present; secondly, a fire that is kept smoldering from evening till morning signifies long life for the couple; thirdly, it is traditional; and lastly, it serves as a ready light for the spirits of the departed ancestors to kindle their tobacco pipes (Sacla 1987:45).

5.1.2 Tolo

Before the man and wife have their first baby, the next stage of ritual, *tolo*, is required. As mentioned in preceding pages, the word *tolo* means three and requires the butchering of three pigs or other animals. These animals are provided by parents of the couple, but if the parents are short on finances, neighbors and immediate relatives help with resources they have, bringing *tapey* (rice wine), *camote* (sweet potato), rice and *gabi* (native food) and firewood. Rituals are performed in the couple's front yard area.

5.1.2.1 Preparation

The preparation of rituals starts with caution. *Tolo* is prepared with the pounding of rice for *tapey*. People in the community come to the host's house to lend a hand. Since this activity is not ordinary but sacred, they are told to be quiet and careful in their conversation. Helping neighbors are told not to babble, throw things, or engage in any unnecessary activities, for it is inauspicious to contaminate the dwelling with imprudent attitudes (Cadangan 1989).

After pounding, people cook the pulverized rice. The cooked rice is placed in the winnower and mixed with yeast. Then, they cover it with banana leaves and set it to stand overnight. The next day the fermented rice is placed in a *koli* or *sopon* (native jar), wherein it is left for further fermentation.

Lastly, they procure sacrificial animals. This includes catching, roping and tying animals from the host's grazing herds. The host family selects animals out of its livestock, raised by the hosts themselves or by their parents. In selection, they look carefully at both size and color, since an animal must be perfect and black.

5.1.2.2 Procedure

Ritual performance takes place at the first quarter of the moon. The host has by now prepared everything for the celebration (Sacla 1987:46). Close relatives, neighbors, and friends are invited to this event. Those who are invited are regarded as honored and privileged. This is also a great occasion for socializing. After most guests appear, the host starts butchering the animals.

Ritual starts with drawing a cup of *tapey* (rice wine) from the *koli* (jar), which is then handed to the parents of the couple. The parents recite the *madmand* (prayer) for offering up the *tapey* to departed *Ap-apo* (ancestors) to come and partake and watch over the ritual celebration.

The prayer in the Kankana-ey version goes:

Umali kayo ay nankatekatey y ap-apo mi,
Umali kayo ay ama ya en ina,
Umali kayo ta enyo ela-en nan anak yo ay nan an-anito
Ta nowada di pankulangan mi ya enyo itonton,
tan dayayo di nan pelti-peltik ed naba-on;
Ela-en yo pay ta magay mabangbang-ag ya man-
ib-ibaw tan nay ang-gay ay ma-peltikan kayo
An nan-kapo-an ya nankatey ay ap-apo;
No waday nalabsan si ga-it yo yan man-asi-aya-ayag kayo
An nan-kapo-an ya nankatey ay ap-apo;
No waday nalabsan si ga-it yo yan man-asi-aya-ayag kayo
Elan yo ta adi mabang-ag nan babalo ay manginom sinan tapey ko (Sacla 1987:46).

The English translation reads:

Come our dear ancestors (invoke the names),
Come father and mother (invoke the names),
Come to witness your children who are going to have a feast of *an-anito*
That if we overlooked some ritual procedures,
We beg you to guide us because you were the performers
of this rice wine offering in the past.
If still, there are other spirits to be mentioned that were missed,
Please call them and advise them not to cause evil to the young
Who are going to partake in drinking this wine.

After the prayer, the pig offering is placed at the center of the performers' yard. Before goring it, two cups of wine, piles of native blankets, garments and coins (preferably the Mexican coins or the old peso coins called *palata*), all contained in the *liga-o* (winnower), are set beside the pig, and the *manbunong* offers them to dead ancestors (*Ap-apo* or *Kakading*) (Igualdo 1989:182).

The prayer that the *manbunong* offers is as follows (Kankana-ey version):

Dakayo ay ap-apo mi ay mangon-ona ay immey (names of dead ancestors),
Dakayo abe ay ama ya ina mi ay en-mey (name of dead parents);
Umali kayo tan nayman-bay-yog din anak yo,
tan nay maikadingan kayo;
Mo wada et di kulang mis na ay Mambunong
bunong ed naba-on;
Elan yo et pay ta mo waday dad-an di na-aya-ayagan
si mapteng ya et ipayag yo sinan ba-ey di nan-sida ta egas-gasat da;
Mo law-lawa yan padagasen yo ed adikaila, ta mankaka-an da;
Ilabalab-ak da pay di lawlawa ya igasat da et si lagbo,
pakan, ya sama, ta wada od di
kai-ngadnga-danan yo ay enme-enmey.

The English translation reads:

To you dead ancestors of long long age (invoke names),
to you our parents (invoke parents of both sides)
Please come because your children who will have a feast,
As that which you offered in this *kadingan* ritual,
So if we, the priests overlooked some ritual
procedures, we beg of you to guide us because
you have performed these prayers before,
We pray that if the invited guests have brought along
some good omen, please leave such good omen in favor of the hosts,
Again, we ask you that if these omens may mean bad luck,
Stop it from coming and instead pass it away to nowhere;
We pray further that any bad omen brought to this
occasion be covered up, by your power, and that
the good will prevail in order that the hosts
Will be lucky in their work, animal and food pursuits,
so that there will be something
For you ancestors to be remembered by (Igualdo 1989:184-185).

When the prayer is finished, the *manbunong* gores the pig with a sharp *iwik* (woodstick). A pointed stick goes through from the side of one foreleg to the center of the heart. While the pig is dying, the *manbunong* and village elders observe omens and signs according to whether or not the pig screams severely in spite of repeated piercing. This omen is referred to the elders and the *mankotom* to see if it has any meaning. The hosts should plan for another ritual if the omen is bad. Additional pigs are required for that.

The pig is singed over the fire and then washed. It is sliced, and the *stey* (liver) is first brought to the *manbunong* and elders to see if its shape is good or bad. Any abnormalities, for instance, *sip-el* (two biles) in the liver, many pockets or many parts, mean good luck, which necessitates another butchering of a big pig as a sign of thanksgiving to the spirits of the dead ancestors and the gods and goddesses.

The pig is sliced into small pieces and cooked in the *langking* (pot). When it is cooked, the pieces of meat are placed in containers in the yard with rice and *tapey*. The *manbunong* calls for the spirits of dead ancestors (*Anito*) and the gods to partake of the food. A separate food offering is given to the spirits of those who have died by accidents, war, suicide, drowning, lightning and other catastrophes or accidents.

The next step to perform is dancing with instruments. Players beat gongs and slap drums, a few pairs of dancers called *mantayaw*, dance with old and native blankets. The purpose of this dance is to honor the ancestors of the celebrating family. In the middle of dancing, wishes are shouted by a village elder. Elders of the village sing in the form of *kulibas* (riddle), *etek* (praise), *solog* (humor), *daydo* (monologue), *alibay* (conversation), and so on. During this activity, wine is continually served to performers and participants (Sacla 1987:50).

The varied instruments, such as *gangsa, pinsak, takik,* and *solibao* (see Wilson 1961:230-233), produce unique and interesting sounds. The sounds make people feel that they are participants in the celebration. Players and dancers are rotated continually. Participants and village people display the moods of excitement expressed in the music.

Such a ritual is an act of worship (Mowinckel 1967:15) to mysterious beings, spirits of varied types. Worship in ritual form thus consists of sacrifices, prayer, chanting, and dancing (Vanoverbergh 1972:73). Relationship with the gods and wishes of Kankana-eys are established through such solemn activity. The above description of one ritual suggests how the Kankana-eys are subject to spirit beings. The people must bring their felt needs to the gods in the form of worship and in living before their presence (Berger 1980:60-62).

5.1.3 Potok

Potok is a special ritual conducted for the pleasure of dead relatives, with the expectation of their blessing upon the couple. For this ritual, only one pig is required. The ritual is performed with singing and dancing, then the offering of animals. Dancing begins in the first stage of the ritual. The *manbunong* directs the gong players to begin to play. Deceased relatives are invited to dance prior to any other dance being performed. The Kankana-eys believe that celestial bodies are made present by invitation, and that they dance as a way of participating in celebration. Instruments are played a long while, until the *manbunong* gives a signal to pause. Then elders, relatives, friends and guests of the couple and their parents are invited to dance. When the dance is over, the chanting of the *bay-yog* (Kankana-ey ballad) is pronounced to invoke the power of the *Kabunyan* and the other gods and goddesses, a way of praising them for their ingenuity and prowess. Chanting with singing is concluded by imploring the *Kabunyan* to give the hosts a prosperous long life, wealth, and a flourishing progeny and blessing for the entire community.

5.1.4 Dasadas

After the completion of a new house, the couple engages in the ritual known as *dasadas,* an expression of thanksgiving to gods and ancestors. The celebration starts with the *manbunong* holding a mother hen and a cup of rice wine. He looks up to the eastern sky, facing the sun, to call for the living spirits of the owners of the house (the couple) to come and occupy the new home. This supplication is followed by the offering of the pig to the ancestors inviting them to come down from the sky. The *manbunong* wishes in his *bunong* (prayer) that if the occupants of the new house get rich, they will perform even greater rituals to honor their ancestors and the *Kabunyan* for blessings. Then a pig is butchered and the entrails of the pig are observed.

The cooked meat and wine are offered to the spirits of dead ancestors (*Anito*). After this procedure attendants are served with foods. The old men remain until the evening, drinking wine and singing the *bal-iw,* which is a native ritual song, to invoke the help and blessing of dead ancestors and all benevolent spirits. Further blessings for good health and an enjoyable life are requested addressed to those who have performed this ritual before.

5.1.5 Liyaw

Rites accompany every phase of the mountain people's agricultural year, from the preparation of the seedbeds through the sowing of the seeds, from the transplanting of seedlings, and danger from worms and drought, to harvesting and storing the yields in the granary (Scott 1969:145). For dead ancestors (spirits) have influence over rain, planting, seed time, first fruits, and other matters (Steyne 1992:84).

Farmers perform the ritual called *liyaw* in hopes of securing blessing upon their harvest. The Kankana-eys believe that the *Kabunyan* have power to control the success or failure of crops. This ritual is popularly practiced during planting and harvesting seasons. It is also conducted when the house of a farmer or a farm itself is struck by lightning. The elders usually interpret such catastrophes as the wrath of the *Kabunyan*. In order to allay any further anger of the *Kabunyan*, the elders advise the owner of house to perform the ritual.

This ritual requires a chicken as a sacrificial animal. The farmers believe that a chicken is sufficient for gaining the spirits' protection against crop infestation until the harvesting season comes.

The *manbunong* first of all, searches for the help of the spirits dwelling within the vicinity of the farms (Sacla 1987:87). The ritual starts with a long prayer and the chanting of the *manbunong*. This chant is a form of ballad, mentioning first of all the many achievements and activities of the twelve gods and the twelve goddesses. The form of prayer expressed is used to supplicate deities for protection and to keep the farm production bountiful (Vicente 1991). In the meantime, the chicken is slowly beaten with a thin stick until it dies. As it nears its death, the *manbunong* continues his prayer and chanting, addressing the two gods, *Lumawig* and *Kabigat*, then addressing all the gods and goddesses, asking them to accomplish the particular wishes.

5.1.6 Benat

Benat is a ritual performed for different purposes and goals: irrigation projects, hunting, gold mining, cockfighting, and so on. As previously mentioned, the Kankana-eys believe that luck comes from deities in response to properly performed designated rituals directed by the priest. The Kankana-eys perceive spirits as controllers of natural resources and bringers of luck and fortune with such resources. The ritual ensures future blessing.

For instance, people in the community or a group of individuals who have a common interest in economic advancement through setting up irrigation projects or pulling more water into an irrigation canal, perform the *benat* ritual.

The elders have a right to designate the day for this ritual performance. The price for purchasing the sacrificial animal(s) is collected by the people in the community. The ritual starts with the prayer of the *manbunong* inviting the *Kabuyan* to come down. Wishes are presented in the form of prayer and chanting. After offering a long prayer, a sacrificial animal is butchered by the people who originally planned the irrigation project. When a pig is butchered, the entrails are examined according to custom. The *manbunong* and elders carefully go through the process of examining the bile and liver. As usual, perfect bile is mandatory;

if it is found to be otherwise, another pig should be killed, and inspection goes on until a pig without defect is found. The meat of the pig is then cut into small pieces and boiled. Cooked meat is offered to the *Kabunyan*, with another set of prayers of the *manbunong*. An entire community attends the ritual performance and participates in the procedure of the ritual. The people join together to invoke the guidance and blessing of the deities on their project. After irrigation is successfully set up and water flows smoothly, the community performs the *benat* ritual again to honor and give thanks to the *Kabunyan* (Inio 1991).

The Kankana-eys trust that their wishes and blessings will be realized through the *manbunong's* proper appeal to the gods and ancestors. They submit to the deities' power to bless and bring good luck upon their lives. The Kankana-eys' every activity is complete only insofar as deities are involved through means of the appropriate ritual performance. Thus, the ritual supplies a meaningful avenue by which the deities are encountered and persuaded to meet the people's needs.

5.2 The Healing Rituals

This section introduces variations on healing rituals and their procedures.

5.2.1 Bay-yog

The *mansip-ok* analyzes information from the sick. If, for instance, the sick person has had bad dreams or signs and omens before becoming ill, the *mansip-ok* affirms that these are causes of illness (Inio 1987). Spirits of dead brothers or sisters are believed to communicate through these means. The *mansip-ok* gets into further analysis and suggests that dead spirits need blankets, clothes, garments, food and animals. The sick person and the family have to meet these needs. The *mansip-ok* also prescribes specific ritual for healing.

The *bay-yog* is one such healing ritual that may be prescribed. The *bay-yog* is derived from the term for the ballad which is chanted in the *bay-yog* ritual. This ritual is performed in a three-part series, including the *kadingan*, the *bay-yog* ballad chant, and the *awang* or *sinoni*. It requires playing native instruments, the *gangsa*, *pinsak*, *takik* and *solibao*, as well as the preparation of ceremonial native blankets, such as the *kuwabaw*, *dil-li*, *pinagpagan*, *tinuwang*, *alad-dang*, *bandala*, *baya-ong*, and *kuba* (g-string). At any rate, the ritual cannot begin if any items are lacking for the spirit beings (Pacyaya 1970:134-135).

The ritual *kadingan* starts with the *bunong* (prayer) and the calling upon *Apapo* (one of the spirits) by the *manbunong*, with the *tapey* (rice wine) as a channel to contact the spirits. The *manbunong* appeals to the dead ancestors of the ritual performer and pleads with the *Kabunyan* to come down from the sky world to partake of the *tapey* and bless the ritual as well as the celebrants.

After the ritual, everybody eats a meal provided by the host. The chanting of the *bay-yog* starts either at night or early the next morning, following the *kadingan*. The *bay-yog* chant starts with the offering of a chicken to the ancestors. The chicken is slowly whipped on the wings and on the neck, until it dies; then, it is singed over the fire. It is cut into small pieces, cooked and served. Then chanting continues with music, the *bay-yog* chanted by the elders and *manbunong*. The *manbunong* holds a young reed shoot called *bel-lang*, or a sugarcane shoot, and directs the singing of the *bay-yog* by moving the *bel-lang's* end. From time to time the tail of the reed is soaked in a cup of *tapey* (called *binagawas*). The same series is repeated until the *bay-yog* chanters finish chanting. The chanting of the *bay-yog* usually lasts for three or more hours, depending upon the tempo at which the chanters sing it and upon how the ritual is performed.

There are numerous spirits to whom the *bay-yog* ballad is offered: ten male gods, *Pati, Lumawig, Kabigat, Gatan, Ballitoc, Suyan, Amduyan, Kalan, Wigan,* and *Lopis*; ten female gods, *Bangan, Bugan, Pe-ey, Yaping, Lingan, Ubbang, Angban, Angtan, Apinan,* and *Daungan*. Chanting is offered to male and female spirits, acknowledging their achievements and exploits, to generate healing power on behalf of the sick person (Igualdo 1989:196). In the *bay-yog* ritual, music with chanting thus plays a significant role in terms of presenting the need for healing.

The chanting to male and female gods is as follows.

Pati (a representative of male gods):

Ginmosad kanos Pati;
Ay banos di kadangyan.
O-oso boliyas yo tan siya;
A-ay inbayad yo si namba;
Inbayas da-lin yo;
O-oso bintawan yo ay mapat-a;
A-ay baliwang yo ay li-nombo,
A-ay baboy yo ay en-melyap.
A-ay san manok yo ay ganak yo,
A-ay sawas esa.

English translation:

Pati came down;
The remnant of the rich and the progenitor of the mighty.
He came down with pigs, your pigs;
The offspring of which are our pigs;
Which you used to pay the person

Who entrusted the pigs to you.
Yes, your fire is brightly lighted;
Now, your yard is warmed with embers;
Your pigs are gone
Your chickens and other stock are gone too;
This is the eleventh.

Bangan (a representative of female gods):

Ginmosad kanos Bangan;
Bangan ed langilangan;
Nay nan-galey si alad-dang;
Ay nangalad-dang tan baknang iman;
Engosad nay maoakan, ay baboy yo.
O-oso boliyas yo etay onmo;
Yay o-oyo ay dal-lin yo;
A-ay baliwang yo, ay sin kabiga-higat yo si mapat-a.
A-ay et baliwang yo ay linombo;
O-oy pay san manok yo ay ganak yo;
O-oy sawas esa;
Ay naktiban san sama yo;
Entengnin di buma-ey ay nan-an-anito.

English translation:

It is said that *Bangan* came down;
bangan from *langilangan* (sky),
Wearing an *alad-dang* blanket because she is rich and mighty;
She came down with stocks of pigs;
Such offsprings are your pigs,
The hosts' stock is given;
Yes, your fire is brightly lit,
From your yard you came out to work in the morning,
You find your yard is warmed with embers;
Your pigs are gone;
Your chickens and stock is gone;
Yes, this is the eleventh;
The fruits of your labors are no more (Igualdo 1989:197-198).

By way of final comment, it may be noted that M. Delson (1990:71) states that Filipinos develop patriotism and national solidarity through the study of the typical Filipino dances and songs, and mountain people, in general, like to show their unique qualities in dances. This affects the beliefs and practice related to rituals and ceremonies (Monroe 1987:220). According to Carino (1988:152), "the animal sacrifices and the dances are expressions of the Igorot's (mountain people) recognition of the need to submit himself (any worldly property) to all-important spirits and gods."

5.2.2 Dipat

Dipat is a ritual aimed to appease an ancestor who has caused sickness. Such affliction may come upon one who, for example, has performed ritual in the past with a single animal, not the requisite pair (Certain rituals require butchering animals in pairs, male and female. When they are taken to the skyworld, they will multiply). If mistakes have been made in this regard, another ritual readily suffices.

In one instance, a sick woman may be bathed by a family member. This signifies an imminent death. Then the sick woman is brought to a female *mansip-ok* (priest). The *mansip-ok,* after hearing from the sick one, says, "Your ancestor in the third ascendant generation performed this ritual. In this ritual, a female and male carabao were to be offered. While a female carabao was the only available sacrificial offering at that time, the ritual was not performed according to conditions requiring a pair of sacrificial offerings to be butchered..." (see Sacla 1987:77-78). The ritual on behalf of the sick descendent is then performed with strict adherence to the wishes of the ancestors' spirits. In this ritual, playing gongs and the *solibao* (instrument for ritual) is prohibited. No native dance is held; only the drinking of *tapey* (ricewine) or commercial drinks is allowed.

A pair of animals is butchered according to the wishes of certain deceased ancestors. Since the purpose of performing this ritual is for comfort and soothing the ancestors' spirits in order to bring the healing of the afflicted, detailed observation of animals' entrails is requisite, in order to detect any omen. The Kankana-eys believe that the performer's ancestors come down for the completion of this offering. G. Rheenen (1991:185) states that the only way dead ancestors can tell their wishes and communicate with the living is by causing such illness and misfortune, or by other similar evil means.

The distinctive phenomenon recurrently revealed in the discussion of rituals is that the spiritual beings favor animals. It seems that a ritual cannot be completed without sacrificing animals. The Chinese hold the same notion for their rites (Wee 1977:34). However, exception is made for poor Kankana-eys who cannot, by any means, afford a sacrifice; then simple prayers are accepted (Vanoverbergh 1953:70).

Healing is expected to occur in response to fulfilling the requests of ancestors by offering a pair of designated animals under the order and direction of the medium, *mansip-ok.*

5.2.3 Pakde

Pakde is performed by a community. The primary purpose of conducting this ritual in the community setting, rather than in an individual one, is to consolidate the people to deter spirits who cause death in a family. Death may spread among people in the community if they do not take measures to prevent such an eventuation.

At the start of what is to be *pakde*, the elders in the village promptly detect current life-threatening phenomena and consult with the priest(s). The host family for the ritual is to be the one which has lost a family member; the same family is responsible for preparing the prescribed animal(s), according to the direction of the priest(s). The selected pig is brought by the host family to a spot where the ritual is to be performed. Wide space is desired to accommodate an entire community, for all the people are expected to participate in the ritual.

The *manbunong* carefully observes the bile and liver of the pig to search for signs and omens. If any defect is in the liver or the bile, another butchering is demanded. This condition applies until the desired bile is found. Until the perfect bile is obtained, one or two members of the family have to oversee this procedure no matter how long it lasts. However, each family member brings a basket of cooked *camote* (sweet potato), rice and soup to eat, for when eating times come.

After the perfect bile is found, half of the pig is cut into small pieces, as in other rituals and cooked, whereas the other half is kept uncooked. Then it is offered to inflicted spirits to soothe their anger. As discussed in the first chapter of this study, the spirits which inflict and cause death usually ask for food, and any lack of sacrificial offering raises the ire of these spirits, who will turn violent and malevolent. There is no chanting, singing, or praying as in some other rituals; but rather, solemn moments are spent waiting for the spirits to come down to partake of the food.

One unusual feature of this ritual is that each family who attends the ritual is given sliced cooked and uncooked meat when returning to their dwelling places. The sliced meat is counted by the *mankotom* beforehand. If there is a piece missing or an extra piece left over from the original counting and distribution, it is reported to the *mankotom* who then declares that the ritual has not been performed in a perfect manner, so another ritual must be performed. The cost of the pigs for this ritual is divided equally among the family heads of the community and collected money is given to the host family.

5.2.4 Bosal-lan

Bosal-lan is a ritual for a normal person who all of sudden has lost his or her sense of hearing, without any noticeable cause. In this case, the older people believe that the affliction is the result of spirits causing deafness. The immediate advice is to conduct *bosal-lan*. In this ritual, first of all, the *manbunong* constructs a replica of a small hut, about one foot wide and a foot high, within the vicinity of the victim's parents' house. Then the *manbunong*, who has shared power with the spirits (Wiber 1989:58), performs the ritual beside this little hut by offering a chicken to appease the deaf-causing spirit. The *manbunong* persuades the spirit to get out of the ear and to transfer to the newly constructed hut which is a better dwelling place for him or her. As the *manbunong* says the prayer, he or she simultaneously plucks wing feathers out of the chicken and puts them inside the small hut for the spirit to follow (Igualdo 1989:231). After this procedure, the chicken is singed, sliced, cooked and eaten.

5.2.5 Maksil/Dawdawak

A few hours after a woman gives birth two rituals are supposed to be performed. One is performed indoors, the other is performed outdoors. The first ritual, performed inside the house of the woman, is called *maksil*; the second is *dawdawak* performed for restoration of health to the mother.

The *maksil* is performed to welcome a newly born member of the family and for him or her to grow in good health. The *manbunong* stakes a *bolo* (big knife) on a log. He beats the *bolo* to produces sound as musical accompaniment to prayer. Simultaneously a chicken is sacrificed. The sound produced out of the *bolo* signifies that when the baby grows up, he or she will have sweet talk like music, which will be pleasant to hear (Sacla 1987:65).

The sacrificed chicken is cooked and eaten by the elders in the village. The elders who eat the meat have to have lived exemplary lives. When the child grows up, he or she, it is hoped, will live a life as worthy as that of the elders so honored.

Dawdawak is conducted outside the house. Another chicken is selected as the ritual sacrifice. When it is killed and offered to the *Kabunyan*, a prayer for quick recovery of the mother and baby is intoned by the *manbunong* (Sacla 1987:65-66). Long prayer is the highlight of this ritual.

In the Kankana-ey perception, invisible malevolent spirits are bound to cause disease and physical suffering (Scott 1969:113), but when the expected rite is performed as a means of soothing them, healing takes place. Thus, the sick are taught to follow ritual precisely, as prescribed by the priest. M. Wiber (1989:48) sees two categories of Kankana-ey ritual: involuntary ritual which includes curing sickness inflicted by a spirit or by ancestral spirits who demand certain rituals; and voluntary rituals, which cover marriage ceremonies, harvests, healing, and irrigation. It is apparent that the Kankana-eys truly believe in the healing power of deities. Under this belief, they practice rituals when needs arise. The Kankana-eys' faith is practiced in performance of the ritual.

5.3 Data Analysis: Ritual Practices

The four analyses – domain, taxonomic, componential, and theme – will be employed here again with respect to ritual. The analyses will address two primary categories: thanksgiving and healing.

5.3.1 Domain Analysis

I examined notes on my observations of ritual practices to determine relevant domains. I found eleven cover terms. Through discussion about ritual practices and based on my own participant observation of rituals, I noted the existence of many rituals applicable to various occasions. They seemed to be intended to meet divergent felt needs. Ritual performance clearly played a prominent part in all aspects of Kankana-ey life. Such were my conclusions after attending a number of the rituals.

A native Kankana-ey informed me that, in point of fact, ritual practice is the most meaningful and valuable activity in Kankana-ey life. Ritual and community involvement are integral and indispensable, because through this activity and only through this activity can people encounter the spiritual beings which are relied upon to meet needs as they arise.

Domain analysis as summarized in Table 8 indicates the various rituals practiced by the Kanakna-eys for any number of given occasions. Table 9 indicates the occasions of ritual.

5.3.2 Taxonomic Analysis

I examined the connection between the two domains (domain and taxonomy) and drew up taxonomies according to my personal understanding of ritual categories. While I constructed taxonomies, I referred back to the domain analysis and to the section of "ritual practice" in order to make further classifications. This effort was designed to ensure validity and accuracy of the taxonomies.

Included Terms	Semantic Relationship	Cover Term
Teteg		
Tolo		
Potok		
Dasadas		
Liyaw		
Benat	is a kind of	ritual
Bay-yog		
Dipat		
Pakde		
Bosal-lan		
Maksil/Dawdawak		

Table 8: Domains of Rituals

Included Terms	Semantic Relationship	Cover Term
Wedding		
Before the first baby is born		
For the pleasure of the dead (expecting blessing)		
After completion of a new house		
Irrigation		
Hunting		
Gold and mining		
Blessing upon harvest	is a kind of	occasion for ritual
To appease an ancestor		
Means of communication of dead brothers and sisters		
To deter afflicting spirits		
For recovering sense of hearing		
After giving birth		

Table 9: Domains of Occasion for Ritual

As an outsider of the culture, I approached the rituals with a set of questions: How are the ritual practices valued? What do the rituals mean to the Kankana-eys? I assumed that the rituals' chief significance was to be found in the fact that, through them, the Kankana-eys maintained relationship with spiritual beings (gods and deceased ancestors). As previously noted, the Kankana-eys believe that spirit beings are not transcendent or removed from human spheres of activity but, rather, they are immanent, close to living human beings. The spirit beings are seen as wanting to associate with living family members and kin. Spirit beings thus approach the living in various ways, whenever they have certain wishes for or expectations of their families. Their means of communicating or getting attention include dreams, causing sickness, omens, and signs. One informant shared with me her own experience. She once had a serious illness without a known cause. She and her family went to the priest to find the cause. The priest diagnosed the illness as one caused by a deceased ancestor who needed clothes and food. Only the priest had the right gift. Performing ritual was prescribed as the only way of fulfilling the ancestor's desire.

Spirit beings not only wish for and demand what they need from their family, but they also want to bless and meet the needs of the family. Spirit beings are believed to obtain power to do so. For instance, the Kankana-eys perform several rituals from the beginning of planting to harvest time. They believe that blessing comes from spirit beings. Thus, my answer to the questions raised above is that ritual performance has a great value in functioning to maintaining intimate relationships with spiritual beings and in securing and meeting felt needs in order to be on the good side of the spirits' power.

My next question was, What sort of value do the Kankana-eys as insiders derive from ritual practices? My answer to this question is based on reading, as well as on my own interaction among and conversation with native people. The Kankana-eys vest the ritual performance with a number of meanings and values. Ritual is deemed essential: 1) to cure sickness, 2) to bring luck and blessings in terms of wealth, family or bountiful harvest, 3) to share one's wealth and blessings with the members of the family and community, and 4) to ward off evil (Casino 1992b:2). It is nearly always believed that, with the performance of ritual, the participants will not face miseries and sickness, but will instead have long life and riches, because of what the *Kabunyan* secure.

A third question asks what impact ritual practices have on other aspects of Kankana-ey life. A few primary sources suggest that the ritual practices reinforce the Kankana-ey perceptions of the universe as being not merely physical but also spiritual in form. Continual communication with spiritual beings of the "other" world establishes socioeconomic, political and religious life for the Kankana-eys.

I have experienced with the Kankana-eys that their life is not as easy as that of other dwellers in the mountains. Every effort is made to till the land for produce, and all energy is invested to reap its bounty. The indigenous concept of the spirit beings does not legitimate the use of a farm tractor to till the land which the *Kabunyan* have given since time immemorial. This doctrine is believed to have been taught by *Kabunyan* (1992:105). When the land produces good crops and harvest, it is interpreted as in line with the cosmic order. When the harvest is poor and pests have eaten the crops, this event is interpreted as the result of chaos in the cosmos. The Kankana-eys find that "human reality is intertwined not only with the creatures of the natural-environment but also with the beings of the suprahuman realm" (Lua 1984:15). Ritual practice is a significant means to the end of a blessed harvest, which is a key to determining their economic situation.

There is further impact on social structure. It is commonly understood among different tribal people, for example, that elite farmers tend to gain their status through commercial activities that are also dependent on repeated ritual. Their local status is firmly rooted in their success in commercial activities. Despite the enormous economic pressure on less-well-off villagers, ritual performance by elite farmers is increased to enhance their status. One importance of this ritual is thus, its role in retaining the elite farmers' status in the community (Russell 1989: 33-34).

The Kankana-eys believe that political institutions and community leadership (see Tabora 1978:494-515) are divine in origin, and were once introduced by gods, *Lumawig* or *Kabunyan* (Scott 1988:97). When the community needs to select a leader, ritual performance is, accordingly, mandatory.

As the above analysis suggests, religion permeates all facets of Kankana-ey life. Ritual practices serve as a basis of an indigenous world-construction and identity formation (Casino 1992a:104). I have observed from both native people and readings that the Kankana-eys also use ritual instruments which are symbolic and meaningful. Specific instruments include cloths or blankets, musical instruments, and jars for rice wine. Dancers for ritual performances wear a native blanket used by a deceased ancestor during his or her earthly life. The rationale is that the dead ancestor is cold and hungry, so ritual hosts express their concern for the ancestor's comfort. A male dancer drapes one blanket over both shoulders as musical instruments are played. A female dancer wraps a blanket around her body. She dances with a hop-and-skip rhythm while the man's arms are stretched horizontally upwards, diagonally, forward and backward. The musical instruments for ritual performance have sacred meaning. These instruments include *gangsa, pinsak, takik* and a pair of *solibao* (drums). A village elder prohibits playing these instruments at any other time, either at home or elsewhere. The kankana-eys have internalized reverence for the instruments as sacred and set aside for use only in appropriate rituals. They believe that, just by the sound of *gangsa*, spirits gather around. So if such sound happens without any ritual, spirits will be offended and will inflict sickness and misfortunes not only upon the players but upon the community as a whole. Thus, these instruments are safeguarded by their owners and brought out only when they are needed. Not all the Kankana-eys are allowed to play these instruments, but only a few rich people and those who frequently perform rituals. Instruments can, however, be borrowed by neighbors. Ritual jars for rice wine are inherited from deceased parents or ancestors. Other jars bought and sold in the market can be used for various purposes. But the jars used for rituals are sacred and kept separate from other jars.

The broad category of thanksgiving ritual includes rituals for blessing harvest, weddings, new houses, irrigation, hunting, gold mining, and first-born babies. Thanksgiving also serves the purpose of expressing gratitude to spiritual beings in response to their protection and guidance. In the other category, healing ritual is performed in response to various illnesses – whether they are diagnosed as being caused by ancestors or natural causes. The Kankana-eys believe that performing healing ritual is the only means by which to secure complete healing.

The taxonomic analysis illustrated by Figure 4 indicates which rituals belong to each of the two major categories.

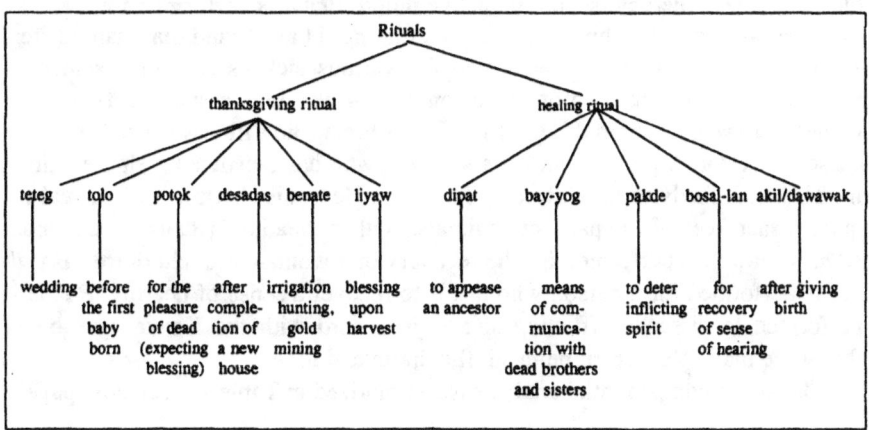

Figure 4: Taxonomy of Ritual

5.3.3 Componential Analysis

In componential analysis, the goal is to contrast data. I referred to the domains of the rituals as a guide to identifying components of meaning in the dimension of contrast.

According to my interview with the native Kankana-eys, these rituals serve as vehicles through which both individuals and community are able to experience healings and blessings.

I learned through my participation in their rituals that, when the Kankana-eys celebrate thanks or expectation of blessing, such as for weddings, they perform the ritual *teteg*. *Tolo* is held before a first baby is born to a married couple, who as new parents expect a healthy baby to be born. *Potok* is intended to give pleasure to the dead and is exercised with an expectation of abundant blessing. *Dasadas* is performed after the completion of a new house. It anticipates particular spirit beings' blessing upon and protection of the house. In this ritual, the *manbunong* holds a mother hen and a cup of rice wine, looks up to sky, and calls for the spirits of the house owners to come and occupy the new home. *Liyaw* is performed in preparation of seedbeds and throughout the growing season, including harvest. The Kankana-eys' profound desire is for the spirit beings to bless them and, thereby, secure their livelihood. *Benat* is performed for the sake of successful irrigation, hunting, and gold mining. I have found that many different rituals for healing are performed for various sicknesses. For instance, if someone is made sick by a dream or omen (for example, a snake gets into the home), *bay-yog* is required. *Dipat* is a ritual for healing illness caused by a deceased ancestor. A person who gets sick and who has sacrificed a single animal in the past is likely to be viewed as having made a mistake, for much ritual requires sacrifice of a pair of animals. Other healing rituals (e.g., *maksil/dawdawak*), is performed for the recovery of a woman after childbirth. *Bosallan* is performed for a person who needs to recover a sense of hearing. *Pakde* is performed to dissuade afflicting spirits, in accord with the Kankana-ey belief that some malevolent spirit beings inflict harm and illness.

The above componential analysis is summarized in Table 10 (see next page).

5.3.4 Theme Analysis

In the final stage of analysis, (i.e., theme analysis), I asked the following question: What connections become apparent in the analysis of the diverse domains of ritual practices? In this analysis a theme did emerge. On the basis of the preceding discussion, tables and figures, I have contrasted the inventory of cover terms, with an eye to finding one theme which spans the data. Through analysis of the divergent cover terms of the domains, the following major theme emerged: "In order to experience healing and to receive blessing, ritual practices of healing and thanksgiving are required."

Means End (X is a way to Y)	Dimensions of Contrast	
Domain	Thanksgiving	Healing
Wedding	Teteg	
To deter inflicting spirits		Pakde
Before the first baby's birth	Tolo	
For the pleasure of dead	Potok	
After completion of a new house	Dasadas	
Irrigation	Benat	
To appease an ancestor		Dipat
Blessing upon harvest	Liyaw	
Means of communication		Bay-yog
Hunting and gold and mining	Benat	
After giving birth		Makil/dawawak
For recovering sense of hearing		Bosal-lan

Table 10: Componential Analysis: Rituals

Componential analysis confirms that the many Kankana-ey rituals fall into two basic categories – healing and thanksgiving. Healing rituals are intended for curing illnesses, and thanksgiving rituals are performed in expectation of or in gratitude for receiving blessings in various aspects of Kankana-ey life.

In summary, the Kankana-eys interact with spirit beings on a daily basis. Spirit beings manifest power on various occasions and in various situations. Spirit beings function to resolve problems arising in Kankana-ey affairs. The roles of priests are important, for priests mediate between the Kankana-eys and deities. Without the priests' assistance, there is no access nor approach to spirit beings. Priestly ability and power to communicate with deities are gifts from spirits. Ritual practice is frequently performed according to people's needs. When they need blessing from deities, thanksgiving ritual is offered. They also perform such ritual for different occasions of thanks. For the Kankana-eys, spirit beings are absolute beings who obtain power to resolve daily problems of the living Kankana-eys.

Part III

Theological Foundation

Chapter 5

Three Encounters

The previous sections (Parts I and II) dealt with two aspects: historical and anthropological. The historical survey traced the works of the major Christian groups and the Assemblies of God. The Kankana-ey people and culture were studied from an anthropological perspective. As described in Chapter 3, the Assemblies of God established its ministry among the Kankana-ey people with a strong emphasis on the power element of God. The power was the key element to penetrate the hearts of people. Chapter 4 discussed religious practices of the Kankana-ey tribal people. They perform rituals for occasions such as thanksgiving and healing. They seek to have their needs met through ritual performances. They perceive spirit beings as possessing power to fulfill the wishes of human beings.

Now, Part III will deal with "the principalities and the powers" and "power encounter." The former will discuss the various forms of dark powers and will focus on power leading to truth and allegiance encounters. After converting from darkness to the light, people grow in the knowledge of God's truth and in Christian maturity. The latter will deal with the power encounter from a biblical perspective; how God revealed his power among his people. The purpose of this study on the role of encounters is to share the gospel effectively with knowledge of God's power gained from a biblical perspective. It is necessary to study "power" in devising an appropriate contextualization of the gospel among the Kankana-eys.

1. Power Encounter

1.1 Dark Powers

The terms "principalities" and "powers" commonly were used in religious settings during the time of Paul. Paul states that powers exist in high places and in the air, or atmosphere, around us (Eph. 3:10). According to James F. Cobble (1988:15), the "powers" were created as aids of the purposes of God in his work over creation, providing structure for life to acquire meaning and order. However, these powers became hostile to God, regulating human existence under the status of gods. The principalities and powers now govern life. Paul says that the reign of death (Rom. 5:14, 17) is a manifestation of the rule and control of sin (Rom. 5:12). Death is thus inescapable, not only for humanity, but for all of creation.

Paul states in Ephesians, "For our struggle is not against flesh and blood, but against the rulers, against the authorities, against the powers of this dark world and against the spiritual forces of evil in the heavenly realms" (6:12). He refers to "principalities" and "powers" to rule, authority, thrones, lordship, world rulers of darkness, the spiritual hosts of evil in the heavenlies, and the authority of darkness. These biblically defined realities of sin and death operate not only in living organisms, but also in structures, institutions, and systems. They are further referred to in Satan and evil.

1.2 Fallen Angels

In Genesis 6:1-4, the ancient myth of the fall of the "sons of God" explains the existence of evil that emanates, not from humanity, but from something higher: not from the divine, but transcendent, suprahuman realms opposed to God and human faithfulness, seeking destruction, damnation, illness, and death. One interpretation of the passage is that defecting angels procreated and bore giants who were drowned in the flood; their spirits live on as demons, evil spirits, or "the powers of Mastema." The angels' leader is variously called Semjaza (*1 Enoch* 6:3; 8:3; 9:7; 10:11), Azazel (*1 Enoch* 8:1; 9:6; 10:4), Mastema (*Jubilees* 10:7; 11:5; 17:16; 19:9), Satan (*Jubilees* 10:11; 23:29; 40:9), and Belial (*Jubilees* 1:20; 15:33) (Wink 1992:23-24). An allusion to the myth of the fallen angels appears in Psalm 82:6-7; "You are gods, you are all sons of the Most High; But you will die like mere men (human beings), and you will fall like every other *ruler*" (LXX αρχοντον). It is also alluded in 1 Corinthians 6:3; 11:10; Jude 6; and 2 Peter 2:4.

In at least some views it may be said that the world sought redemption from these powers. "Deliver me from the hands of evil spirits who have dominion over the thoughts of men's hearts, and let them not lead me astray from thee, my God," cried Abraham for himself and all who, through him, would subsequently believe (*Jubilee* 12:20; 1:20; *1 Enoch* 8:4; 9:2-3) (Wink 1992:24-25). 1 John 3:8 declares, "The reason the Son of God appeared was to destroy the devil's work."

Jesus regards his healings and exorcisms as an attack on the Kingdom of Satan and an indication of the Kingdom of God breaking in (Mt. 12:28; Lk. 11:20; Mk. 3:22-30). Thus, the gospel is concerned with a cosmic battle in which Jesus delivers humanity from the dominion of evil powers.

1.3 Demonic Power

J. McDowell and D. Stewart (1982:47-49) denote characteristics and activities of demons depicted in the Bible: they are spirits without bodies (Eph. 6:12); they are numerous (Mk. 5:8, 9); they are organized (Mt. 12:24); they have supernatural power (Rev. 16:14); they are allowed to roam the earth and to torment people (Mt. 12:43-45); they can inflict sickness (Mt. 9:32-33); they can posses or control animals (Mk. 5:13) and human beings (Lk. 5:12); they do oppose God's people (Eph. 6:12); they do attempt to destroy Christ's Kingdom (1 Pet. 5:8); they know that Jesus Christ is God (Mk. 1:23, 24). They are seen as disembodied spirits with total control over the possessed. Demons exert power in various human activities and in other phenomena. Their aim is to destroy and conquer the world, but God promises to judge demons at the last judgment (2 Pet. 2:4).

1.4 Satan

Paul defines Satan as the personified leader of the powers. Satan is a supernatural being; although limited in power, he is still greatly effective in fulfilling his malicious purpose (Simpson 1990:117). Satan is called "the devil" (Eph. 6:11), "Belial" (2 Cor. 6:15), "the evil one" (2 Thes. 2:3), "the tempter" (1 Thes. 3:5), "the serpent" (2 Cor. 11:3), "the god of this world" (2 Cor. 4:4), and "the ruler of the kingdom of the air" (Eph. 2:2).

According to Henry Chadwick (1971:49), the word "Satan" is purely a Semitic word, meaning, "to oppose" or "to be an adversary." As stated above, "Satan" refers to the personified ruler of evil (Zec. 3:1; Job. 1 and 2; 1 Ch. 21:1). Some passages regarding Satan (the adversary) are found in the Old Testament. In 1 Samuel 29:4, we read, "Send the man back, that he may return to the place to which you have assigned him; he shall not go down with us to battle, lest in the battle he become an adversary (Satan) to us." First Kings 5:4 says, "But now the Lord my God has given me rest on every side; there is no adversary (Satan) or disaster." Numbers 22:22 notes, ". . . the angel of the Lord stood in the road to oppose him (Satan)."

Satan is understood as an enemy but, in further detail, as an enemy with respect to the law, the adversary raised up against Solomon (1 Ki. 11:14). The role of Satan is also exercised as prosecutor in the heavenly court. Furthermore, Satan can be sent to carry out the purposes of God.

1.5 Spiritual Warfare

In Ephesians 1:3, Christians are said to be blessed "in Christ with every spiritual blessing in the heavenly places"; in 2:6, Christians are described as already raised up with Christ and made to "seated us with him in the heavenly realms. . . ." These passages imply that "the heavenlies" is a sphere in which Christians, with one foot in each of two worlds, already experience the risen life in Christ. It is understood that "the heavenlies" are a dimension of reality into which believers have already, while on earth, been admitted, yet in which unredeemed powers still exercise dominion and must be fought with (Wink 1992:90). Satan tempts humans to sin, brings oppression, and renders people demonized. S. Malek expounds on this warfare:

> Satan does not calmly watch the demise of his Kingdom. He intimidates Christians who attack his domain. He spreads fear, a morbid preoccupation with weakness, and an unwholesome attitude of deferential humility. He utilizes all means available to counterattack his assailants (1991:191).

According to Paul, heaven is integrally implicated in this present evil age, and war in heaven and war on earth will continue until the final victory of God brings the new heaven and new earth (Eph. 1:4, 18, 21; 2:7; 4:30; 5:16, 27; 6:8). However, Christians already experience the powers of the new age at the present in union with Christ, and use them to fight against evil. Satanic power can be defeated only by the power of Christ who has won victory over the powers, in the cross.

2. Truth Encounter

Charles Kraft (1991b:4, 9) postulates that any power behind a power demonstration must be true power, not an impostor. Knowing truth from a scriptural point of view has a relational rather than an intellectual basis. Knowledge of truth is an instrument through which understanding is brought about. Knowledge and scriptural understanding are relational and experiential. The truth encounter, thus, is basically a personal encounter, not merely a matter of words and or cognition.

2.1 God as Source of Truth

God has been revealed as the ultimate source of truth. In the Old Testament God spoke his words to his prophets and servants in different events and so it was manifested. His people experienced the truth of a reliable God, and the true God worked through power encounters. This following section accordingly explores personal experiences of truth encounters as revealed in the Old Testament.

2.1.1 Victory of Hezekiah

Second Kings 19:1-35 speaks about Hezekiah's fervent prayer and his anxiety about the threat of Sennacherib. The Assyrian king caused Hezekiah to be disheartened so that he tore his clothes and put on sackcloth and went into the temple of the Lord. Putting on sackcloth was a common way of expressing repentance, remorse and despair. So Hezekiah dramatically expressed his enormous disappointment (Hobbs 1985:274).

Isaiah's distinctive role as a prophet is also stressed here. Isaiah intervened in the matter just described and lifted up the king's soul by pronouncing the response given from Yahweh: "Do not be afraid" (v. 6). The first statement of Isaiah was reassurance that God would be on the king's side. Verses 5-7 say,

> Isaiah said to them, tell your master, this is what the Lord says: Do not be afraid of what you have heard – those words with which the underlings of the king of Assyria have blasphemed me. Listen! I am going to put such a spirit in him that when he hears a certain report, he will return to his own country, and there I will have him cut down with the sword.

In alignment with the prophecy of Isaiah, the Lord answered Hezekiah's prayer (v. 20). The response of God to Hezekiah's plea was positive. God spoke his will against Sennacherib. For the faithful Yahweh, nothing other than Yahweh was ever to lay claim to his people's allegiance. The word of God was straightforward in reaction to the false claim. Sennacherib failed in his attempt to take Jerusalem. Yahweh appeared as Protector and true God who keeps his word to his servant.

2.1.2 Victory of Elijah

First Kings 18:34-38 tells about the people of God who confused the God of Israel with Baal. Yahweh was their ancestral God, yet they could not tell Elijah which god really was God. The obstacle was the strong influence of the Baal religion among the Israelites. Thus, Elijah attempted to prove who was indeed the living God. Elijah's prayer in vv. 36-37 had two purposes: 1) to proclaim Yahweh as truly God in Israel; and 2) to attest Elijah as his true servant. Further action of Elijah led to the contest between Yahweh and Baal, by which means Yahweh's true and authorized prophet was authenticated. Elijah was struggling, because the people had doubted his authority. Therefore, Elijah claimed, "If Yahweh is God, follow him; if Baal, follow him."

Part of Elijah's demonstration was intended to say that belief in truth must produce an action (Devries 1985:230). The contest was arranged by Elijah's initiative. Elijah was the only one of the Lord's prophets left, while Baal had four hundred fifty prophets. The true God was to respond by igniting the sacrifice on the altar. "Get two bulls for us. Let them choose one for themselves, and let them cut it into pieces and put it on the wood but not set fire to it. I will prepare the other bull and put it on the wood but not set fire to it. Then you call on the name of the Lord. The god who answers by fire, he is God" (vv. 23-24). Such was Elijah's challenge.

Fire was the power which legitimated the sacrifice. Here the issue was sharp because both Baal and Yahweh claimed to rule over power of fire (for Yahweh, Gen. 15, 19; Ex. 3, 19; Jud. 6, 13; Amos 1:4, 7, 10, 12, 14). Early Israel believed not in a theoretical but in a practical monotheism which meant to them, "the god who answers by fire is God." The issue was to be left entirely up to the rival gods. The outcome would finally eliminate the confusion of the people of Israel (Devries 1985:228).

The result of the competition between Yahweh and Baal was decisive. The Baalists took practically the whole day crying out to their god. Yet hardly any time elapsed in response Elijah's call to Yahweh (vv. 25-29). As a result, Baal suffered a major defeat (v. 29). All the people who watched the fire acknowledged that "Yahweh is God" (v. 39).

Through this contest, the Israelites were renewed in the truth that Yahweh was the living and true God whose power far exceeds that of Baal. They acknowledged the authority of Elijah who proclaimed the truth of God. Through this tremendous experience, their faltering faith was strengthened.

2.2 Christ as Exemplar of Truth

Jesus says in John 14:6-7, "I am the way and the truth and the life. No one comes to the Father except through me. If you really knew me, you would know my Father as well . . ." Jesus proclaimed Himself as the truth and promised freedom in this truth. John 8:32 says, "you will know the truth, and the truth will set you free." Kraft (1991a:12) comments that Jesus sought to involve experiential and relational components of his truth at nearly all moments of healing, casting out demons, and performing miracles.

2.2.1 The Man with Leprosy

On Jesus' approach to a Galilee one time, a man came along who was covered with leprosy (Lk. 5:12-13). Leprosy was one of the most dreaded diseases. Two kinds of leprosy were found in Palestine. One was simply a bad skin disease, whereas the other started with the aggravation of a small spot and ate away the flesh until the victim was left with only a stump of a hand or leg. Lepers were isolated from society. They lived in caves or tombs. They were not allowed to come nearer than one hundred feet from a well person. When anyone approached, the leper was required to give warning, calling "Unclean!" The affliction was also regarded as coming as a consequence of sin. People believed that the leprosy could be cured only by God (Hobbs 1966:100).

This man with the worst of the two types of leprosy approached Jesus for healing. He addressed Jesus as Lord and knelt down before him, asking the Lord to make him clean: "When he saw Jesus, he fell with his face to the ground and begged him, 'Lord, if you are willing, you can make me clean.' Jesus reached out his hand and touched the man. 'I am willing,' he said. 'Be clean!' And immediately the leprosy left him" (Lk. 5:12-13).

At the word of Jesus the leper was healed. The man not only was healed, but he was saved, as was signified in his becoming "clean." Life came through Jesus. The Son fulfilled what the Father was to fulfill through Himself. So Jesus further claimed elsewhere, "I tell you the truth . . . Yes, to your amazement he will show him even greater things than these. For just as the Father raises the dead and gives them life, even so the Son gives life to whom he is pleased to give it" (Jn. 5:19-20). Jesus lived an exemplary life in power and in fulfilling truth.

2.2.2 Overcoming Satan in the Wilderness

It seems to be a common experience for Christians to endure testing and temptation in the world. Jesus was no exception. Right after he was anointed with the Spirit for the ministry, he had to confront evil (Mt. 4:1-11). The attack of the devil in the wilderness was intended to overthrow the Messiah at the opening of his public work as the Savior of the world. If Jesus was fully conscious of his Messiahship after being baptized, then surely he knew what was waiting for him in the wilderness, for Jesus' particular task given from the Father was "to destroy the works of the devil." Indeed, the second Adam, Jesus, withstood the temptation, whereas the first Adam failed (Plummer 1953:35).

Jesus suffered three specific temptations of the evil one: 1) "If you are the Son of God, tell these stones to become bread" (v. 3) ; 2) "If you are the Son of God, throw yourself down" (v. 5) ; and, 3) "All this I will give you, if you bow down and worship me" (v. 8). He cast off the temptation of the evil one by the word of power. He proved that the ultimate source for overcoming evil was the Lord God.

Jesus himself exemplified how to conquer temptation with the word of truth. Jesus displayed his own power, with the purpose of teaching and bringing hearers to the saving knowledge of Christ. The primary function of the truth encounter, similarly, is to enable people to gain information to be able to correctly interpret events (power to disclose, or other related powers) and to bear witness of the Savior Jesus Christ.

2.3 Truth Encounter in the Book of Acts

In the Book of Acts, most truth encounters are based on a previous knowledge of the Scriptures, and the truth is manifested by witness to Christ. Acts 6:8 recounts the persecution of Stephen by the Jews. Stephen was filled with the power of the Holy Spirit and the wisdom of God's word to speak against his opponents. By an opposing plot, he was brought before the Sanhedrin (6:8, 10, 15). Stephen was full of knowledge of the Scriptures and was thereby able to speak persuasively of God's work and power and the presence of the Holy Spirit in whom he believed.

Paul likewise manifested the truth of God in Damascus. Acts 9:20-21 says, "At once he began to preach in the synagogues that Jesus is the Son of God. All those who heard him were astonished. . . ." Paul (Saul) exerted more and more effort to prove with the word of God that Jesus was the Christ. Paul preached to Jews, to mobs, to people in Caesarea and to Jewish leaders in various cities. He preached about Jesus Christ, invoking scriptural messages drawn from the Old Testament. He worked in Pisidian Antioch (13:14-42, 45-47, 50f), Thessalonica (17:1-3, 5-8), Athens (17:16-33), Corinth (18:1, 5f, 12f), Rome (28:17-29), and Caesarea (24:10-26; 25:23-26).

Prominent people of God experienced truth encounters in diverse situations. When they shared the living word, God's power was manifested. When truth was encountered with wisdom and knowledge, hearers were convicted and converted to Christ.

2.4 Freedom in Truth

The path to freedom is laid by believing the truth and walking according to faith. Faith should be practiced in following the truth; renouncing old ways – involvement with the occult, cults, and other religions, and forgiving and confessing sins (Anderson 1990:132, 148). The truth sets people free (Jn. 8:32; 16:13; 15, 17) from bondage of darkness and from Satanic captivity. People are thus healed (physically, emotionally, and otherwise) when they experience a truth encounter. The truth is unchanging and universal (Holmes 1977:31). The truth is found in an unalterable logical structure of what is ultimately real. The truth, in many respects, transcends temporal and transient human thought patterns. God's truth remains forever unchanging. This unchanging truth gives people freedom when they believe and obey it.

2.5 Role of Truth

First Timothy 4:6, 13 describes the "good minister of Christ Jesus," that is, the one who is "brought up in the truths of the faith and of the good teaching." This definition implies that sound teaching brings people to spiritual maturity. This same part of 1 Timothy says, "some will abandon the faith and follow deceiving spirits and things taught by demons" (v. 1) which come through hypocritical liars. Subtle spiritual attack will confound the unaware. The motive of Satan is to dismantle and destroy the believers' faith. Adam and Eve fell into temptation by way of a partial truth. In order to stand firm in Christ, believers have to grow in the truth.

In 2 Corinthians 4:4, we read, "The god of this age has blinded the minds of unbelievers, so that they cannot see the light of the gospel of the glory of Christ." Evil spirits try to prevent people from coming to Christ and to distort their hearing of the word of God.

However, Jesus demonstrated right teaching of the Word of God. Luke 4:14-15 notes, "Jesus returned to Galilee in the power of the Spirit" after being tempted in the wilderness. This text hints not only at his works of power to be displayed, but also of the words of power that would come from the lips of Jesus who would teach in the synagogue (Packer 1993:209). Luke cites Jesus as identifying himself with the prophetic word of Isaiah:

> The Spirit of the Lord is on me, because he has anointed me to preach good news to the poor. He has sent me to proclaim freedom and recovery of sight for the blind, to release the oppressed, to proclaim the year of the Lord's favor (4:18-19).

Good news is accompanied by the work of the Holy Spirit in the depths of the life of the hearer. The ultimate task for all Christians is to bring to the world this truth (Eph. 1:13). In witnessing of Christ, God's Word, which is empowered by the work of the Spirit, is the key to its own success.

2.6 Process of Truth Encounter

Teaching is a key vehicle for interpreting powerful truth. The truth encounter plays the role of providing an overall context within which other understanding takes place. Jesus continually sought to bring hearers to an understanding of the plan of God (Kraft 1995:39). The Spirit is the agent of aid in leading people into this truth (Jn. 16:13).

Jesus leads his hearers in their involvement with him, from an initial awareness and then onto building an understanding of the truth through communicating knowledge. A power exhibition is indeed not significant unless it fosters accurate understanding of the Truth who is the Source of that power (Kraft 1995:39-40). Truth and power must always be united, because the truth of the gospel and the power of it come from the same Jesus Christ (Well 1987:67). J. Wimber and K. Springer (1991:9) postulate that "when experience of God is separated from knowledge about God, people fall into various errors: Eastern mysticism, pantheism, even the occult." When knowledge is neglected, erroneous interpretations corrupt the intent of the Lord.

Truth encounter is primary for initial allegiance to God and for developing relationship with God, which then grows into maturity in a life-long process. Allegiance is tightly associated with truth, and it is contextualized within the truth encounter.

Start		Process		Aim
Awareness	→	Leading in knowledge	→	Understanding of Truth

Figure 5: Truth Encounter (Kraft 1995:40)

3. Allegiance Encounter

Of the three encounters, allegiance is the most important, for "without allegiance to Christ, there is no spiritual life" (Kraft 1991a:9). Allegiance requires entire submission to the will of God after one turns toward Jesus and away from what is evil in the world. This is the lesson of Paul and his companions, who brought many souls to God, as is indicated in the Book of Acts. When they arrived in Philippi, for example, a woman named Lydia and some other hearers were converted and baptized (Acts 16:11-15). Hearers of the gospel gave over their allegiance after having a truth encounter. The sign of their allegiance was baptism and multiplication in their lives of other legitimate and sincere disciples.

3.1 Darkness to Light

It is necessary for hearers to be aware of the fact that there are two kingdoms, not of equal strength: God's Kingdom and that of evil. Ezekiel 28 and Isaish 14 clearly draw distinctions between the two kingdoms and between what is involved in submitting to either one. Gospel bearers need to present a message of good news by way of indicating that converting to Christ means moving from darkness to light, giving up allegiance to evil and committing allegiance to God. E. Nida and W. Smalley (1959:63) make the same point: "there can be a definite move away from basic mistrust of an irresponsible spirit world to a confidence in an eternal, loving and just God." A. Tippett (1975:484) says that neither the animist nor anyone else should be allowed to drift into Christianity. The passage from animism to biblical faith is to be a definite clear-cut act, a specific change of life, a "coming out of something," and an "entry into something" quite different.

When people accept Christ, their motivation must be considered and dealt with. Motivation for conversion colors one's view of Christianity, one's reception of the gospel, and one's new, Christian sense of responsibility (Tippett 1975:849). Often times people "accept" Christ as Lord and Savior in a manner deemed consistent with conversion, but they do not give their hearts in complete allegiance to God.

John 8:12 says, "I am the light of the world. Whoever follows me will never walk in darkness, but will have the light of life." Jesus is light (Jn. 1:5) and the light shines in the darkness. When people are brought in Christ, they no longer belong to darkness but to the light (Eph. 5:8). "Light" marks the one who has made a new allegiance to Christ.

3.2 Worldview Change

Jesus challenged believers to change their worldview when they followed him. He said, "You have heard that it was said, love your neighbor and hate your enemies. But I tell you: love your enemies and pray for those who persecute you ... if someone strikes you on the right cheek, turn to him the other also" (Mt. 5:39, 43, 44). Whereas, people tend to naturally to seek their own needs and profit. Jesus taught, "seek first his kingdom and his righteousness, and all these things will be given to you as well" (Mt. 6:33).

C. Kraft (1994:22) writes of planting the seeds for change at the deep worldview level, noting that such reorientation requires practice in an integrated Christian life. If followers believe in the word but do not practice belief in their lives, they remain in the old life.

Paul posed a challenge to Philemon (Col. 4:1) who used to be a slave owner before becoming a Christian. Paul knew that Philemon was concerned about how to treat a runaway slave. Paul's advice was to accept the slave back, but to recognize him as a Christian. This advice pressed Philemon in the direction of a worldview change, which inevitably would issue in a difficult change of habit and life practice. Followers of Christ are all expected to change basic values and perspectives. Conversion requires change in both worldview and behavior.

3.3 Growth in Faith

Spiritual growth and personal transformation involve growth in faith. In Colossians 1:10, Paul says that a life lived fully pleasing to God is one that is continually "growing in the knowledge of God." Growth in faith and obedience builds on our intellectual grasp of Christian belief (Wimber and Springer 1991:5). Allegiance to God goes hand-in-hand with faith. K. Kantzer and C. Henry (1990:34) stress that faith is "relational" as well as "rational." Since faith is "relational," it must be conjoined in "practice." Any disjunction between faith and practice generates hypocrisy.

Paul was delighted with believers in Colosse who put their faith in Christ Jesus and demonstrated love for all the saints (Col. 1:3).

Paul, in Colossians 1:5-6, remarks on,

> ... the faith and love that spring from the hope that is stored up for you in heaven and that you have already heard about in the word of truth, the gospel that has come to you. All over the world this gospel is bearing fruit and growing, just as it has been doing among you since the day you heard it and understood God's grace in all its truth.

In an Old Testament example, we may recall that God recognized David as a man after his own heart, one who would "do everything I want him to do" (Acts 13:22). David obeyed God in practice, demonstrating that faith is a matter of what we do (Jas. 2:18, 26; 3:13). Romans 2:13 says, the righteous are "not those who hear the law," but "those who obey the law."

Believers need to have a relationship with God in intimacy: trust, dependence, giving ourselves fully to God, and personal encounter (Jn. 17:3). Jesus says that to really "know" the truth is not just to believe it, but to "obey" it, practicing in faith.

3.4 Maturity

Spiritual growth is a process. According to 2 Corinthians 3:18, believers continually are being transformed "into his likeness with ever-increasing glory." Paul says that baby Christians need one type of spiritual food – milk – but mature Christians need solid food (1 Cor. 3:2; Heb. 5:12-13). These will continue to be the needs of Christ's own until his Second Coming (1 Cor. 15:35-58). Mature Christians keep increasing in maturity.

Jesus did not treat God's will as something vague. Mature Christians look for the specific will of God. Emphasis in this regard should be on the way of life. John 6:38-40 quotes Jesus as saying,

> For I have come down from heaven, not to do my own will, but the will of him who sent me; and this is the will of him who sent me, that I should lose nothing of all that he has given me, but raise it up at the last day. For this is the will of my Father, that everyone who sees the Son and believes in him should have eternal life; and I will raise him up at the last day.

To discover the will of God, believers must personally encounter the living Christ. This encounter is not based on a blueprint for living. It does, however, require that Christians be enlightened about a way of life which is embodied in Christ and empowered by the Spirit. James F. Cobble elaborates:

> The knowledge of God's will is to be used to lead a life worthy of the Lord. Knowledge must be translated into and manifested by good works. Kingdom values and commitments characterize this new life which is based on a lifestyle that bears fruit in every good deed. Knowledge and action yoked together manifest God's will through good deeds (1988:58).

The will of God becomes clarified through the process of transformation. God became a human being not simply to produce better people of the old kind but to make a new kind of people. His intention was to transform human beings. Our own transformation involves both study of the Scriptures and participation in the life of the church. Daily decisions and commitments increasingly are to reflect growth toward Christian maturity as defined in the New Testament.

3.5 Commitment

The Old Testament notion of life is that human beings and the world are God's creations, and the human beings find satisfaction only in total allegiance to and dependence upon God. People in Israel are thus required to live based on a covenant relationship with God, or in other words, to commit themselves to God. Then God who redeems his people's life heals their diseases and satisfies their desires with good things (Ps. 103:3-5). God promises to give his people long life (Ps. 34:12) along with salvation (Ps. 91:16). In short, life and prosperity can be achieved if the people of God carefully follow his commands. Thus, it was important for the Israelites to keep the covenant, even as God keeps his promise: "if you pay attention to these laws and are careful to follow them, then the Lord your God will keep his covenant of love with you, as he swore to your forefathers. He will bless the fruit of your womb, the crops of your land ..." (Deu. 7:12-13).

The New Testament sees Jesus as setting the standard for our commitment. When Jesus faced death, he prayed, "Father, if you are willing, take this cup from me; yet not my will, but yours be done" (Lk. 22:42). C. Kraft (1991b:261) sees allegiance to Christ, by way of a commitment encounter, as the defining feature of the Christian church. "Jesus sought to lead people into the most important encounter, the commitment encounter," for the clear reason that "only a commitment to God through Christ really saves."

J. Moltmann makes another comment worth quoting here:

> The name of church gives itself - the church of Jesus Christ – requires us to see Christ as the subject of his church and to bring the church's life into alignment with him. Thus ecclesiology can only be developed from christology, as its consequence and in correspondence with it.
>
> But on the other hand the history of the Christian faith since its beginnings in the New Testament shows that the titles given to Christ, in which the churches express their faith and their hope, are historically conditioned, varies from time to time and change in substance ... (1977:66).

Individual Christians and churches must fully avow allegiance to Christ in order to receive the salvation of Christ. A further task, beyond being saved, is bringing the gospel to the lost, which is the ultimate goal of the church. The apostles in Acts (1:7-8) were committed to carrying out their commission assigned by Jesus. They made solid allegiance to God by obedience.

4. Relationship of the Three Encounters

Each encounter has its own role, but interaction of the three encounters is also needed. Power encounter frees from the bondage of darkness. It serves as a catalyst for people who are interested but have not yet experienced salvation. Teaching is a reliable means for undergirding understanding of what power encounter means and further to help converts develop a relationship with God. Allegiance encounter is indispensable to the Christian at any stage of maturity in experiencing power and truth.

4.1 Integration

Jesus displayed his power demonstrations within teaching contexts, rather than merely performing them without reference to his teaching. Teaching is a matter of transmitting knowledge and truth. Those who are converted to Christ are required to encounter truth both in relationship with the other two encounters, as well as in continual experiences through which they move toward maturity in Christ.

Experiential truth has to be centered in a relationship with Christ. This encounter plays the vital role of interpreting both of the other two encounters (Kraft 1991a:3). This relationship involves a constant experience of God's power to and personal touch. Truth and power of God together bring freedom in all aspects of life, ministry, and allegiance.

4.2 Interworkings of the Three Encounters

The three basic encounters should interwork with one another as Christians grow. Each helps to sustain growth and assurance. A diagramming of the interworkings of three is seen in Figure 6.

Each stage indicates a different aspect of the process and its own result is distinctive. In the first stage, after being freed, people make a commitment to God. In the second stage, through teaching, people grow in knowledge and develop in relationship with him. In the third stage, the role of people who have grown in truth and God is to witness to those at the first stage as well as to those who do not yet know Jesus Christ. None of the three encounters can be neglected along the Christian journey toward vitality and maturity. By these means and their display in believers' pilgrimages, God's people deepen their relationship with God and with others.

	Start	Need	Process	Result
	Satanic captivity	Freedom to understand	Power encounter	
Stage I	Ignorance/error	Enough understanding	Truth encounter	Commitment to Jesus
	Non-Christ – making allegiance	Challenge to commit to Jesus	Allegiance encounter	
		Spiritual warfare to provide protection, healing, blessing, deliverance		
Stage II	Commitment to Jesus	Teaching	Truth encounter	Growing relationship to God and his people
		Challenge to greater commitment and obedience	Allegiance encounter	Witness to those at the beginning of stages of Christianity
		Authoritative prayer	Power encounter	
Stage III	Growing in relationship to God and his people	Teaching	Truth encounter	Witness to those at the beginning of stages of Christianity
		Challenges to commitment	Allegiance encounter	

Figure 6: Interworkings of the Three Encounters (Kraft 1991a:13)

In summary, it is noted that Christians experience spiritual warfare as they live in this world. Dark power rules the world and attempts to fail believers. But those who come to Jesus Christ experience God's power enabling them to overcome the power of the principalities. People who have been converted to Christianity not only experience God's power but also grow in truth. God is the source of truth, and Christ is the exemplar of truth. There is liberty in truth. The truth makes people free from the bondage of sin and from Satanic power. People experience healing (physical, emotional, and otherwise) through truth encounter. People who come to the Lord pledge their allegiance to God. It is a commitment that they will not return to old religions and a traditional belief system. As they live according to his Word and will, they continue grow in Christian maturity.

Chapter 6

Power Encounters in Scripture

Christians are commissioned to be witnesses of Jesus Christ. Good news of salvation is the primary message of Christianity. Being a witness is a critical matter in the Kingdom of God, as the Lord Himself has demonstrated (Mt. 28:19; Mk. 16:15). The same commission was given to the Israelites – that is, they were to be light for the Gentiles (Isa. 42:6). They were assigned the task of letting the Gentiles know God. This is one reason why God frequently demonstrated his power in the history of Israel.

One can simply state that to evangelize is to communicate or proclaim the good news. In further analysis one realizes that sharing the gospel involves three encounters: power, truth, and allegiance. In order to effectively evangelize, the dynamics of these encounters should be recognized and employed. Sobhi Malek (1991:181) states that the Spirit of God acts in power through the gospel, while the Christian witness proclaims the gospel and seeks to honor Christ's name, acting on God's promises. The power of Christ is manifested through answers to immediate needs. Signs and wonders confirm the word of God and authenticate the witness. Demonstration of the power of God may help people to take a step of faith toward Christ and ultimately bring them to allegiance to God. Christians should practice engagement in these three encounters throughout their Christian lives.

1. Manifestation of Power of God in the Old Testament

God manifested his power among the ancient Israelites. He revealed His power on different occasions and in diverse situations: healing, war, punishment, and life and death.

1.1 Healing

The power of healing took place through the intercession of a servant of God, and it appeared as an outcome of repentance of people who had committed sin (Num. 12, 21:4-9, 2 Ki. 5, 1 Ki. 13:4). An individual's earnest and faithful prayer might also lead to physical healing (2 Ki. 20:3). Various passages in the books of the Old Testament give accounts of healing.

1.1.1 Naaman's Cure

In 2 Kings 5 is an account of a power demonstration by the prophet Elisha. One intention of this passage seems to focus on the issue of whether or not Elisha would heal the sick, thus making known a prophet's capabilities. The story retells the lesson of Naaman's rage against what he perceived as the prophet's humiliating order, noting how rage-turned-to-acquiescence benefited the patient and led to his healing (Hobbs 1985:58).

Naaman is described as being a valiant warrior but an unfortunate leper. According to T. R. Hobbs (1985:63), Naaman's disease was a skin disease and resulted in whiteness of his flesh. It was dryness of the skin tissues which modern medicine has diagnosed as leprosy.

A young girl, who was a captive from Israel, served as an attendant for Naaman's wife. This little girl bore witness of a prophet in Samaria. She suggested going to Samaria for help with the critical condition. The girl appears in this story as a key witness who connects two persons for the unfolding of the word of God. Upon hearing news of the prophet, Naaman went to his king to report the testimony and to receive permission for a journey to Israel. The king's response was positive, and he sent a letter of introduction and request to the king of Israel (v. 5).

The reaction of the king of Israel was negative. He recognized his own inability to work a miracle of healing. However, Elisha got word of the incident and asked for Naaman to come to him. When Naaman came, he was offended by Elisha's suggested means of healing (v. 11). Elisha proposed that Naaman wash himself in the Jordan seven times, as a means of restoration and cleansing. Ritual washing in rivers such as the Jordan had its origin in the primitive worship of river gods in the ancient Near East. But none of the Semitic gods of healing is associated with water. In this context, water is a symbol for cleansing (Hobbs 1985:64-65). However, the symbolic act was misinterpreted as an insult and disgrace. Naaman thus was enraged at this ridiculous idea (v. 10).

This seems to have presented a moment of crisis, or of testing Naaman's faith. Naaman ultimately stepped out in the faith of obedience. As pronounced by Elisha, Naaman was completely healed after dipping himself in the Jordan seven times. The power of God was revealed in this work on behalf of Naaman. God's miracle seemed to be readily available when one exercised faith.

1.1.2 Snake Bite

Numbers 21:4-9 records a crisis which developed as a result of grumbling and complaining against God. Divine anger was roused and punishment was meted out, but the healing followed through the imploring prayer of God's servant.

The Israelites were exhausted and discouraged by the long journey around Edom. So they complained and spoke against God, questioning his purpose for them. Their complaint is noted in verses 5-6: "Why have you brought us up out of Egypt to die in the desert? There is no bread! There is no water! and we detest this miserable food!"[2] Grumbling against God met with the chastisement of fiery snakes. Scores of grumblers were killed by the snake bites. People trembled in the threat of this incident and reacted immediately by confessing their sin and human weakness. They sought the singular leadership of Moses, whom they could approach to request intercession, to seek for God's anger to stop and for healing to come. Moses, as the leader, responded to the people and beseeched God on behalf of his chosen ones. Moses' prayer resulted in obtaining a way of healing from God. The solution, fraught with salvific symbolism, was as follows: make a bronze snake. Those who looked at it would be cured, but those who did not were killed. These results occurred exactly as God had prescribed and pronounced them through Moses. Moses actually used a similar technique when he handled the calf incident in Exodus 32:1-35. Regarding the snake symbol, K. R. Joines (1968:245-256) argues that the background of the snake symbol is Canaanite, whereas H. H. Rowley (1939:113-141) proposed that the snake symbol refers to Nehushtan, the bronze serpent destroyed by Hezekiah (2 Ki. 18:4).

From the New Testament vantage point we see similarities between the crucifixion and the glancing at the brass snake. Both means of salvation display divine power which is exercised on behalf of an undeserving people who God, nevertheless, wills to save according to their response to his plan.

1.2 War

A prominent theme of Israel's national formation and security was that "God fought for Israel" (Hamlin 1983:95). Vivid accounts of God's fighting are found in the book Exodus. God showed his mighty power to rescue his people from Pharaoh. God's mighty intervention was needed because the king of Egypt would not otherwise relinquish his grasp on the Lord's people (Ex. 3:19). The

---

2 Quotations are taken from *New International Version*.

words, "God fought for Israel," mark a long series of interventions of God's absolute power on behalf of his people.

1.2.1 Fall of Jericho

Having been confirmed and fortified in the covenant with God, as memorialized in the observance of Passover, Joshua committed himself to persevere in the land of Canaan (Jos. 5:10) (Keil and Delitzsch 1950:61). The town of Jericho was encompassed by the strong wall erected to withstand any foe approaching from the east (Jos. 6:1).

Joshua 6 records a strange method of Yahweh's conquering Jericho. There were armed men, seven priests blowing rams' horns, the ark, and the rear guard. These were the instruments used for destroying the city. God instructed the people to circle Jericho each day, seven times on the seventh day. Chapter 6 mentions the ark nine times (vv. 9-15). The ark is presented as the presence of God Himself in the midst of his people. This element of the story recounts Yahweh's presence and how passive were God's people. It seems that God sometimes insisted on bypassing his people's activity in order to enhance His own glory among them. His ordinary pattern was to work through the instrumentality of his people.

Yet, throughout the history of the Israelites it was God who fought for his people. The people of God were rescued and were empowered to overcome their enemies by the overwhelming power of God, not the strength of humans (2 Ch. 4:7).

1.2.2 Battle with Canaan

In yet another text, Judges 4:1-15, a testimony of victory through God's divine power is set forth. This story is about Israel fighting with Canaan. Canaan is pictured as a strong nation with a strong military (Cundall 1968:88). The Israelites were, for a long period of time, cruelly oppressed by Canaanites. Severe persecutions of Canaanites eventually caused the Israelites to cry out to the Lord (Jud. 1-3). The courageous judge Deborah, the woman who led Israel in this period, decided to act by engaging Canaan in battle. Deborah commanded Barak, son of Abinoam, to take ten thousand men of Naphtali and Zebulun and lead them to Mount Tabor. An intriguing element of this narrative is the human conspiracy combined with God's plan. According to Deborah, God said, "I will lure Sisera, the commander of Jabin's amry, with his chariots and his troops to the Kishon River and give him into your hands" (v. 7).

Deborah significantly demonstrated faith, courage and wit, all of which enabled success. She assured herself and Barak that God would lead the victory. Deborah commanded Barak, "Go! this is the day the Lord has given Sisera into your hands. Has not the Lord gone ahead of you." In accord with Deborah's prophecy, God indeed, routed Sisera, the commander of Jabin's army of Canaan, and all his chariots and army. Sisera abandoned his chariot and fled away on foot (vv. 14-15).

Deborah's spiritual leadership prevailed in the course of this battle with Caanan. She, besides assuring people of God's power, used human wisdom as a means to victory. God was with his people and fought for them with his mighty power.

1.3 Punishment

One distinctive means employed by God for divine punishment was catastrophe. Occasionally, such a punishment was accompanied by an uproar in the order of creation (Zakovitch 1992: 47). Parties who received punishment were both individuals and groups, as a consequence of their part in improper cultic acts (Lev. 10:1-2; 2 Ch. 26:16-26; 2 Ki. 17:26) and for unintentional violations of sanctity (1 Sam. 6:19-21; 2 Sam. 6:6-9). Individuals who transgressed God's word were punished (Gen. 19:26; 1 Ki. 13:24-25, 28), as were groups that complained against God (Num. 11:1-3, 4-34).

1.3.1 Nabal's Death

In 1 Samuel 25:1-38 is presented background on a wealthy but arrogant man, Nabal, who died by being divinely stricken. Verse 3 describes Nabal "as churlish and ill-behaved." His name Nabal (fool) characterizes his attitude and behavior accurately. Nabal thought of himself as self-reliant and believed that "there was no God" (cf. Ps. 14:1), no neighbor, and no social implication for being. He did as he pleased. He neither feared nor respected any other, nor did he care for anyone (Bureggemann 1973:175). The same passage contrasts Nabal's personality with his wife Abigail, who was understanding and beautiful (v. 3). Abigail's tactful way with words had the power to alter bad situations. Nabal was "foolish" but Abigail was "wise" (1973:176).

The story of Nabal begins with David, a servant of God hearing that Nabal was in the vicinity to shear sheep. David sent messengers to him to ask for provisions. David's delegation of ten carried forth a respectful word from him. When David's people delivered the message, however, Nabal reacted negatively, as if he had never heard of David, even though God had anointed David through Samuel (v. 10). The "son of Jesse" title that Nabal used in reference to David was probably derogatory (Klein 1983:249).

When David heard of the rejection, by word of his messengers, he attempted to retaliate against Nabal. Upon hearing this, Abigail's wise action prevented David's revenge. She intended to save her husband's life and her wealth. Her wise word to David was pivotal in saving her household. Nevertheless Yahweh took vengeance into his hand on behalf of his servant David. God smote Nabal (v. 38), and David regarded the death as vindication for himself and his own restraint.

1.3.2 Catastrophes upon Egypt

Divine punishment by means of catastrophe is told in the narrative of Exodus 7-11. Moses and Aaron demanded that Pharaoh release the Hebrew people. Pharaoh rejected their request because his heart was hardened. In fact, part of this story was that God also made Pharaoh stubborn so God's miraculous signs and wonders would be displayed against the backdrop of the ungodly ruler (Ex. 7:3).

Exodus 9-11 tells of ten different plagues brought about by divine power. Whenever Pharaoh found his magicians able to mimic the wonders, he concluded that Aaron's activity was magical deception. It is intriguing, indeed, that the magicians of Egypt were as skillful as Moses and Aaron. God's last plague struck Pharaoh with a force which compelled release of the Israelites: "At midnight the Lord struck down all the firstborn in Egypt, from the firstborn of Pharaoh who sat on the throne to the firstborn of the prisoner..." (Ex. 12:29). "During the night Pharaoh summoned Moses and Aaron and said, 'Up, leave my people, you and the Israelites! Go, worship the Lord as you have requested'" (Ex. 12:31-32).

In a certain sense, Pharaoh had attempted to ascertain whether or not he had to obey the source of the power that was displayed by Aaron. So also he had called his magicians to replicate the signs (Jamieson 1945:296). However, Pharaoh eventually was forcefully persuaded to acknowledge the power of God, which surpassed the power of the magicians in Egypt. Through these horrific miracles of judgment, the God of Israel, through his ambassadors, proved his supreme power over all the gods of Egypt.

1.4 Life and Death

Some biblical miracles directly or indirectly link with life and death (Zakovitch 1992:852). The life-miracles are counted as an achievement of immortality (Enoch, Gen. 5:24; Elijah, 2 Ki. 2:11-12) and as revival of the dead (1 Ki. 17:17-24; 2 Ki. 4:32-37; 13:20-21). Thus, God proves he is capable of bringing forth new life. Another prominent biblical miracle is that barren wives bear children (Gen. 21:1-2; 25:21-26; 30:22-24; Jud. 13:2-24; 1 Sam. 1:11-20; 2 Ki. 4:14-17).

1.4.1 Elijah Taken up to Heaven

Second Kings 2 contains a pair of stories which attest to Elijah's ascension to heaven by the power of God; in conjunction with this event, Elisha is given the role of replacing his master Elijah (Hobbs 1985:15). It seems that significant parallels are drawn between the two. Further, Elisha is to succeed Elijah (v. 13), as Joshua was to succeed Moses (Num. 27:12-23). For example, Joshua was ordained by Moses and was "full of the spirit of wisdom" (Deu. 34:9); Elisha received a double portion of Elija's spirit. Joshua performed actions similar to those of Moses (Ex. 14; Jos. 3-4), and Elisha performed actions similar to those of Elijah (vv. 9-14).

What happened to Elijah is well described in 2 Kings 2:8, 11: "Elijah took his cloak, rolled it up and struck the water with it. The water divided to the right and to the left, and the two of them crossed over on dry ground . . . . As they were walking along and talking together, suddenly a chariot of fire and horses of fire appeared and separated the two of them, and Elijah went up to heaven in a whirlwind." At this scene, fifty men who most likely were prophets, stood at a distance and witnessed the spectacular moment of Elijah's ascension. One readily comprehends that, since Elijah was understood as a distinguished miracle performer in the works of divine power, the power of God was displayed within Elijah himself at the moment of his separating from the earth.

1.4.2 Birth and Revival of the Shunammite Woman's Son

Second Kings 4:8-10 draws attention to a Shunammite woman's hospitality for Elisha. It appears that she detained him, or "persuaded" him to stay in her place. Her hospitality to the servant of God ultimately worked to her own credit and brought her to a point of receiving God's blessing (Gray 1970:443-444).

As pronounced through Elisha, she became pregnant and the next year, about that same time, she gave birth to a son (v. 17). The son grew, but of a sudden he had a bad pain in his head and, sitting on his mother's lap, he died. She was in bitter distress. Her immediate decision was to bring him to the servant of God. Upon hearing this sad news from her, Elisha went into a room and shut the door. He stretched himself over the boy, matching him limb for limb. John Gray (1970:469, 497) has observed with others that this gesture was an unusual act in an attempt to retain the spirit of the boy. The boy miraculously revived. God's power was laid upon the boy through Elisha. Notably, Elisha had capabilities the equivalent of, or even greater than Moses and Elijah. Hobbs (1985:54) has remarked that this was, indeed, the most spectacular miracle on the part of Elisha. In order to experience such a miracle, there had to be a confluence of an act of faith believing in God and the ability of God's servant with the will and power of the God of Life.

2. Manifestation of Power of Christ in the Gospels

In the New Testament is shown how Jesus Christ established the reign of God through his ministry with accompanying signs of miracles. He was the One who came to demonstrate through power the fullness of God's sovereignty. With the power of the Spirit that descended on him during John's baptism, Jesus was vested with power to carry out a divine mission in fulfillment of God's promises (Lk. 4:18) (Remus 1992:862). Through this power, God's new reign was launched. Christ wondrously fed multitudes of hungry people (Mt. 14:15-21; Mk. 6:30-44; 8:1-9); walked on the water and stilled winds and waves (Mk. 6:45-51); he compelled Satan's forces to obey him (Mk. 1:23-26, 34; 3:11); and he raised Lazarus from the dead (Mk. 5:42; Lk. 8:56; Jn. 11:1-46). However, Jesus Christ was not merely a miracle worker. He had a messianic role to fulfill. In order to accomplish the task, he had to suffer and pay the price of death. Thus, Jesus Christ was God's promised Messiah (1992:863). So, Jesus Christ served two universally significant purposes. One was to demonstrate the reign of God and God's sovereignty through performing miracles among various people according to their needs. The other was to fulfill the messianic role through suffering and death.

The following sections deal with four different types of miracle accounts: healing the infirm, exorcising demoniacs, life and death miracles, and nature miracles.

2.1 Healing

Jesus employed his healing authority not for personal benefit but in his work as the servant of God. Matthew quotes Isaiah 53:4, saying, "he took our infirmities and carried our sorrows." This reference reminds readers that he used his power for the purpose of serving people (Mt. 20:28; 26:28) (Smith 1989:133). The Gospels attest the abundant healing ministry of Christ (Mk. 1:29-34, 40-42; 2:1-12; 3:1-6; Jn. 4:46-54; 9:17; Mt. 8:1-4; 12:9-13). Another purpose for the healing ministry of Christ seems to have been to bring people into the Kingdom of God. When people saw and experienced the power of healing, their attention was arrested and they were more likely to believe that Christ was who he claimed to be (Lk. 10:1-9).

2.1.1 Restoring a Centurion's Servant

Matthew 8:5-13 talks about the healing by Jesus of a centurion's servant in Capernaum. The centurion, a Roman officer, commanded a hundred men in a Roman legion. He was likely a Syrian Gentile in the service of Herod Antipas, stationed at Capernaum with a small garrison of troops because of its location as a border city (Gardner 1991:146). The servant of this centurion was terribly sick in bed. The centurion approached Jesus on behalf of his servant.

This is a picture of an admirable and magnanimous personality. At the same time, the centurion had faith in Jesus (vv. 3, 7, 10), that he would be able to heal the slave with power and authority. Among leaders of the Jewish community, the centurion was regarded as worthy because he loved the Jewish people and had even built a synagogue for them (vv. 3-5) (Craddock 1990:94). But the centurion felt himself unworthy of Jesus' presence in his home (vv. 6-7), simply because he was a Roman Gentile.

The centurion believed in the power of Jesus' word, even apart from the touch of the servant's body (v. 8). Jesus was absolutely amazed at such faith – faith in Jesus the Lord, not in Jesus a magician. The healing immediately took place in response to the centurion's faith.

The authority of Jesus to heal was never confined to a certain group, but it was demonstrated to whomever believed in his healing power and word. Through revealing such power, his authority as universal Son of God started to become known in surrounding areas.

2.1.2 Restoring Deaf and Mute

Mark 7:31-37 talks about the power of Jesus on behalf of a deaf and speech-impaired man. After staying in Tyre temporarily, which is described as a purely pagan city (Earle 1957:97), Jesus returned to the Decapolis located near the Sea of Galilee. As usual, people surrounded Jesus; they brought a person who was completely deaf. They "begged him to place his hand on the man" (v. 32). This dramatic picture indicates that, wherever he went, marginal people such as the poor and the sick followed after him for help (v. 32). Jesus intended to respond to their imploring but took the deaf man away from the crowd, an unusual, uncommon way for Jesus to handle the sick. He may have intended to avoid excitement from the crowd, or else to focus especially careful attention on the man (1957:98).

Jesus performed an unusual act in the process of this healing. He made the motions of putting his fingers into the man's ears and touching his tongue with saliva. Then Jesus looked up to the heavens, sighing, and commanded the ears of the man to "open" (v. 34). As declared, "the man's ears were opened, his tongue was loosened and he began to speak plainly" (v. 35). The work overwhelmed and amazed the crowd.

Jesus had compassionate affection for this man. The affection which moved his heart motivated his healing of the man. He blessed the man not only physically but spiritually as well. Jesus' compassion for humankind was as dynamic as was the power availed him.

2.2 Life and Death

Jesus frequently encountered critical situations. He could neither avoid people's agony nor ignore his own human engagement with them in their sufferings. Jesus incarnated the compassion of the loving God. The power of God, accordingly, was released through him even to raise dead (Lk. 7:11-16; 8:49-56, Jn. 11:1-16).

2.2.1 Raising the Daughter of Jairus

An event of raising the dead is displayed in Luke 8:49-56. Jesus was amid a crowd and performing miracles. When Jesus was somewhere near the house of Jairus, a synagogue official, someone came from the house of Jairus, saying, "Your daughter is dead, Don't bother the teacher any more" (v. 49). It was a mournful message and Jesus was regarded as too late to heal the infirm one. Yet he heard the plea for him to do something (Ironside 1968:276). Jairus came to Jesus with earnest purpose of heart, probably believing even that Jesus was able to raise his daughter. Jairus believed in the mighty power of Jesus to do anything in which other humans were short handed. Jesus comforted him with the assuring word, "Fear not: believe only." The word assured Jairus that the Lord would undertake to solve this matter (1968:277). With anticipation of seeing the girl, Jesus entered the house where the girl lay. Hired mourners were already ceremonially mourning with musicians' assistance. When he looked at the girl, strangely enough, Jesus said, "The girl is not dead but asleep." Of course this announcement did not persuade the crowd. Nevertheless, Jesus intended to imply that God's power could awaken the dead from death (Gardner 1991:159).

In order to give full attention to her, Jesus drew the people outside and left Himself alone with the child. Then he took her by the hand and said, " 'My child, get up!' Her spirit returned, and at once she stood up. Then Jesus told people to give her something to eat" (vv. 53-55).

Jesus continually demonstrated his dramatic power to give deliverance to those who never believed in his word as the word of the Lord. The faith of Jairus invited the power of Jesus to bring back life to the girl. Putting faith in him was, again, a primary element alongside of which Jesus performed the miracle.

2.2.2 Raising Lazarus

The death of Lazarus and his resurrection through the power of Jesus is retold and expounded in John 11:1-16. Bethany, where the incident occurred, lay on the east side of the Mount of Olives, less than two miles from Jerusalem, along the road toward Jericho (Carson 1991:405).

Mary, who was a sister of Lazarus, is further made known to the reader when she is depicted in a later episode in which she pours perfume on Jesus' feet and wipes them with her hair (Jn. 12:1-8). The same family also has appeared in Luke 10:38 as extending hospitality to Jesus and his disciples to rest along their way. It seems that the gospels have sought to establish that Jesus and the family of Lazarus enjoyed a close fellowship generated in the love of Jesus among the family members (v. 3). This love and affection of Jesus is, in fact, one of the key factors of the raising of Lazarus. We see the love further displayed when Jesus lingers for a time after the healing.

A significant message in the account of Lazarus is Jesus' intent to prove God's glory; not only that God may be glorified or praised but also to reveal the glory of God specifically through the Son Jesus (Jn. 11:40). Through this event, Jesus intended to accomplish two important things: 1) to powerfully demonstrate Himself as the resurrection and the life (v. 25) and 2) to affirm the faith of his disciples (v. 15), of some Jews who were onlookers (v. 45), and of the family of Lazarus itself (v. 22).

2.3 Nature

In nature are seen some of the most profound expressions of the revelation of God. Jesus likewise reveals his power through nature. The ancestors of the Hebrews grasped the world with amazement and wonder; they felt in natural phenomena a sense of awe and reverence. This orientation structured people's involvement with the world from one generation to another.

2.3.1 Water Turned into Wine

The first miracle that Jesus is seen to perform occurs at the wedding in Cana in Galilee (Jn. 2:1-11). It appears that wine was of particular importance in this setting. In the ancient period, wine was diluted with water to between one-third and one-tenth of its fermented strength (Carson 1991:169). If in the middle of the wedding banquet, all the wine were consumed, asking for help from the guests would not be appropriate nor expeditious. In this situation, Mary immediately demonstrated concern for such a situation and asked for help from the Son. In other words, she counted on Jesus to perform a miracle. He ordered the servants to fill up the six water jars, each containing from twenty to thirty gallons. Then, he asked the servants to serve some of the freshly made wine from the water jars to the master of the banquet. "Master" probably referred to a chief steward who was in charge of catering (Carson 1991:174). This first miracle signified inauguration of Jesus' ministry in the earth, and it fittingly introduced the starting point of the messianic age. This miracle was not just a perfunctory ministry of Jesus in public but, rather, it had implications of the beginning of the messianic age. Through this miraculous sign, he revealed his glory.

2.3.2 Feeding Five Thousand People

Luke 9:10-17 depicts a biblically prominent miracle, the feeding of five thousand people. It echoes the feeding of the children of Israel in the wilderness, through the miraculous provision of God. This was what God had done in the course of rescuing his people from Egypt by the great act of salvation, the basic foundation of Israel's history (Nineham 1968:178).

The story begins with the disciples' reporting to Jesus on their mission (vv. 1-6). Having heard the report, he wanted to take them away from the crowds.

Withdrawal was needed, for Jesus wanted rest from the following crowd and, perhaps, he sought to spend time in prayer and renewal (Mk. 6:31). But it was impossible to hide from the people, because they were eager to see him. Jesus preached to them the Kingdom of God, and he healed the sick (Lk. 9:11). The sermon probably went long, until late afternoon, so that some people got hungry. Hearing a report to this effect from the disciples, Jesus ordered the disciples to provide for the need (Mk. 6:37). The order was, perhaps, a means to test their little faith (Lk. 8:26). Jesus apparently knew and intended to demonstrate that ultimate provision was his responsibility. Eventually, Jesus gave thanks to God and consecrated a meager one-person lunch of bread and fish (Gundry 1982:293). Then the miracle took place as the crowd partook of the bread and fish after the prayer. It was enormously multiplied.

The crowd and the disciples had either seen or heard that Jesus could cast out demons, heal the sick and raise the dead. Even in such a remote area, they probably expected him to do something for their hunger. Their expectation in him met with power that fed them. So the feeding of the multitude was comprehended by the Gospel writers (Mt. 14, Mk. 6, Lk. 9) as one key event within the full range of Jesus' ministry and revelation.

2.4 Demoniacs

Jesus overcame Satan in the wilderness (Mk. 1:12-13). He fully exercised his authority by compelling Satan's forces and overcoming temptation. After this testing, Jesus continually exerted his power to drive out demons which afflicted people (Mk.1:23-26; 5: 1-20; Lk. 4:33-36; 11:14-15; 8:26-39; Mt. 12:22-37).

2.4.1 Driving out an Evil Spirit

Many times Jesus cast out demons, and afflicted people returned to normal. No ordinary person could drive out evil spirits, but only the One who had power in the heavenly realms. Luke 4:33-36 specifies two distinct authorities: teaching authority and authority over the power of evil (Earle 1957:36). In the ancient context, the Jewish believed that demons inhabited deserts, water, air, and subterranean regions. When they entered a person, the person became blind or mute, and all kinds of physical as well as mental disorders plagued the person (Craddock 1990:65).

While Jesus was teaching in the synagogue, a demon-possessed man cried out (v. 33). In Greek, "in an unclean spirit" meant that he was under its power. The demon-possessed man all of sudden acclaimed Jesus "the Holy One of

God," thus referring to the Messiah (cf. Jn. 6:69). Then, he uttered more: "What is there between us?" In other words, "What business have you with us?" These expressions indicated that the demoniac, or the unclean spirit, feared the approach of Jesus. These types of spirits, evidently, were conscious of the superiority of divine power. The expression, "the Holy One of God," is used in contrast to the demon's own uncleanness (Earle 1957:36).

Jesus turned on the unclean and surly spirit and with a stern rebuke, and said, "Be quiet!" which literally meant, "Be muzzled" (Earle 1957:37). The demon threw the man down before the onlookers and came out without injuring him (v. 35). This event amazed people and it turned them to search for the source of this power (v. 37)

Jesus taught not merely words about God but that in God was power. Hence, the demon cried out against the authority Jesus claimed in his teaching. "The Holy One of God," as uttered by the demon-possessed man, attested to the identity of Jesus. This incident announced the great power of Jesus which, in turn, motivated his driving out the demon.

2.4.2 Devils Cast out of a Man

Mark 5:1-11 tells of Jesus' dramatic encounter with another demoniac among the tombs. This man was so severely possessed by demons that no one could bind him in chains. ". . . he tore the chains apart and broke the irons on his feet." As previously mentioned, when evil entered into a person, he or she behaved abnormally (vv. 4-5). Strangely enough, this episode unfolded in the Gentile territory called Gerasa, which was thirty miles southeast of the Sea of Galilee (Gardner 1991:152). This was the first time in the Gospel that Jesus had been in Gentile territory. The occurrence probably bolstered legitimacy of support for Gentile mission in the early church (see Nineham 1968:151).

The demon-possessed man rushed down the hill toward Jesus and the disciples. The screaming terrified the disciples, for the man also screamed and cut himself with stones day and night (v. 5). On reaching Jesus, he prostrated himself before Jesus. This body language may even be interpreted as "worship" or "adoration" (Earle 1957:71). Then, the man voiced, "What do you want with me, Jesus, Son of the Most High God?" (v. 7). The demons, now known to be legion, speaking through the man beseeched Jesus not to torment them. Evidently these thousands of demons realized their inevitable doom. Here, "legion," which referred to "soldiers," means "thousands" (1957:71). The demons begged Jesus to allow them to enter a large herd of hogs (vv.11-13) rather than being bound forever. Jesus permitted their request. The result was that the afflicted man was seen again in his right mind, and appropriately fully clothed.

The demons acknowledged Jesus by falling before his feet. They knew the great authority he had. This authority could not only drive them away from the man but could bind them. Hence, they begged him to send them into the pigs. The Son of God revealed that he was the One with the authority granted from God for releasing those who were under bondage of darkness and evil power. Through such authority, his ministry and reign unfolded extensively.

3. Understanding of the Power of Christ in Pauline Literature

Paul understands the power of Christ in multiple ways. It seems that in Pauline thought, every possible spiritual work is known to be done only by the power which derives from Christ. In general, Paul lays emphasis on present living experiences of the revelation of God's might. He understands power primarily in view of the power which raises the dead in the last days and the new creativity of the Holy Spirit. This power of God, which is at work in the last days, is perceptible in Christ who has risen and now serves the body of Christ. The exalted One is the bearer and mediator of this power.

God's invisible power can be deduced from the works of creation (Rom. 1:20). But the raising of Jesus from the dead represents the central eschatological proof of God's might (Rom. 1:4; 1 Cor. 5:14). One obvious visible demonstration of power is revealed in the resurrection, which goes with exaltation (Eph. 1:20), whereby Christ becomes the "power of God" (1 Cor. 1:24). Resurrection is the constantly available source of God's power for his church. Paul uses the verbal form ενδυναμω, "to strengthen," to describe this work of the exalted Christ in the lives of individual believers (Phil. 4:13).

Christ's mediating work seems to involve a double revelation of God's eschatological power: 1) Word which brings salvation; and 2) the Holy Spirit who creates and makes new. Yet, this analysis may be broadened as the following discussion suggests. The discussion thus deals with four major highlights of Paul's many illustrations regarding power.

3.1 Power of Salvation

The power of salvation is established through communicating the gospel. But it is only possible because the word of God grants salvation (Rom. 1:16; 1 Cor. 1:18). From a human standpoint there is nothing to hope for, and one does not obtain power to save his or her fellow human being. Furthermore, no human law directs the way of salvation, nor does human behavior naturally incline toward it.

However, within God the human can find true eternal life, because he gives life to the dead and calls being into existence even from non-existence. He serves as a true second Adam by overcoming death through the power of resurrection.

Then, what is the meaning of this salvation? T. M. Snider defines it as follows:

> Salvation is responding in complete trust that God will do what God has promised to do. It is relying on God's presence, care and loving guidance and even when outward circumstances and inward experience may not confirm these things. Furthermore, it carries a deep meaning that the salvation is no longer being a slave to the destructive powers in life. And sin is no more the controlling factor. It does not mean that one will no longer sin, but that sin is no longer in control of one's motives and behavior patterns (1942:42).

One aspect of power which comes from God enables one to throw off the shackles of slavery and bondage. That is, the human can have power from God to deal in open and creative ways with temptations (Snider 1942:42). One soon figures out that the power that is available to his people is recognizable in the church as strength, enablement, and power to stand at God's side.

Is the power of salvation limited to a "spiritual" sense of life? Evidently not. When the saving power comes, it encompasses body, mind, and spirit. Having been saved, renewal effects are given outward expression (Rom. 15:19-20). Paul's apostolic task is not only to preach the gospel, but also to demonstrate signs and wonders through the power of the Holy Spirit. In order to complete his task of the preaching the gospel, he never sat complacently in one place. Rather, he went out with great ambition to impart the salvation of the Word of God to all, to the Jews and the Greeks alike.

According to the Pauline theory of atonement, through the crucifixion of Christ, reconciliation of God was extended to sinners (Rom. 5:8). In the gospel itself, then, is the power which effects freedom and salvation. This power and its consequences are accepted and recognized by faith (Rom. 1:16). So faith is the core factor of securing salvation unto life.

This power of salvation through Christ's atoning work should be shared in word and deed among all people, as the apostle Paul has set his example. As the gospel or good news of salvation is preached, demonstrations of its power will follow, even to break physical bondage and to heal, so that the salvation experience encompasses and enfolds the whole being of a person. This truth, through the work of the Lord, is to meet with faith, as Paul indicates in Romans 1:16.

3.2 Power of Love

Paul admonishes Christian congregations to attain to mature and sincere love. Romans 12:9 expresses how believers should radiate their love and what kind of attitude ought to go along with it. Paul does not neglect to teach them to grow in the Lord in the right way. He is always mindful about instructing growing Christian people. He teaches love in which there is power to keep and embrace the charisms (Dunn 1988:752).

How does this love function in the church? J. Dunn (1988:752) addresses it in 1 Corinthians 13, stressing that love is the indispensable medium through which the charisms must be exercised; otherwise they are useless. In Romans 12:1-2, Paul accentuates that the charisms are simply the functions of the body of Christ; for his teaching moves in an accustomed sequence of thought from charism to love. It is not because they are opposites or alternatives, but because both are indispensable. Even more importantly, love determines the character of the body's functioning. Charisms without love are counterproductive to their purpose and are rendered graceless. The call for genuine love functions as the core element, summarizing a mutual relationship, acceptance of brothers and sisters and even enemies as God in Christ has accepted us who "belong" (1 Cor. 5:6-10).

Paul warns that the charisms become merely mechanistic if they are exercised without love. Furthermore, he warns that if there is a pretentious claim, it is as manipulative as any coercive charism with an outward form of a judgmental and condemnatory spirit, the body falls into the danger of degenerating in spirit and in society (Dunn 1988:752).

In terms of the quality of love, the entire chapter of 1 Corinthians 13 stresses it in a graphic manner. This dynamic indeed shows the distinctiveness of the Christian way of life. For example, 13:4-7 denotes the quality of the love on specific content: "love is patient, love is kind. It does not envy, it does not boast, it is not proud. It is not easily angered, it keeps no record of wrongs. Love does not delight in evil but rejoices with the truth. It always protects, always trusts, always hopes, always perseveres."

The verb used in the first phrase, "love is patient," is μακροθυμεο and the opposite of "short-tempered." It denotes patience with people rather than with circumstances. It thus points to a God-like quality. The next description of love says it is being kind. Love reacts with goodness towards those who deal out ill-treatment; it gives itself in kindness, in the service of others. Next follow the qualities of not being envious and nor boastful. Love is God's special gift by which every believer may possibly overcome destructive tendencies. Because love is not rude, one is expected not to act in a disgraceful, dishonorable, or indecent way. Furthermore, genuine love is not self-seeking. It is not self-centered, egoistic. This love keeps no record of wrongs. The verb used here is $λογιζομει$, in the sense of reckoning righteousness to believers; it conveys an eloquent poetic description of love. Love does not carry a negative memory of the past, or a grudge. Love does not respond to any offense catalogue and deduct from another's merits. It takes no account of evil. Love never harbors a sense of injury (Morris 1989:736).

The power of the love in Christ is far greater than any other force. As stated above, this is an essential factor that every believer ought to seek. In fact, love is the basis upon which the Christian community should be built. Community is not nurtured in self-serving knowledge and boastful charisms.

As the above poetic descriptions and personifications of love indicate, love transcends everyday language. There is in love a clear and undivided sense of human commitment to godly living. Yet, love cannot be humanly self-generated. The ultimate source of this love is God, in the mystery and revelation of his sending his begotten Son to die for sinners. It is also manifested in the love of Christ toward his church, which leads believers to live this life of unselfish love. The power of love cannot keep hidden within itself. It ignites and courageously embodies the life Christ has exemplified and given. It is undeniable that Paul had a strong desire to urge on his beloved fellow Christians life within this love, because this divinely originated love has power to win the world and to overcome evil.

3.3 *Power of Justification and Reconciliation*

Paul also stresses the power of justification in the blood of Jesus. All sinners are under condemnation and subject to the wrath of God. But, in Christ, "peace with God through the Lord Jesus Christ" replaces the wrath (Rom. 5:1-5). Here "peace with God" connotes blessing coordinated with justification and acceptance as a righteousness with God (Murray 1973:158-159).

Romans 5:1-2 declares: "Being therefore justified by faith, we have peace with God through our Lord Jesus Christ; through whom also we have had our access by faith into this grace wherein we stand; and we rejoice in hope of the glory of God." These verses plainly indicate that all sinners are alienated from God. But, justification and the resultant relationship with God come as consonant with secure status. The mediation of Christ is not dispensed with in the bestowal of the privileges which proceed from justification, and dependence upon the mediation of Christ is never suspended. Jesus Christ indeed becomes a reconciler between sinners and God. His mediation also promises joy of being justified (Murray 1973:159).

Then what are specific ways for reconciliation? Ralph P. Martin (1986:153-154) identifies three aspects of reconciliation: 1) God reconciles the world to Himself; 2) God reconciles the world through Jesus Christ; and 3) God in Christ reconciles the world. God is in Christ reconciling the world; also, Paul expresses in one epistle that "it was only because God in all his fullness had chosen to dwell in Christ" (Col. 1:19) that reconciliation was accomplished.

It seems that God makes an earnest initiative to deal with the obstacles erected by sin of humankind. It was he who made peace with humanity. This act prevails upon human conscience to believe in the seriousness of his will and to lay aside distrust. Apparently, it is God seriously dealing on his own side with obstruction which constitutes reconciliation. The story of this work is "the word of reconciliation" (Rom. 5:10) (Martin 1986:154). "Reconciliation," in the New Testament sense, is not something which humans accomplish when laying aside enmity to God, but it is something which God accomplishes in the death of Christ. God puts away everything that, on his side, has meant estrangement, so that he can come and share peace with reconciled or unobstructed sinners.

Consequently, Paul conceives the gospel as the revelation of God's wisdom and love, in view of a certain state of affairs subsisting between God and humankind (Martin 1986:155). Paul is well aware of the work's completion, and he serves as a preacher of this peace. Paul's own ministry is best described as a setting forth of the "word of reconciliation" so that his hearers can also experience the gospel of reconciliation.

3.4 Power of Perfection in Resurrection

In Philippians 3:10, Paul articulates his keen interest in knowing Christ's resurrection: "I want to know Christ and the power of his resurrection and the fellowship of sharing in his sufferings, becoming like him in his death, and so, somehow, to attain to the resurrection from the dead." In his early writing, Paul expresses his determination to treat every worldly thing as rubbish and willingly to throw it away (Phil. 3:8). His one and only desire is "to gain Christ" and "to know him better." Paul trusts that, in Christ, all the treasures of wisdom and knowledge are hidden (Col. 2:3). Coming to know Christ outweighs the value of everything that the world can offer. In a most specific sense, knowing Christ results in a growing knowledge of Christ (Hawthorn 1983:143).

That this knowledge of Christ is personal and relational is made clear by the awareness of the power of his resurrection. Paul seems to equate the two: "to know him and [to know] his resurrection." Paul is a man who is not merely content to know Christ as a fact of history, but who must know him personally as the resurrected ever-living Lord of his life. The power he wishes to know is not something separable from him, but the power with which the risen Christ is endowed. He wishes to know Christ "by experiencing the power he wields in virtue of his resurrection." Paul whole-heartedly wants to know Christ alive and creatively at work to save and transform human beings. This existential knowledge propels forward a life of service so that others can see inaugurated in them "newness of life," by the Spirit and in the word. This word of God contains the power of resurrection, which moves a person from death in sin to life, to quicken and stimulate her or his whole moral and spiritual being (Rom. 6:4-11) (Hawthorn 1983:144).

Hawthorn, commenting on the second phrase, "and the fellowship of his sufferings," makes an astute grammatical observation (1983:144). The word "fellowship" shares the same definite article with the word "power." This suggests that the power of the resurrected Christ and the fellowship of his sufferings are not to be thought of as two totally separate experiences, but as alternate aspects of the same experience. But Paul is not thinking of his own physical sufferings as in any way completing the full take of Christ's afflictions (Col. 1:24); nor does he here have in mind the principle he enunciates elsewhere: "to suffer with Christ is to be glorified with him" (Rom. 8:17-18; 2 Cor. 4:7-11). This phrase in its context, rather, illustrates Christ clothed with his righteousness, and this reminds readers of Romans. 6:4. Thus, knowing Christ in the power of His resurrection is an inward experience that can be expressed in terms of being resurrected with Christ (Rom. 6:4). Knowing Christ in following in His suffering is equally an inward experience that can be described in terms of having died with Christ (Rom. 6:8; Gal. 2:19-20).

To the preceding argument, Romans 5:12-18 lends support. It reads:

> Therefore, . . . sin entered the world through one man, and death through sin, and in this way death came to all men, because all sinned, for before the law was given, sin was in the world . . . But the gift is not like the trespass. For if the many died by the trespass of the one man, how much more did God's grace and the gift that came by the grace of the one man, Jesus Christ, overflow to the many. Again, the gift of God is not like the result of the one man's sin: The judgment followed one sin and brought condemnation, but the gift followed many trespasses and brought justification.

Paul thus calls Christ the second Adam who embodies the whole of humankind. Jesus completely identifies Himself with human beings in the state of sin and helplessness. Followers likewise might be equally identified with Christ in his resurrected life. In Christ's suffering and death, the old humanity finds the end of itself. In resurrection, the new humanity begins (2 Cor. 5:14-17). Therefore, for Paul to say that he wishes to know Christ and the fellowship of his sufferings is not to say that he seeks to know Christ and to experience physical sufferings of martydom. Rather, to know Christ who suffered and died for him is to know that he therefore has suffered and died in Christ, to be resurrected in him to a new and superlative life (1 Pe. 3:18).

Then what treasures does Paul obtain? Paul attains to belief and hope in Christ. His desire is to acquire the knowledge of Christ, the only purely worthy and valuable treasure. So he abandons every single worldly treasure. His encouragement of the same is extended to all believers who imitate his faith; his theological argument is that every believer may expect ultimate perfection in the power of resurrection.

In concluding the study of power in Pauline theology, it seems apparent and noteworthy that Pauline ideas of the power of Christ are more abstract than the images set forth in of the Old Testament, or even of those in the Gospels. None of the wonderful works which Christ has brought into the life of believers can be accomplished by any power in the world. Superior power belonging only to God is at work only through Christ Jesus, the risen Lord. This power is absolutely incompatible with any other power in the universe.

It is tremendous that all the sinners no longer need be bound over to slavery but now may fully realize the redemption of Christ. Being saved by the blood of Jesus Christ, the very expression of God's love, has to be at the center of Christian life. The same love compels Christians to share the love with others.

God puts away the condemnation and wrath, and willingly provides a universal way of reconciliation through his initiative of love. Such is the basis of the present new status and future hope. Finally, the power of the resurrection is what Paul eagerly awaits as the ultimate eschatological hope. Without this great expectation, believing in Christ is hopeless and absurd. Paul wants to attain to this knowledge and to dispense it among fellow human beings. For Paul's life is centered around this affirmation and the security of everlasting life.

In summary, in the Old Testament God directed his people and revealed his presence by supernatural power. Jesus launched his ministry through displays of power, and the gospel of good news was effectively promulgated and signified by this means. The apostles in the Book of Acts preached the gospel in the same manner . . . with power and in God's truth.

God delegated Christians, as practitioners of his power and authority, to exercise in preaching the gospel, casting out demons, and healing the sick (Lk. 9:1). God's power is also intended to supply daily needs as they arise. In 1 Corinthians 2:4, Paul exemplifies the Christian life, "My message and my preaching were not with wise and persuasive words, but with a demonstration of the Spirit's power."

Part IV

An Ethnological Analysis of Kankana-ey Christianity

Chapter 7

Kankana-ey Understanding and Practice of the Christian Faith

In Part III, I discussed the role of encounters from a biblical perspective and this affirmed the importance of God's power in Christian experience. The power which was manifested during ancient times and the earthly ministry of Christ is still demonstrated among the Kankana-ey people. Because of the power experience, many people were converted to Christ. After conversion, they learn that the Christians' God is different from the gods they formerly served. God blesses them without demanding a sacrifice. There is the gracious promise of salvation and eternal life in God. He is a loving father who meets their needs and helps them solve their problems. God, thus, is not merely transcendent but is immanent and approachable, allaying their fear and hesitation. The people see major differences between their previous religious life and the life afforded by Christianity. What remains for them in the course of this Christian life is the task of establishing their own ethnic theology: a distinctively Kankana-ey way of thinking about God. The following discussion is based on interviews with Assemblies of God church members in Benguet Province. These interviews were conducted in June-July 1995.

1. God

I examined two areas in the category of God: blessing and curse. The Kankana-ey Christians understand and experience God largely as God is perceived in these two dynamics. The Kankana-ey Christians' understanding of God is developed through their experience in daily life.

1.1 Blessing

It is commonly accepted as fact that when the Kankana-eys were pagan, through means of performing ritual, they sought to receive blessing from the gods. After conversion, they learned that the one Lord God is the ultimate source of blessing. A loving Father wants to bless his people when they ask. Learning of this promise of God's blessing and abundance, they earnestly sought his blessing and favor. The following discussion attempts to explore the diverse ways in which people have experienced and sought to experience blessing. These various approaches to God are focused on *receiving* blessing.

The majority of Kankana-ey Christians are farmers and miners. Through farming and mining, they tend to experience God's blessing and favor, particularly in terms of what they meet with in their work. They earnestly seek for God's help and blessing from God, particularly when they meet with disaster.

1.1.1 Failure of Crops and Plants in Farming

Q. "If your crops and plants were destroyed by a strong typhoon so that there were no way to recover, what would you normally have done when you were not yet Christian, and what would you do now?"[3]

1.1.1.1 Female Respondents

In the twenty to thirty-four age group, 19 out of 120 said that before they were Christians they would have been immensely disappointed. They would have been angry and bitter. They would have lain under great stress for many months. They would not have found any solution for such crisis. Thirty would have blamed and even cursed their ancestors and become rebellious. Their ancestors would be despised because they did not protect their people's property. Forty-five, however, would have expected their ancestors to restore their plants, and accordingly they would have gone to a priest for consultation. The priest would have prescribed a certain ritual to perform, and these informants would have followed the order. Twenty-six would have borrowed money from their neighbors to start a new work. They would not leave their farms, but would seek new work. Land was endowed by their ancestors, so they would feel compelled to maintain responsibility for it.

Having become Christian, said 41 of the 120, they would put their faith in God, hoping that God would open a way to recover what they had before. They expressed belief in his promise in the Bible, that he would never forsake them, and that he would answer their prayer. Thirty would give thanksgiving, even in the midst of trial, to God who is the provider for their needs and the source of blessing. They would not want to fail their faith in difficult situations but would seek to have victory in Christ. Twenty-five would have peace and joy in their hearts, because joy is their strength. Their simple trust would make them peaceful. They would believe that he would be faithful to provide for their needs. Ten would borrow money and start over from scratch. They would employ human

---

3 Q. stands for an interview question in English translation.

resources for a quick recovery. Fourteen would regard it as a trial and a testing period and accordingly would draw near to God and be strong and firm in the Lord.

In the thirty-five to forty-four age group, in pre-Christian times, 30 of 130 would have borrowed money for capital to start work again. Twenty would have been in great anxiety as complaints piled up in their hearts. They would be in grief. They would not find any way to recover but would have to endure the dire situation. Thirty thought that there would be no hope in life, so they would be brought to the brink of killing themselves. Their hearts would have been broken. Fifty described this common reaction: in order to solve the problem, they would have sought the priest, listened to their priestly advice and received comfort. The priest's final order would be to butcher and offer an animal sacrifice to appease angry ancestors (ancestors neglected by their descendants and thus angered enough to cause the disaster).

In current Christian times, 41 out of this 130 said they would ask God who has power to rescue and give relief from the circumstance. God is able to help them resolve such problems with his power. They indicated that they know that God's power is unlimited. Twenty-three believed that such crop failure affords a time to test their faith and to learn to trust God more. Although it would be difficult to go through the trial, they would strive to endure it and thereby see their faith strengthened. Twenty-four would be encouraged by Scriptures and lifted up through prayer. Through reading the word of God, they would more deeply believe in the promise of God's blessing, because God never fails to keep his promise. Twenty-five said that they would regularly gather their family members together for family devotions and prayer. Through times of prayer, they would be strengthened in their faith and increasingly put their hope in God, believing that ultimate blessing comes from God. Seventeen would be at peace and attempt to rejoice in the Lord even in their time of trial.

In the forty-five to sixty (and above) age group, prior to Christian faith, 49 out of 110 would have sought help of spirit beings, believing that their gods could bless them again. They stoutly believed that their ancestors could bless and restore their losses. Twenty-six would have borrowed money to resume farming. This work afforded their only means to live their lives. They would have had to deal with their miserable lot and suffer until their loans were repaid. Twenty-five would have suffered both economic and mental depression in such circumstances. Such emotional depression would have caused them to get sick, thus further delaying their economic recovery. Ten would have lost hope in the face of destroyed plants and crops and would have seen no way to be restored.

Now, 60 out of 110 would pray, because it is the only way to overcome failure. They would hold to the belief that God has power to bless. Through prayer, they would want to present their needs and ask for blessing. Thirty said that the pastor's role would be important. They would also expect a pastor to hold particular times of prayer in the church and to give encouraging words from Scriptures. They would want to be encouraged from the message to believe in God's power of blessing and enabling. Twenty would see such a time as one which tests trust-levels in relation to God. They would want to discover how much they believed in and trusted God's promise.

1.1.1.2 Male Respondents

In the twenty to thirty-four age group, before Christian conversion, 45 out of 115 performed ritual to obtain blessing. They sought to have consolation through such ritual performance. Their ancestors were regarded as potential comforters, providers, and problem-solvers. Thirty-seven would have gotten drunk in order to forget the critical situation. Stupor was the only way to ease or to mitigate their depression. Twenty-six would have exploded and directed their anger against their wives, losing self control. They said it would be the toughest time they had had to go through. Seven would have sought from their friends or relatives advice for future plans. Those with prior experience would give helpful advice.

Now, 45 out of 115 believe that God would help to restore their farms. They would trust him who is the only source of blessing and who has supreme power to help. Twenty-six would see such crisis as a time for examining their faith and being strengthened in the Lord. They would try not to lose their faith. Through continuing prayer, they would find some solution to the destroyed farm. Their only hope would be that God intervenes in situations and helps and guides. Twenty would want church elders and pastors to give encouraging words and to pray for them. By their own strength, they would not be able to handle the situation. Twenty said they would put their hope in God. Through such a trial, they would spend more time than ever before in prayer.

In the thirty-five to forty-four age group, before becoming Christian, 55 out of 125 would have lost hope and desire to survive. Their situation would have been difficult to endure, so they would have sought consolation from the priest. The time of consulting with a priest would have been also a time of release from anxiety. The priest would have prescribed appropriate ritual for receiving blessing from spirit beings. Twenty-two would have been depressed due to disastrous occurrences and would have required a long time to recover from their mental anguish. Thirty-five would have borrowed money to start over on the farm, anticipating that they could thereby regain what they had lost. Fourteen would have grown restless and taken to drunkenness as a means of alleviating their pain.

Now, 12 out of 125 say they would learn a lesson from God in such circumstances. They would glimpse something of God who attempts to teach something in the circumstance of disaster. They would also apply their own best effort to try to recover the farm. Along with human effort, they would anticipate that God's blessing may lead to restoration. Twenty-four would try to look for other business. They would borrow money from their neighbors or friends to start a new work. Their reasoning is that this way would be easier than sinking money and time into restoring the destroyed farm. Twenty-three would seek God's hand to help. Their simple faith would not lead them to search other methods, but would learn them to wait for divine help. Forty-nine would simply expect that they would see God's blessing through believing in his promise, for God is a source of blessing for his children. Seventeen would try to be encouraged by fellow church members. They would share their heavy burdens and request prayer.

In the forty-five to sixty (and above) age group, before being Christian, one man who used to be a pagan priest said that whenever such a thing happened he immediately consulted with spirit beings and performed suitable rituals for recovery. Since he was a priest, he was able to communicate with spirit beings. Twenty-seven out of seventy consulted the priest and followed what the priest ordered, which would have been a ritual that required a certain number of pigs for sacrifice. Twenty-two would have lost their hope and become depressed. Such trial would have caused more distress than what they thought humans could bear. Twenty-one would have borrowed money to either start a new work or to attempt recovery. Borrowing was the only means they could employ to go on with their work.

Having now become Christian, the man who was the priest confessed that he would never think of performing ritual, no matter how difficult were the moments he might encounter, but rather, he would go to the Lord for help, and he would do so even in the circumstance described by the question. He believes that God is the only one who can help and restore losses. Forty-seven out of seventy would come to the same point, praying to God alone, believing that he would bless his children. They reflected on their previous experiences in learning how God led and guided them when they were in difficult circumstances. Recalling God's goodness would enable them to trust him more in a crisis such as this. Ten said that it would be a time of trial, so they would strive not to fail in their faith. They would try to be firm in prayer and to be shored up by the word of God. Thirteen would borrow money to recover their farms. They expressed belief in the need to pull human resources together to reestablish what had been lost.

1.1.2 Low Productivity in Mining

Q. "If, in spite of hard work, your production of gold was still disappointingly low, what would you have done when you were a pagan, and what would you do now?"

1.1.2.1 Female Respondents

In the twenty to thirty-four age group, 22 out of 120 said that before becoming Christian, they would have given up this job and looked for new work. They could not be sustained in this situation and would have to survive by means of other work. Thirty-four would have tried to endure and anticipate better production. This would demand harder work of them. Forty-one would have gone to the pagan priest. As usual, the priest's final say would have been to perform a ritual to make production. Twelve had actually heard advice of old folks in the village who had been through this kind of experience before. They would have followed what the old folks advised. Eleven would have trusted spirit beings (their ancestors) to bless their business, for such was their only hope to ensure production.

Being Christian now, 25 out of 120 would want to hear encouraging words from their pastor. Their pastor would thus strengthen them and help sustain them in this circumstance. Although they could give up this business and find other jobs, they would prefer to keep the one they had. The business would have been inherited from their ancestors. Sixty-four would pray to God for higher yields of gold. They would anticipate God's blessing on their business, for God enabled their mining work to be successful. Fifteen would look to church members for comfort. They said their faith was still growing and dependent upon other people's prayer and comfort. Sixteen would seek the word of God as strength for faith and continued work in the mine.

In the thirty-five to forty-four age group, before becoming Christian, 31 out of 130 would have been disappointed. Low production would shrink their regular incomes and hamper their survival. So they would have closed their businesses temporarily and worked in other places. Twenty-nine would have lost their hope and advised their husbands to seek other work. They would regard finding another job as better than staying attached to the failed one. Thirty-three would have gone to the village priest for advice and would have tried to find a reason why this had occurred. They would have followed what the priest ordered – performing ritual. Eighteen would have taken a chance and repaired and expanded their mining to increase production. They would have tried to employ any possible means to improve production. Seventeen wives would have told their husband not to lose hope. The wives would have found a job and worked hard to support the family while production was low. Twenty-two would have continued the work, expecting good production in the future. They would have needed enormous patience.

Now that they are Christians, 45 out of 130 would want to trust God for help. They would ask church people to pray for them, believing in the power of prayer. God would be the only hope for them. They would believe in his promise of blessing. Thirty-nine would want to keep their jobs in hopes that there would be good production someday in the future. This would require endurance and diligent working. Twenty-nine wives would advise their husband to close the mining business and look for another job, because they would run out of patience. Seventeen would go to their pastor for some suggestions, because they would not be able to recognize any other solution. In a crisis like this, their pastor would play multiple roles as comforter, encourager, and advisor.

In the forty-five to sixty (and above) age group, before becoming Christians, 49 out of 110 indicated they would have searched for another job with better means of earning income. Fifty-seven would have sought the priest regarding ritual performance. Through this means they would have thought they could ensure good gold production by the help of their ancestors. Four (older persons) who had not had mining experience could not respond to this question.

Being Christians now, 39 out of 110 would earnestly seek the help of God. They would beseech God for directing their businesses and blessing them. Hoping that God would bless, they would keep mining. Thirty-two would share their critical problem with church people and ask them to pray. They would want to be strengthened through prayer of fellow Christians. Thirty-nine would anticipate divine intervention in this situation, believing that everything is under God's control and care and that he secures ultimate blessing. Based on what they have experienced of God in the course of their Christian journey, they would anticipate that God would undertake to clarify and bring resolution to their situation.

1.1.2.2 Male Respondents

In the twenty to thirty-four age group, before becoming Christians, 23 out 115 would have gone to the *sari-sari* store with friends and drink beer to alleviate frustration. They would have been emotionally paralyzed with the stress of low production. Thirty-four would have felt guilt feelings in the face of the family, due to having no income for them. This would have caused them to spend more time away from home rather than with their own families. Twenty-four would have sought village elders to hear their advice. Thirty-four would have gone to the village priest who would prescribe ritual for this unfortunate occasion.

Given that they are now Christians, 34 out of 115 would want to keep the jobs and work diligently. They would anticipate that God would secure their good production. Twenty-nine expressed belief that God can turn a bad situation into a better one. They would simply put their hope in him, reflecting on God's goodness as it has been experienced through their Christian lives. Twenty-seven would want to leave the business and find another job. They would think that they had gone through enough suffering. Continuing such work would further their distress. But they would expect God to direct their paths. Twenty-five indicated the response that although they would be going through tough times, they would want to give thanks and praise to the Lord. They would remain attached to their jobs claiming the promise of God's blessing.

In the thirty-four to forty-four age group, before becoming Christians, 49 out of 125 would have attributed their misfortune to their own lack of care for their ancestors. So they would have performed ritual. They would have butchered as many animals as the priest ordered. They would have even borrowed to buy sacrificial animals. Ritual offered to their ancestors would be trusted to secure further blessing upon their mining business. Thirty-six would not have kept mining, but instead would have looked for other available jobs in order to go on with their lives. Fifteen would have continued this work but not as a total income source. They would have searched for other jobs to guarantee a large portion of support, but would have still anticipated good production. Twenty-five would have stayed in that job and worked harder in waiting on "for better days."

Being Christians now, 23 out of 125 would regard their circumstances as a trial and a time of testing. They would want church elders to pray for them. Thirty-five would invite the pastor to lead devotions and give inspirational Scriptures. Through the pastor's encouragement, their faith would grow. Forty-five who indicated they were strong in faith said they would trust God and keep their businesses. They would want to experience God's blessing through this trial. They believed that God would never forsake his people but would always care for them. Even in this circumstance, God would reign and remain in control. Twenty-two would reflect on God's blessing as revealed through characters in the Bible, believing that if they endured the hardship the Lord would bless them even more.

In the forty-five to sixty (and above) age group, fifty out of seventy responded that before becoming Christians, they would have offered ritual to their ancestors in order to win blessing. Four would have discontinued the mining work and found other jobs. They would have been concerned about their families' suffering. Sixteen indicated that they never had mining experience but, if they had been miners and were in this difficult situation, they would have given up mining and found other jobs. They would have been convinced by the crisis that there would be no hope in continuing that type of work.

Being Christians now, thirty-four answered that they would want to endure in the mining business, seeking God's help and guidance. They would believe that God would never forsake them but would guide them as they trusted in him. Twenty-three indicated that they would need someone else's prayer, because theirs alone would not be enough to strengthen them to keep on mining. However, thirteen of the oldest respondents said they would not want to keep this job, because it is burdensome. They would want their children to look after the mining work. Their desire would be to find peace the rest of their life.

1.2 Curse

Cursing is an accepted practice among people of pagan tribal communities. Believers are sometimes cursed by non-believing family members and relatives for going against tradition. Persecution intensifies when one shares the gospel. However, through such trial these believers experience God in his power and goodness. They attest that this type of experience makes them grow in faith. It affords a time and place for them to practice their Christian faith.

1.2.1 Hatred from Non-Believers

Q. "If your uncle were to die due to illness, according to Kankana-ey tradition, the funeral is to be accompanied by a series of rituals. All family members, relatives, friends and neighbors are expected to attend them. If, in this situation, you decided not to go but to stay at home and, as a result, they severely cursed you, what would be your attitude? What would you do to counteract the cursing?"

1.2.1.1 Female Respondents

In the twenty to thirty-four age group, 43 out of 120 would pray to God to convict them that someday the taunters would come to God and realize that the traditional funeral rites were wrong and against God's way. Despite being cursed they would still want to show the love of Christ. These people would try to overcome hurt feelings from the curse. Thirty-eight would trust in God's protection, knowing that the devil would not harm them. They would want to counteract the curse with prayer so that no harm would befall them. Twenty-nine would rebuke the cursing parties in the name of Jesus and would pray for their salvation. They would not argue with non-believing friends and relatives. Ten would want to bless those who cursed, as the Bible instructs. They would pray for their jobs continually to be blessed, not cursed.

In the thirty-five to forty-four age group, 27 out of 130 would pray to God for his help to endure in this situation. They would want to pray to God to reveal his power over those who cursed. Forty would want to stand firm in their faith and be faithful in God even though they were badly cursed. They would want to show people their unwavering faith. Thirteen would explain to these non-believers why they do not attend such funerals. Although these people might be mad at them, they would still want to display the love of Christ. Forty-six would want to consult with a pastor about this problem and get help. At the same time, they would request that church members pray against the curse. They would believe in the power of prayer warriors to prevent the curse. Twenty-four would have compassion on the cursing relative or neighbors, hoping that they would pray to receive salvation. The respondents of this group would show what they considered to be a right Christian attitude by remaining silent, so that the curse would become a blessing to them. Twenty would rebuke the curse and pray to God to keep them from becoming involved in any wrongdoing. Rebuking them would mean not personal confrontation but rebuking the devil in prayer.

In the forty-five to sixty age group (and above), 35 out of 110 indicated that, although it would be hard to take the harsh words hurled at them, they would want to display God's loving kindness. They would pray to God that no harm would come upon them. Twenty-four would rebuke the attacks of the devil which had come to them in the form of curses, believing that the best way to counterattack is to ask their pastor and church members to pray. They alone would not feel sufficient to overcome the curses from a group of non-believing friends, relatives, and family members. Thirty-one would want to set up special times of prayer to prevent the curses from befalling them. They would want to overcome the curse by God's power. Through that power they would keep their faith in him. Twenty would seek Scriptures for encouragement. They expressed belief that through reading Scriptures, they would overcome feelings of offense and would thereby gain strength.

1.2.1.2 Male Respondents

In the twenty to thirty-four age group, 21 out of 115 would ask for God's protection. They would stand on the promise of God that he keeps his people from evil spirits. Although non-believers might curse them, their ill will would not be fully realized because of God's protection. Thirty-eight indicated their desire to be witnesses of Christ through any such opportunity. They would attempt to share the gospel with those who had them. Twenty-nine would want to remain at home and spend time praying and reading the Bible. They indicated that they believe this is the only way to counteract curses from non-believing people. They further acknowledged that without the help of God, they themselves might fall into the temptation of attending the rituals.

Twenty-seven would go to a pastor whom they would want to have prayer for them and who would be able to suggest how to counteract the curse. They would want to share their feelings and disappointment.

In the thirty-five to forty-four age group, 28 out of 125 expressed belief that God would protect them from the non-believers' curse. They would rather bless those people who curse than confront them. Thirty-six would regard the circumstance as a trial for which they would want to devote time in prayer. Through prayer, they would be strengthened and experience the power of the living God – protection, peace, and joy. Forty-one would want to delve into the Scriptures related to manifestations of the power of God in order to rebuke the cursing. They indicated that they believe that God's power is much greater than any force of evil, so God's power would function as a weapon to counteract the curse. Twenty would want to ask their close church friends to pray for them to overcome any curse that might threaten them. They would even want to set up a time for gathering on a regular basis during the series of ritual performances.

In the forty-five to sixty (and above) age group, 32 out of 70 indicated some sense of fear about being abandoned by friends, relatives, and even family members, but they said they would not join in the rituals for the funeral. However, they would acknowledge the curse and in response, pray to God to bless the people who had cursed them. Twenty-nine would pray to God to forgive people's sin and see them to salvation. They would never believe that the curse would find fulfillment because God would always keep them in safety. Nine expressed a sense of affection and hope for souls of their cursers to be saved. Although the non-believing people might curse badly, the victims of hate would not return ill will toward them, but instead would bless them and pray for God's salvation for them.

1.2.2 Rejection of the Gospel

Q. "Consider the following hypothetical scenario: When you try to evangelize your pagan neighbor, she shows her interest in knowing the Gospel. However, her father, being a staunch pagan, curses you as well as his daughter. What do you do?"

1.2.2.1 Female Respondents

In the twenty to thirty-four age group, 31 out of 120 would want to continue sharing the gospel, praying for the conviction of the Holy Spirit upon and salvation for the father. They expressed belief that even if the father cursed them, the curse would find no further eventuation in their lives because God would keep and protect them with his power. Twenty-four would not fear the father's curse but would be concerned for the daughter. So they would want to encourage her not to fear the curse. They would want to explain to the daughter that if she were to accept Jesus Christ as her personal Savior, he would keep her from danger and risk. Thirty-nine would want to devote themselves to prayer for courage to continue witnessing to her without fear. They indicated that prayer is a weapon available to them to fight against evil powers and principalities. They said they would not care what the father said, because God's power is greater than threats. Twenty-six would want to read Scriptures to help themselves overcome the harsh impact of people's cursing. They noted that they would undoubtedly suffer pain and hurt feelings, but they would not give up witnessing to her. They expressed belief that God would strengthen their faith to enable them to stand firm.

In the thirty-five to forty-four age group, 21 out of 130 would want to show the father the love of Christ and be friendly. Through kindness, the father would feel the love of God. He might then be interested in Christianity. The curse from the father would not do any harm as long as the Holy Spirit kept the witness safe. Thirty-seven would boldly continue to approach the daughter and even the father. Regardless of what the father said, they would share the good news of Jesus Christ. They would have compassion for his soul. Forty-one would pray for both the father and the daughter to turn to Christ, overcoming the curse. They would believe that human wisdom and power are limited, but God's are not. They further indicated that they would not have enough strength to stand alone against the strong man, but if God would help them, they would boldly keep sharing the gospel. Thirty-one would be rendered slightly despondent by the curse and persecution from the father. They would need encouraging words from some sincere church members. They would seek the help and prayer of those church people.

In the forty-five to sixty (and above) age group, 37 out of 110 would want to have a personal conversation with the father. This means they would want to persuade the father. They would believe that if the Holy Spirit intervened in their conversation, the father would turn his heart to Christ. Twenty-eight would pray in a group, believing that the power of God would enable them to keep bearing witness. They would not want to discontinue evangelizing the daughter even though they were cursed. Thirty-five would want to concentrate on praying for the father to be convicted by the Holy Spirit about Christ. They would know that this would not be easy work but they would desire to face him, telling him the truth of God. They would not worry over what was the father's curse, but rather would see it as just an outburst of anger. Ten would discontinue witnessing to the daughter until the father's anger subsided and then would go back to her. They would encourage her not to be affected by nor afraid of the curse. They would attest to God's power for protection over her as she came to the Lord.

1.2.2.2 Male Respondents

In the twenty to thirty-four age group, 23 out of 115 would want to keep sharing the gospel with the daughter in the midst of the curse and persecution from the father. In fact, they would desire to bring both of them to Christ. They would comfort her to allay her fear of the curse. Thirty-eight would pray for the father not to curse anymore and would ask in prayer that his heart be changed. If he persisted in hindering them from coming to see his daughter, they would not witness to her anymore. Forty-one would pray for the father to accept Jesus Christ as his personal Savior. They would further request that church elders and members unite in intercessory prayer. They expressed the belief that if he were to come to Christ by any means, many village people would likewise turn to God. They noted that it happens among pagan Kankana-ey communities that if a devoted pagan or priest becomes a Christian the village majority tends to convert to Christ. Meanwhile, they would keep going to visit the daughter to share with her the living word of God. Thirteen would show loving kindness to the pagan father despite his cursing. Through love manifested in their life, the father's heart would soften and perhaps be led to find Christ in them. The daughter would, perhaps, also see the attitude of Christians as different from that of pagans.

In the thirty-five to forty-four age group, 36 out of 125 would try to be patient with and forgive the father. They would understand that he is a sincere pagan who wants to keep his daughter from being affected by Christians. However, these witnesses would not back away due to the curse, but rather, would keep sharing the gospel. Forty-two would pray for the father to be saved. They would feel powerless to convict him, but would trust the power of Christ to effect some change. They indicated that prayer is their only way to expect miracles to happen. Twenty-seven would pray for the father not to curse. If he kept on cursing, they would not visit his daughter anymore. They indicated that they would be more concerned for witnessing to her than about what the father would say. They would never fear the curse. Twenty-two thought they might be quite disappointed. They would seek the advice of their pastor. They would want to follow the pastor's advice.

In the forty-five to sixty (and above) age group, twenty-nine out of seventy would never give up sharing the good news of Christ with the daughter. They spoke of having burning hearts not only to share the gospel but also to lead regular Bible study if she would permit it. They would not distance the father simply because he cursed them. They would, rather, try to contact him. In a friendly exchange, the father might open his heart and perhaps even accept Christ some day in the future. Thirty-five would pray to God that the curse would not fall upon the daughter nor themselves. They had experienced as pagans that, if a sincere pagan cursed, something disastrous happened; yet they would not believe this would happen to them anymore. However, they would ask God to protect them, their households, and their businesses. Six were not sure if they would continue evangelizing her or would instead, postpone witnessing if the father strongly opposed them and kept on cursing. They would find it difficult to share the gospel in this climate. They would refrain from witnessing for a certain period of time, then go again to see her.

2. The Holy Spirit: Healing

The Kankana-ey Christians believe in the work of the Holy Spirit. They indicate that they have often experienced the healing power of the Holy Spirit upon themselves and their families. They frequently claim the power of the Holy Spirit in situations in which they may otherwise be rendered powerless.

The Kankana-ey believers often hear the preaching of pastors on the healing power of the Holy Spirit. They also have chances to hear testimonies of the healing experiences of fellow Christians. I believe that most of the Kankana-ey believers have had empirically verifiable healing experiences in their Christian lives. This section analyzes more responses from the Kankana-ey church people, with an eye to how they practice their faith in the healing power of the Holy Spirit.

2.1 Infants' Sickness

Q. "If you had a little baby who started coughing and the cough became so severe that the baby suffered a whole night with cough and fever, what would you do?"

2.1.1 Female Respondents

In the twenty to thirty-four age group, 27 out of 120 would seek divine power of the Holy Spirit for healing. They would invite the presence of the Holy Spirit and ask the Spirit to touch their baby. They claimed a solid faith that God would never fail them when they approached him in faith. Forty-two would invite some church members to come and pray for the baby. They would feel an urgent need for the people's prayer for the sick baby, given that the baby had coughed the whole night. They indeed would anticipate the touch of healing power of the Holy Spirit. Thirty-five also would seek the help of the Holy Spirit but, additionally, would want to use medicine along with the prayer, believing that God can heal their baby through the medicine. Sixteen would want to bring the baby to a nearby clinic. They emphasized that such action would not signify that they neglect praying nor deny the power of healing, but rather that they would, in love and compassion, employ any possible means to stop the baby's coughing. As parents, they too would suffer pain when the baby suffered.

In the thirty-five to forty-four age group, 69 out of 130 would pray for the baby to be healed by the power of the Holy Spirit. They would earnestly seek the Holy Spirit to heal the sick child. They would maintain a strong faith. Bolstered by past experience, they would remain convinced that the Holy Spirit would reveal his power by healing the baby. Thirty-five would bring the baby to a pastor to be prayed for. They would trust their spiritual leader to undertake bearing the burden of the parents, doing so with prayer. Through the prayer of the pastor they would be encouraged. Twenty-six would anticipate a healing touch of the Holy Spirit and also use medicine if they have it. They would desperately utilize any means available. However, these people in dire need would hardly be able to purchase medicine; they would need outsiders or missionaries to dispense it free of charge.

In the forty-five to sixty (and above) age group, 68 out of 110 would hold the baby in prayer, believing in the healing touch of the Holy Spirit. They would earnestly desire to see the extending of God's merciful hand upon the baby. They attested belief that such would be a moment in which to measure their faith in him. Forty-two would beseech the Holy Spirit for healing, but they would want to use all possible means to alleviate the baby's cough. If they were able to bring the baby to a hospital, even at a great distance, they would do so. Or, if they had appropriate medicine, they would be willing to use it. They would not want the baby to suffer.

2.1.2 Male Respondents

In the twenty to thirty-four age group, 76 out of 115 emphasized the need for strong faith in the healing power of the Holy Spirit. They would want to reflect on the goodness of God as it had been administered throughout their spiritual lives, realizing afresh that he answered their prayers and met their needs. So, in times like those, they would not panic but would silently seek God's face. Thirty-nine would consider this moment a time of measuring and testing of their faith. Their experience of God was (in years) less than that of the older respondents. They would expect the Holy Spirit to be revealed in such a critical moment to touch the sick child so that their shallow faith would be strengthened.

In the thirty-five to forty-four age group, 69 out of 125 would trust the healing power of the Holy Spirit. These respondents, having already had years of experiencing God's healing touch, at this time would all the more anticipate the Holy Spirit's healing power. They indicated that through the experience of God's healing, their faith would be solidified. Forty-two would request that some close church members join in prayer. They noted belief in the power of intercessory prayer. They alone would not be sustained but, with assisting prayer, they would abide the trial. Fourteen said they would pray for the baby before taking him or her to a hospital. They would not want the baby to suffer from the cough any longer than was avoidable. They would try to use any possible means to stop the cough and bring down the fever.

In the forty-five to sixty (and above) age group, thirty-nine out of seventy would pray for the healing touch of the Holy Spirit. At the same time, they would want to administer appropriate medication. They would believe that the baby would be healed by the power of Holy Spirit, and that this power would not be diminished by the allopathic aid of medicine, which is ultimately given from God. Thirty-one would want to approach God alone to let him manifest his complete healing power upon the baby. They would believe in the absolute power of the Holy Spirit, which manifests when his people earnestly seek it. They see this response as an exercise of what the Bible teaches.

2.2 Temptation of "Shortcuts" to Healing

Q. "You have been ill for a long period of time, when village people and relatives visit you. Many of them are non-believers and encourage you to return to your roots in the old belief system and its practices. They believe it to be a quicker way to recovery. Presented with this attempt at persuasion, what would be your response?"

2.2.1 Female Respondents

In the twenty to thirty-four age group, 57 out of 120 would never think of reverting to traditional ways of healing. They would never believe that the sick could be healed by performing ritual, now that they have become Christians. They claimed to truly believe that they are saved by the blood of Jesus and that, thereby, they have become God's children. Forty-six would have no desire to reclaim the old belief system for healing. However, if temptation were to come over and over, they would pray to God to be able to resist it. They would ask the Holy Spirit to convict non-believing relatives and friends so that they would turn to the Lord. Twenty-three would not give up praying to God for healing. They would want to be patient with the Lord, knowing that personal experience with the healing power of the Holy Spirit would be a persuasive testimony in the future. They said they would rather suffer with disease than listen to misguided advice of non-believing people.

In the thirty-five to forty-four age group, 49 out of 130 would explain to non-believing people that they would not go back to the old system. These people displayed a unique understanding about sickness – that physical sickness relates to spiritual ailment, so they would have to check on their spiritual life. They would try to renew their spiritual life through prayer and reading the Bible. They believe that God would not fail them. Fifty-two would explain to the defenders of the way of tradition that performing ritual would not do them any good. These people expressed belief that illness results from sin. If they repent of their sin, God forgives, and healing will take place. They further note that sometimes healing does occur, not quickly, but slowly. Twenty-nine expressed the tenacious conviction that they would rather die in the hand of God than revert to old religious practices. Although they had pagan backgrounds, they would never think of compromising their faith. They would cling to their faith in any crisis.

In the forty-five to sixty (and above) age group, 55 out of 110 said they would not go back to rituals for healing, even though they may have suffered long with illness. Through physical suffering, they indicated, they would come to know more of God, even as their intimate relationship with him has been developed already. Forty-five would stand on their faith to overcome temptation. They would ask the Holy Spirit to help overcome physical suffering. They would want to hold onto the promise of God, that he never leaves nor forsakes his children. The word of God would serve as a strong defense and a weapon against temptation and vexation.

2.2.2 Male Respondents

In the twenty to thirty-four age group, 71 out of 115 would want to explain to the non-believing relatives and friends that they are already Christian and have no intention of turning their backs on God. God, in whom they believe, is the living and the most high God. God may have a particular purpose in permitting the physical illness, and accordingly, he would heal in his own time. Forty-four would ignore people's urging to seek traditional ritualistic ways of healing. These respondents would want to demonstrate their Christian faith to their non-believing contenders. They would not fail in their trust and faith in God, so that when non-believing relatives and friends saw their faithfulness, some of them might even be touched by and converted to Christ.

In the thirty-five to forty-four age group, 82 out of 125 would never accept any such urging. Their understanding is that backsliding means fleeing from God. If they were to go back to pagan practices for healing purposes, they would not feel able to come back to God because of their heavy guilt feelings. They would avoid this alienation and, therefore, keep their faith in any circumstance. Forty-three would witness that they had already become children of God and thus, belonged to the one who saved them. They would never renounce their faith and turn to pagan religion. They would endure suffering from illness with prayer and the word of God.

In the forty-five to sixty (and above) age group, fifty-two out of seventy would explain to the non-believing people about God's goodness and faithfulness, that he is always good and does take care of them. They would add that they no longer belong to the pagan belief system, but, rather, are alive to God who created the universe and desires to free human being. They would see the need to trust God through this experience. Faith would prove stronger than ritual-traditions. Eighteen would not accept any encouragement from non-believers on this issue of believing that healing comes from ritual performance. They would see the system as deceiving the people. They would wait on the Lord and expect that in his time, he would heal them.

3. Revelation

The Kankana-eys are sometimes bothered by bad omens and dreams in the course of their Christian life. Often they meet a strange occurrence when they make a trip. Or sometimes a deceased father or mother appears in a dream and express his or her wish. If they were still non-believers they would perform ritual to fulfill the wish.

3.1 A Bad Omen

Q. "One day when you are about to leave for a trip, you see a strange animal crawling in your way, an event which is commonly considered a bad omen. What do you do?"

3.1.1 Female Respondents

In the twenty to thirty-four age group, all respondents (120) would not postpone their trip but would take off. Yet, they would pray to the Lord against bad feelings about the strange animal. They would ask God for a safe journey and pray that nothing would happen on the way to their destination. Even while they would do their business, nothing unfortunate would occur, and their job would be successful by God's help. They expressed confidence that such an event would be an interruption from dark powers aimed to create spiritual turmoil. They would thus rebuke the bad omen, considering it Satanic activity.

In the thirty-five to forty-four age group, 81 out of 130 answered that they no longer believed in bad omens as pagans do. They belong to the world of light where Jesus Christ is the Lord in their life. They would go on the trip with joy and would invite the presence of God along the trip. Forty-nine would try to dispel the force of the old notion. They would be quite conscious of the animal and its sign. So, before the trip they would pray to the Lord to remove the wrong understanding about the strange animal and help them to believe that it is merely one of God's creatures. With prayer they would take off on the journey.

In the forty-five to sixty (and above) age group, 62 out of 110 would go on the trip as it had been planned but, before leaving, they would ask a church pastor and some others to pray for them to not feel uncomfortable about the experience. They would continue going to the Lord to ask for a safe journey and pleasant business. They would recall verses of the Bible to combat uneasy feelings. Forty-eight would share this experience with some close church members and listen to their advice. They would suspect that it had come from an evil spirit attempting to disturb the trip. They would want to be encouraged with prayer of fellow Christians.

3.2.2 Male Respondents

In the twenty to thirty-four age group, 62 out of 115 would not care about any strange animal crawling into their home. They no longer believed what non-believers believe about bad omens. Fifty-three would go on the trip with the faith that nothing would happen on the way. They would trust that God would be with them wherever they were to go. They expressed belief that it would be an act of faith that should be demonstrated in a situation like this.

In the thirty-five to forty-four age group, 52 out of 125 would try not to be bothered by the strange creature. If the notion of a bad omen lurked in the back of their minds, they would rebuke it with the power of the Holy Spirit. They would try to stand in a position as children of God who do not fear anything. Thirty-eight would go the Bible and find peace and comfort from the living Word, knowing that God always keeps his children safe from danger. This promise would serve as a refuge on which to dwell in their minds, and they would peaceably proceed with the journey. Thirty-five would pray before leaving for the destination. They would ask God to bless the trip. They would not have an unfortunate experience but would safely return home. Prayer would go along with their travel.

All of the forty-five to sixty (and above) age group indicated they would not be bothered by a strange animal. They would not regard that animal as a bad omen. Many of these respondents were senior members in a church whose faith had firmly been built. They were the Bible-believing people of God, knowing God as one who directs them on a good path.

3.2 A Terrible Dream

Q. "When you plan to visit your sister's home, you have a terrible dream the previous night. Would you go on the trip or not? If you needed to go, what would you do?"

3.2.1 Female Respondents

In the twenty to thirty-four age group, 51 out of 120 would pray against the bad dream and ask for God's protection on their trip. The terrible dream might bother them on their way, but they would try to get over uncomfortable feelings with prayer. Thirty-nine would go and visit their sister's home as well. They would discern that an evil spirit was attempting to discourage them with the terrible dream, but they would not give in. Rather, they would declare the victory of Jesus gained by the resurrection. They testified that even though they had had this kind of experience before, they were now immune to it. Thirty would put off plans for visiting the sister's home. They would not want to leave with uneasy feelings but would rather stay at home and pray.

In the thirty-five to forty-four age group, 62 out of 130 would go on the trip to visit the sister's home. They would expect the presence of the Holy Spirit to be with their journey. They would keep on praying to God to grant peace and comfort. Sixty-eight would proceed to visit the sister. They would try not to be affected but would also rebuke the memory of the bad dream coming to the mind. They would believe that God allows pleasant trips, and he would let nothing tragic happen. They would try to practice their faith in such a case.

In the forty-five to sixty (and above) age group, 53 out of 110 would pray that nothing harmful would occur on the way to their sister's home. They would constantly go to the Lord to ensure a peaceful and joyful journey. Thirty-nine would go and visit the sister, trusting God to protect and guide them on the trip. They would know that God is good and he would keep them unharmed and safe. Eighteen would try to remove uneasy feelings before they departed. In order to ensure God's protection, they would pray and read the Scriptures. They would try not to attach their fears to the dream but would get over them with spiritual power.

3.2.2 Male Respondents

In the twenty to thirty-four age group, 79 out of 115 would go and visit the sister. They would not be affected by the dream. They said that Christians do not believe what they used to believe as pagan people because they are children of God saved from darkness. Thus, the bad dream would not hinder them from going on the trip. Thirty-six would have discomfort because of the bad dream. The dream would be something unusual, so that they might recall it over and over. In order to forget the dream, they constantly would go to the word of God and through this means, they would overcome all negative feelings creeping in. However, they would go on the trip after settling down their hearts.

In the thirty-five to forty-four age group, 65 out of 125 would go ahead with the trip as planned. They would have faith that God would grant them a safe journey. He would not let them meet with any unfortunate incident but would guide them, even until they returned home. Thirty-two would rebuke the bad dream. They expressed that such a dream would be an attempt to dishearten them and threaten to hinder to their spiritual life. They would not put off visiting the sister but would continue as arranged. Twenty-eight would leave for the trip, believing that God would protect them. They would try not to dwell on the dream. They would refer to the word of God to counter the bad dream.

In the thirty-five to sixty (and above) age group, forty-seven out of seventy would rebuke the dream. They would see it as a Satanic work, aimed to impair their spiritual life. They would not give up their plans to visit the sister. They would have firm faith that God is always with them and that he keeps his children from attacks of evil spirits. Twenty-three would go and visit the sister's home, and they would bless their trip and believe in God's protection. They would try to have a joyful journey. They would trust that the trip would transpire with God's presence.

4. Spiritual World: After Death

Non-believing Kankana-eys believe in life beyond death. Spirits of deceased ancestors are believed to be roaming around the community and associating with the affairs of living people. Kankana-ey believers' understanding of the spiritual world is entirely different.

Through two questions, I attempted to observe what the Kankana-ey believers have been taught to believe about the world in relation to the dead. Their changed notions of existence after death are detected through their answers.

4.1 Understanding of Spirits

Q. "Before your conversion, the priest in a ritual would say that an ancestor's spirit had come. Now what do you think it was that had come?"

4.1.1 Female Respondents

In the twenty to thirty-four age group, 57 out of 120 thought that it was an evil spirit in disguise. They denied that the ancestor's spirit had come to help solve their problems and needs. Thirty-two believed that it was an evil spirit; the ancestor's spirit was in an unseen world and never roamed around the world. What they had done before, they now thought was entirely wrong. Thirty-one understood that it was a work of Satan. Before conversion they had lived in a realm of dark power and under control of Satan. After becoming Christians they were freed from bondage of darkness.

In the thirty-five to forty-four age group, 45 out of 130 believed that it was a devil who was disguised as an ancestor's spirit. They were deluded by the evil spirit. What they had believed about the visitation of the ancestor's spirit was wrong. Eighty-five said that it was an evil spirit. They were surrounded by dark power and were driven by the evil spirit. Their old belief system was a way of serving evil spirits. They had fallacious understandings of ancestors' spirits.

In the forty-five to sixty (and above) age group, all respondents (110) understood the manifestation to have been an evil spirit, so they were deceived by the evil spirit. What they believed about the power of spiritual beings (ancestors' spirits) was wrong. It was by evil power that they anticipated healing, blessing, and having their needs met.

4.1.2 Male Respondents

In the twenty to thirty-four age group, 47 out of 115 believed that it was an evil spirit revealed in the form of the ancestors' spirit. After becoming Christians, they came to learn that there was no existence of spirit of ancestors but only of evil spirits. Sixty-eight also indicated that they were held in the bondage of darkness and worship of evil spirits, rather than having real relationship with an ancestral spirit. They now realized that spirits of ancestors do not obtain power to meet their descendants' needs. Spirits of ancestors were viewed as dysfunctional in that they had no ability to do their kin favors.

In the thirty-five to forty-four age group, all of the respondents viewed such manifestations as evil spirits disguised as spirits of ancestors. After conversion, they never believed in such an existence of an ancestor's spirit, nor in an ancestor's ability to cure or solve problems. The Christian God, they indicated, is the only living God who can release power for healing and meeting needs.

In the forty-five to sixty (and above) age group, people unanimously agreed that it was an evil spirit. The pagan Kankana-eys, they said, are spirit-filled people in the sense that spiritual beings dwell in an underworld and skyworld. They associate with living people's affairs and daily activities. This notion has been imbedded in them since childhood. However, such orientation to spirits of ancestors no longer has sway over the minds of these Christian people. The God they now serve and worship is the only living God who answers prayer and provides for their needs.

4.2 Perception of Spirit World

Q. "Where do you think all the deceased spirits are now?"

4.2.1 Female Respondents

In the twenty to thirty-four age group, people identically answered that deceased spirits of believers are with the Lord, while spirits of unbelievers are in hell. They believe in two different worlds after death, heaven and hell. Those (spirits) who have accepted the Lord as their personal savior and become true Christians go to heaven, but those who are in bondage to darkness go to hell.

In the thirty-five to forty-four age group, respondents indicated that they thought the same way as the above group. Deceased souls of believers would go to heaven, whereas non-believers' souls would go to hell. They indicated belief in the existence of an unseen world to be met after death. However, they do not believe that spirits roam in the spheres of the visible present world.

In the forty-five to sixty (and above) age group, all respondents answered that deceased spirits of Christian, would be with Christ, while spirits of non-Christians would fall into hell. They indicated belief in the existence of an invisible world where two different sorts of people's spirits go after death. They obviously believed that these spirits never traveled to the earth nor associated with activities and affairs of living people.

4.2.2 Male Respondents

The three different age groups, twenty to thirty-four, thirty-five to forty-four, and forty-five to sixty (and above) gave identical responses concerning their understanding that believers' spirits would be with Christ, while non-believers' spirits would be in the darkness of hell. All of them had clear representations about the unseen world to be met after death. Heaven was seen as the final world in which Christians will dwell, while non-believing people's spirits will be destined to hell and to suffering forever.

In summary, through the above summaries of my data, I see that a majority of Kankana-ey tribal Christians have been exposed to the exercise of faith and trust in God in various crises. Their faith is that he will never forsake his children, but will bless and help them restore their businesses.

In comparing their pre-Christian with post-Christian lives, it appears that pre-Christian Kankana-eys customarily sought village priests to consult with them about their problems and routinely followed the priestly advice. Others borrowed money from their relatives or friends to re-establish their farm. Still others lost their control and often drunkenly vented their anger. After becoming Christians, however, they seem to deal with crises in totally new ways. They seek God to intervene in their problems. It is not because they are lazy but because they trust in God. They strive to maximize their faith in him. In such crises they have no idea how to reestablish their destroyed garden. Although they want to borrow money to repair it, often the high interest rate forbids many from doing so. Some Christians are eager to seek new work. Whatever job may be available, they want to work to survive.

The Kankana-ey Christians express firm belief in the healing power of the Holy Spirit. They seem to desire personal experience of this power whenever someone in the family gets sick. I noticed that many of them recounted personal events that occurred as healing experiences of God along their Christian life. My analysis of the data leads to the conclusion that many people in different age groups earnestly seek the power of the Holy Spirit, especially in the trials of a sick baby.

Though past pagan ways are largely discarded, I notice that some believers feel uneasy about making a trip after having a terrible dream. Some members do not make their trip after experiencing a bad omen. Their reaction does not seem to be because they hold onto notions of pagan fears; rather, it may reflect a tendency of human nature. Most of the believers would make an effort to pray and read Scriptures to allay fears caused by such a dream.

The Kankana-ey Christians believe in the spiritual world. After becoming Christians, they discover that what they believed about the existence of ancestors' spirits was misguided. It was not ancestors' spirits but evil spirits that were manifested in ritual. They had erroneously perceived that spirits of their ancestors had power to bring good and bad luck to enable the living to deal with affairs of everyday life. However, with conversion, this notion was entirely changed in their minds.

They now seem to unanimously believe that spirits of Christians go to heaven, but spirits of non-Christians are destined for hell. Deceased spirits do not wander the world and harm people or make people sick. Yet, the Kankana-ey Christians do believe in existence after death.

Chapter 8

A Comparative Theological Analysis of Traditional Kankana-ey and Pentecostal Practices

In Chapter 7, I have dealt with the Kankana-eys' own ethnic theology, built through their Christian experience. After becoming Christian, their worldview changed, including their understanding of God, blessing, and healing. This chapter endeavors to compare and contrast the worldviews of Pentecostals, Kankana-ey Pentecostal Christians and animists (native Kankana-eys) based on the studies done in the previous chapters. The chapter further analyzes aspects of traditional Kankana-ey practice over against Pentecostal practice, in the light of the above comparison. For a clear point-by-point comparison, the four categories are again enlisted in this procedure. That is, I attempt to describe how each group views God, the Holy Spirit, revelation, and the spiritual world. Identifiable commonalties may be indicative of potential contact points for further evangelism among these people.

On the worldview of the native Kankana-eys, versus the Kankana-ey Pentecostal Christians, Chapter 4 (on religious practice of the Kankana-eys) and Chapter 7 (on ethnic theology of the Kankana-ey Pentecostal Christians) will be referenced. For the Pentecostals, I have based my analyses on practical Pentecostal theology – theology that is not necessarily learned through literature, but rather is lived by Pentecostal Christians in their everyday affairs.

1. God

This section will discuss the three groups' worldviews on God (spirit beings), especially in terms of blessing and curse notions. Each group's distinctive experience with God (spirit beings) will be delineated.

1.1 Blessing

In most religions both fortune and misfortune are ascribed to the will of the deities. The Pentecostals view God as the loving father, faithful, and good. The loving father blesses his children as they present their desires to him. God is faithful to meet their needs. Kankana-ey Pentecostal Christians likewise experience God's blessing and believe in God's provision. They believe that God cares for his people.

1.1.1 Native Kankana-eys

The native *Kankana-eys* not only believe in spirit beings, but also in these beings' intimate involvement in the daily activities of their life. The deities thus function in roles which are significant for people. The most relevant and tangible expression of divine power is felt in the forms of blessing and curse endowed or inflicted by the deities. The gods are believed to be the ultimate source of blessing. Thus, the Kankana-eys frequently perform rituals to receive blessings. The gods are sought in order that the people may obtain power to meet their needs and resolve conflicts.

As mentioned in Chapter 4, the Kankana-eys perceive that spirit beings have arbitrary power to bring fortune or misfortune to human beings. In every aspect of their life, from bountiful harvest, prosperous family life, increasing herds, to successful business, spirit beings are involved with their power. The Kankana-eys assume that the ancestors have power to grow the crops, raise the animals, and govern in daily works (Russell 1989:24). This notion is so deep in their mind set: if they expect more blessing, they offer more sacrifice.

The following discussion, also mentioned in Chapter 4, describes several occasions on which the pagan Kankana-eys attempt to receive blessing from the gods. A newly married couple, for instance, is encouraged to perform a ritual for a couple of days following the wedding festival. The priest prescribes an appropriate ritual in several stages for the new couple to have a successful and happy married life. Through performing the ritual, they expect blessing and good luck from spirit beings.

Ritual performance is also required before a baby is born. The young couple desires safe delivery for the baby. This wish is fulfilled only through performing a ritual. The villagers are invited for the occasion. The priest carefully observes the liver of the sacrificial animal to determine if the shape is auspicious or ominous. For example, the presence of two biles in the liver, many pockets, or many parts, means good luck will come upon the baby. The priest then orders the young couple to butcher a large pig as an expression of their thanksgiving to the gods.

A native Kankana-ey family, upon the completion of a new house, is expected to perform a ritual to express their gratitude to and to secure more blessings from the deities. The priest (*manbunong*) offers a prayer of blessing. His typical prayer is that the family would offer even greater rituals to honor the gods, especially if the occupants of the new house become rich.

The Kankana-eys also believe that the gods have power of control over success or failure of crops, the people's primary source of sustenance. Rituals during the planting and harvesting seasons are thus the most commonly celebrated. Various smaller rituals are likewise offered for occasions such as mending irrigation channels, hunting, gold mining, cockfighting, and so on. The Kankana-eys perceive the gods as having control over natural resources. For community projects such as irrigation work, village people or groups of individuals agree on an appropriate performance of ritual.

The Kankana-eys trust that their wishes and blessings will be realized through the community priest's proper appeal to the gods along with the proper performance of ritual. They recognize the gods' power to bless and bring good luck to their lives. Every activity of the Kankana-eys is complete only insofar as the deities are invoked to intervene. This invocation is achieved solely through the appropriate means of ritual performance. The ritual provides a meaningful avenue by which the people have their felt needs met.

1.1.2 Pentecostals

Pentecostal theology of blessing is not much different from that of traditional Christian theology. However, Pentecostals believe that God intervenes tangibly when they ask, and specific blessings are therefore expected. That is, the Pentecostal belief is characterized by an expectant and experiential dimension in Christian life.

What characteristics of God assure the Pentecostals of God's blessing? First of all, God is faithful. The Hebrew word *amen*, "truly," is derived from one of the most outstanding Hebrew descriptions of God's character, reflecting his certainty and dependability. The Pentecostals use *amen* to express their assurance of God's ability to answer prayer (Joyner 1994:125). God reveals his faithfulness by keeping his promises: "Know therefore that the Lord your God is God; he is the faithful God, keeping his covenant of love to a thousand generations of those who love him and keep his commands" (Deu. 7:9). The psalmist confesses, "You established your faithfulness in heaven itself" (Ps. 89:2). Pentecostals frequently confess God's faithfulness saying, "mercies are new every morning; great is thy faithfulness" (Lam. 3:22). The verbal pronouncement is more than a mental exercise. They anticipate in the expression that they will experience his faithfulness. Paul contrasts the human and the divine natures as follows: "If we are faithless, he will remain faithful, for he cannot disown himself" (2 Ti. 2:13). God's dependability is absolute, because God is faithful (Deu. 32:4; Ps. 89:8; 1 Th. 5:23-24; Heb. 10:23; 1 Jn. 1:9). The dependable and faithful God keeps the promise of his blessing as his people ask and seek for it.

Secondly, God, by his nature, is good. During the days of creation, God periodically examined his work and declared that it was good, in the sense of being pleasing and well-suited for his purpose. The psalmist expresses the same thought: "The Lord is good and his love endures forever" (Ps. 100:5). Another Psalm expresses praise for this goodness: "The Lord is gracious and compassionate, slow to anger and rich in love. The Lord is good to all; he has compassion on all he has made" (Ps. 145:8-9). Pentecostals often celebrate his goodness in praise and worship. They believe that God, who is good, will meet his people's needs. In fact, he is willing to bless and provide for his people (Acts 14:17).

Thirdly, God is love. He is God who loved the world so that he gave his only begotten son. This reveals God's particular kind of love – giving sacrificially. God lavishly displays his love also by providing for his people rest and protection (Deu. 33:12). Yet, the highest form and greatest demonstration of his love is found in the cross of Christ (Rom. 5:8). Because of his love and grace, the world is redeemed and sinners are saved.

The expectation of God's blessing has as its basis God's own character, which is exhibited in his relationship with his people. The character of God discussed above is formed of integral dimensions and dynamics, and these features never change. God promises his blessing to his people based on this divine integrity. His blessing is intended for his people's experience in daily life. It is not meant only to be transcendent, but also to be immanent, tangible and empirical as well. For this reason Pentecostals do not hesitate seeking such blessing of God. Experience enhance their relationship with God as they are drawn closer to him, and this leads them into deep faith.

1.1.3 Kankana-ey Pentecostal Christians

The Kankana-ey Pentecostal Christians want to experience God's blessing in the whole spectrum of their daily life. When any unexpected disaster strikes them, they are immediately brought earnestly to seek God's help and blessing. During the monsoon season, for a period of six to eight months, a series of typhoons pummels the region, and the people often suffer great losses and destruction. Their farm products, for use in deriving their major source of sustenance, are most significantly affected. In such critical situations, the Kankana-ey Pentecostals intensely look for God's help and blessing.

Through the interviews of this study (discussed in Chapter 7), conducted among the Kankana-ey Pentecostal Christians, questions were asked so as to register their views of God's blessing. Interviews revealed a simple yet profound understanding of God's blessing. Their theological view has been established primarily through empirical, daily life experiences, where they exist as Christians in a pagan community.

They, first of all, view God as Provider of their needs. They have learned to request of God what they need. After conversion, they come to know that their provider is no longer the whole array of pagan gods, but rather the one God who created the universe and humankind. The Kankana-ey Pentecostals hold to what the Bible says: he never forsakes nor neglects his children, but he always cares for them. Thus, when they encounter disasters in their business, they prioritize seeking the Provider for help and blessing. They confess, "We want to exercise our faith in such a difficult circumstance." Practicing faith typically leads them to endurance and further experience of his blessing.

Secondly, they have an immanent orientation to God. He is believed to be able to supply the basic needs of his people. When the Kankana-ey believers face financial crisis, they earnestly beseech God for help. They frequently expect that God can and will improve farming and production mining. They actively believe and anticipate that God will intervene in their circumstances and assist in their affairs. They express their trust in various ways. In a time of crisis, they seldom wrestle with problems by themselves. They often broadly share their concerns. It is thus not uncommon to have an hour-long time of testimonies during any given service. They freely share their thanksgiving as well as their prayer needs. Considering their traditional timidity, this is a rather unusual scene. They often call together fellow Christians for corporate prayer. This practice clearly expresses their oneness in the face of being surrounded by "persecuting" relatives and neighbors. They simply believe that blessing will truly come when they ask for it.

Thirdly, they believe that God is the source of all blessings. Prior to receiving their Christian faith, they indicated they would believe that the pagan gods were the ultimate source of their blessing. Facing calamity, they would seek the village priest to prescribe an appropriate ritual for blessing, and thus secure their future. After becoming Christian, they came to believe that God is the only One who can bless. God is trusted as the One who is in charge of their lives. One Kankana-ey Pentecostal Christian stated, "he [God] cares for us and brings blessing to us when we look for it." Thus God is viewed as the abundant Blesser.

Fourthly, God blesses because he is faithful. The Kankana-ey Pentecostals' experience of God in his faithfulness may be dramatically contrasted with their former relations to gods who were unpredictable and who constantly changed their demands. The capricious and demanding nature of the gods is reflected in one of the rituals in which the number of sacrificial animals increases, beginning with one, then three, five, seven, and so on. They also understand God's faithfulness as supplying the needs of his children. As they believe in his faithfulness, they wait on his blessing. This perseverance results in their growth in faith and trust in God. Some of them articulated their view of God as follows: "We frequently recall the experience of God's faithfulness in his blessing," or "It helps us to wait on what is anticipated to come."

To summarize, the Kankana-ey Pentecostals view God in terms of his blessing. He primarily is considered as the Provider who is faithful and as the source of all blessing. It seems reasonable to assume that their firsthand experience of God's blessing has contributed to the formation of such a view of God's blessing. They particularly believe that God's power is manifested through blessings. Their concrete minds further seem to generate simple belief and trust. God is higher than any other gods, and his power is greater than any other gods' powers.

1.2 Curse

Whenever non-Christian Kankana-eys experience disaster or difficulties, they attribute it to the gods and spirits. The acts of the gods are considered either as curses or judgment. Calamity occurs, according to their understanding, when they offend any of the gods or spirits. The gods are able to discern if a person is guilty or not, and they will curse a community's offenders. The Pentecostals similarly believe that in God's judgment, they may suffer when he is offended. God is the Lord of love and judgment. Judgment is to be expected when one commits sin. The Kankana-ey Pentecostals experience curse as it is embodied by non-believing members of the community, especially when the Christians no longer participate in traditional religious practices.

1.2.1 Native Kankana-eys

The native Kankana-eys hold to a notion that the gods bring a curse when a ritual is not properly offered or if it is omitted. The offended and angered spirit beings bring affliction as a form of curse, causing poor harvests, illness, hearing problems, sleepiness, drowsiness, headache, inability to procreate, or the like. Sometimes the spirits, the Kankana-eys believe, cause acute depression for an extended period of time. This affliction naturally keeps one from normal activity and renders a victim unproductive in daily life. The only way to counter such affliction is to appease the offended deity. The requisite appeasement involves careful execution of an animal sacrifice, or the appropriate material offerings. This activity is not voluntary worship, but rather is acquiescence to and appeasement of anger, whims or caprice. Since the purpose of performing this ritual is to comfort and soothe the angry gods in order to expect healing of the afflicted, detailed observation of animals' entrails is requisite in order to detect any omen. The Kankana-eys believe that the performer's ancestors come down for the completion of this offering.

The curse normally comes upon the offended party from *Adika-ila*, the highest god and god of justice and fairness. If an individual is suspected of stealing someone's animal, the owner brings the suspect to the members of the village council. The priest presides over the council and proceeds with the case. The priest first offers a prayer to the deity. Then a council member interrogates the accuser as well as the accused one. The first question is addressed to the accused: "Do you believe that the guilty party will be cursed by the highest spirit?" The suspect answers, "Yes." It is implied that he asserts his innocence. Then the council asks the accuser, "If there is no truth in your charge, are you willing to suffer the curse of *Adika-ila*?" The farmer indicates this willingness. The council then asks the final question of the suspect, "You claim your innocence, while the accuser is positive in his accusation. In this case, we cannot give judgment but leave the case to *Adika-ila*." Then the council presents to the suspect a selection of several curses that he or she should suffer. In this particular case the selections are: 1) that he or she shall live a very poor life; 2) that lightning will strike him or her; 3) that a snake will bite him or her; or 4) that he or she may not live long (Sacla 1987:16).

In summary, the pagan Kankana-eys perceive the gods as having power to bring curses. It is, therefore, of crucial importance for them to avoid offending the gods in any degree. Appropriate avoidance and appeasement will prevent them from unfavorable occurrences, and will secure favor. Offering sacrifices restores normal states of life. The gods are also capable of discerning whether a person is a guilty or not, and they will curse society's offenders.

1.2.2 Pentecostals

The Pentecostals understand God as the God of justice (משפט). The justice of God includes judgmental penalty (Deu. 7:9-10). His character is dependable in ethical and moral realms. "Rightness" (in Hebrew, צדקה) is a feature of his character and action (Joyner 1994:130). He judges his people in righteousness and justice (Ps. 72:2).

According to the biblical worldview, the shape of which is reflected in the Pentecostal worldview, there are several types of guilt (He. אשם, Gen. 26:10; Gk. ενοχος, Jas. 2:10). Individual or personal guilt may be distinguished from the communal guilt of societies. Objective guilt ascribes to actual sin, whether realized by the guilty or not. Subjective guilt refers to the experience of guilt as it is perceived by a person. Subjective guilt may be honest, leading to repentance (Ps.

51; Ac. 2:40-47; Marino 1994:286). God's justice does not compromise with sin (Ps. 11:5; Rom. 1:18). Penalty or castigation inflicted by an authority on sinners is the just result of sin, a chastisement predicated on guilt.

Scriptures further teach that the impact of sin is apparent in nonhuman creation. The curse pronounced in Genesis 3:17-18 marks the beginning of this evil. Romans 8:19-22 elaborates on the continuous state of frustration in nature. The creation groans expecting the consummation of Jesus Christ. The Greek ματαιοτες, "frustration," "emptiness" (Rom. 8:20), describes the incessancy of corruption that is set in motion when something is separated from its original intent, epitomizing in one term the overall futility of the present state of the universe itself. The condition may range from plants and animals to quarks and galaxies (Marino 1994:285).

Judgment, however, renders the guilty motivated to replace what has been taken or destroyed. This can be a witness of God's work in a life (Ex. 22:1; Lk. 19:8). Deterrence, for example, includes using castigation of the guilty to discourage others from behaving similarly. Such deterrences may often be seen in divine warnings (Ps. 95:8-11; 1 Cor. 10:11). Remediation enables the guilty not to sin in the future. It is an expression of God's love (Ps. 94:12; Heb. 12:5-17).

Issues of justice are to be dealt with in the church over against the reality and problems of sin, as part of the truth of love. God's justice and love resides at the center of Christian worldview concern, wherever the uncompromised gospel may be practiced among the authentic body of Christ and further shared among non-believers. Pentecostals accordingly transmit the good news of Christ as containing both justice and love. The Pentecostal preachment is that the world should hear a balanced, two-edged message of Christ.

1.2.3 Kankana-ey Pentecostal Christians

The Kankana-ey believers frequently are cursed by non-believing relatives and neighbors when the former do not follow Kankana-ey traditional religious practices. Sharing the gospel also elicits curses from non-believers. According to the interviews for this study, the Kankana-ey Pentecostal Christians typically counteract cursing with prayer. They say, "We trust God to prevent and protect us from the curse of the non-believing people." "We believe in the power of prayer, that the curse from the pagans will not occur."

Although they are cursed these believers still return the love of Christ. This response is possible only through the help of the Holy Spirit. The Kankana-ey Pentecostal Christians know that love is an essential element of Christianity and that they have to show it to pagan people. They continue to demonstrate the lovingkindness of Christ to those who curse. Cursing is not something Christians are taught to do. The Kankana-ey believers are taught instead to bless the non-believers who curse. To bless those who curse is a sign of spiritual maturity. They believe that they demonstrate a biblical pattern when, as Christians, they do not return cursing for cursing. They do rebuke the curses of pagan people, invoking the power of God. However, rebuking does not mean that they confront unbelievers. Rather, they exercise spiritual power granted to them so that they will be protected from the curse. This typical behavior shows that they indeed take cursing seriously. It also implies that they rely upon God's authority. In this sense, the Kankana-ey Pentecostal believers are verbally bold to declare the power of God. One states, "Whenever we need to proclaim God's power, we do so."

The Kankana-ey Pentecostal Christians also counter the curse with the word of God. They understand that God's word is a great spiritual weapon availed to their use. They constantly read the Bible to gain strength in God. They stress that "God is with us when we go through suffering and difficulty." They believe that God's word literally provides a "refuge."

They believe that God, with his power, is able to protect them from the curse. They trust that he would never allow his children to be cursed, because God's power is greater than that of any other god. He is viewed as capable of keeping his children from any harm. Accordingly, for instance, they regularly pray as they travel that the blood of Jesus will cover their ways.

2. The Holy Spirit: Healing

The native Kankana-eys believe in an absolute power of spirit beings. They resort to costly ritual ceremonies to meet the need. The Pentecostals believe in the healing power of the Holy Spirit. The Kankana-ey Pentecostal Christians experience the power of Holy Spirit throughout the Christian life and continually experience the Holy Spirits' healing touch.

Healing is one prominent area of concern for all three groups involved in this study. The pagan Kankana-eys, as any other animists, are spirit-conscious people. They perceive the spirits as responsible for diseases and that ancestors' spirits have also obtained power to heal. They also believe that human beings can induce the healing power of the spirits via ritual performance. Pentecostals acknowledge healing as the work of the Holy Spirit. They frequently invite the presence of the Holy Spirit when his healing touch is needed.

2.1 Native Kankana-eys

When a family member becomes sick, pagan Kankana-eys seek the counsel of the priest, (*mansip-ok*), who is gifted in discernment. The priest analyzes all the information supplied by the sick person. Often, dreams and/or omens around the time of the onset of sickness bear significance to the cause. The *mansip-ok* determines the cause of illness from them (Inio 1987). Often the spirit of a deceased brother or sister communicates to family members through these means. The *mansip-ok* determines which specific spirit is responsible for the sickness. One example of interpretation is this: a certain ancestral spirit needs blankets, clothes, garments, food or animals. The family of the sick person has to meet these demands. The *mansip-ok* also prescribes a specific ritual for healing.

As discussed in Chapter 4, in some instances a normal person suddenly loses his or her sense of hearing without knowing the reason. The immediate advice is to conduct a ritual called *bosal-lan*. Before starting actual ritual, the *manbunong* makes a replica of a small hut, about one foot wide and a foot high, near the house of the sick person's parents. Then the *manbunong*, who has partaken of power with the spirits (Wiber 1989:58), conducts ritual beside this little hut. He offers a chicken as sacrifice to pacify the spirit who caused the deafness. The *manbunong* induces the spirit to come out of the ear and to move into the hut, for the hut is a better dwelling place. While the *manbunong* offers a prayer, the sick person plucks wing feathers of the chicken and places them inside the hut to lead the spirit to come in. After finishing this process, the chicken is singed, sliced, cooked and eaten (Igualdo 1989:231).

The spirits of the deceased are not totally separated from the visible world, their families or their descendants. Rather, they intimately interact with them. Since the spirits have no direct means of communication with living kin, they employ dreams and sickness to tell what they want. It is believed that, although the spirits are out of body, the spirits still need for their use the items listed above – blankets, clothes, garments, food, and animals. The spirits obtain power to heal the living who comply with their demands. The spirits are figured as power, and power that the Kankana-eys believe is released when living people approach the presence of the deities through mediums in the worship of ritual.

2.2 Pentecostals

It appears that healing is one of the Pentecostals' distinguishing messages. According to the Pentecostal worldview, when the Holy Spirit moves, healing takes place. Instances of healing frequently are recounted among Pentecostal believers. Such testimony often serves to bring souls to Christ.

Pentecostals believe that the healing ministry was an essential part of Jesus' ministry during his earthly life. His healing authority was revealed as a sign that the Kingdom of God had come in him and through his work. Matthew quotes Isaiah 53:4, saying, "he took our infirmities and bore our diseases." This reference reminds listeners that he used his power for the purpose of serving people (Mt. 20:28; 26:28; Smith 1988:133). The Pentecostals rightly argue that the Gospels attest the abundant healing ministry of Christ (Mk. 1:29-34, 40-42; 2:1-12; 3:1-6; Jn. 4:46-54; 9:17; Mt. 8:1-4; 12:9-13).

Pentecostals also argue that the healing ministry of Christ is intended to bring people into the Kingdom of God. When people see and experience the power of healing, their attention is arrested and they are more likely to believe that Christ is who he claims to be (Lk. 10:1-9). This evangelistic significance is well attested in Jesus' commissioning of the seventy-two (Lk. 10:1-2). They were equipped with power and commanded to "heal" (Lk. 10:9).

Pentecostals further note that baptism in the Spirit was necessary before the first disciples were to leave Jerusalem or even begin to fulfill the great commission. They needed power to witness (Ac. 1:8). The concept of the Holy Spirit in the New Testament and that of the Spirit of God in the Old Testament are intimately connected with power. Considering the pattern of Jesus' ministry after the appearance of the Holy Spirit in his baptism (Mt. 3:16), it is not difficult to assume that the "power" is more than dynamic verbal capability. It includes power to heal. The healing account in Acts 3 is taken by Pentecostals to be a typical case. This event immediately drew a large crowd, and Peter was given an opportunity to present the message of Jesus and his salvation.

The history of the mountain Pentecostal churches in the northern Philippines is replete with accounts of healing and miracles. These occurrences are particularly frequent during the early stage of the Pentecostal ministry (1947). As discussed in Chapter 3, the power of the Holy Spirit was revealed through healings of various sick people, through the work of one missionary woman working on her own, Elva Vanderbout. Her burning desire to bring souls to Christ impelled her boldly to share the gospel among the pagans. Her first revival meeting was held in Tuding, Itogon, Benguet Province. In this meeting, the Holy Spirit moved mightily among the people. Many were saved, and more than 150 were baptized in water. A countless number of people, young and old, including small children, shared wonderful testimonies of the power of God. Primarily, they referred to God's power by referencing his miraculous work to save souls and to heal sicknesses (Soriano 1948).

At every subsequent Sunday night service more people were also baptized with the Holy Ghost and fire, in the pattern of to Acts 2:4. It was like old time Pentecost. With a tremendous sense of anticipation people came to services to hear the message of Christ. God's power was displayed through the message and through prayer. The power the people experienced was something different from the power of ancestral spirits mediated by pagan priests.

Vanderbout held a revival meeting for salvation and healing in Baguio City. During the revival meeting one girl, eighteen years of age who had suffered as a deaf-mute for twelve years, was instantly healed. During each morning and evening service, the sick lined up for healing (Vanderbout 1955). The Holy Spirit moved mightily among the people and many sick people were healed. The blind were enabled to see. Paralytics were healed. People suffering with tuberculosis and many other diseases were healed. One woman was healed who was suffered for a long period of time a large goiter. It became smaller when she was prayed for on Saturday night, smaller still when she came back to the services on Sunday morning, and it all disappeared later (1955).

Healing and salvation characterized Vanderbout's eight-day crusade. In fact, healing and miracles not only drew large crowds, but also convinced them that God, through the Holy Spirit, is the Miracle Worker. Through healing manifestations many pagans turned to Christ and abandoned their traditional beliefs. The healings continued to take place by the power of the Holy Spirit throughout the mountain ministry. It is likely that the people's religious expectations contributed greatly to the frequent manifestation of the healing power of the Holy Spirit. As a result, the Assemblies of God opened many works and erected numerous churches throughout Benguet Province and beyond. The successful penetration of the Assemblies of God into the animistic mountain region thus is largely attributable to the active manifestation of the power, frequently of healing, of the Holy Spirit.

2.3 Kankana-ey Pentecostal Christians

The Kankana-ey Pentecostal Christians expect the regular working of the Holy Spirit in their lives. They believe that the Holy Spirit readily works when people of God urgently beseech him. The Kankana-ey Pentecostals, when a family member gets sick, intensely pray for the intervention of the Holy Spirit. It is believed that, when the Holy Spirit is present, healing will take place. Peace and consolation come along with it.

The Kankana-ey Pentecostals say, "God never fails us when we approach him in faith." This phrase reflects their strong faith in abiding in God. The

Kankana-ey believers frequently convene for corporate prayer. They customarily make their prayer requests known to fellow Christians. When prayer is answered, they publicly share their testimonies in a church service. Testimony time is the part of a church service allotted for anyone to stand up and share such testimonies.

Experience of healing power leads them increasingly to rely more on the power of the Holy Spirit. The Kankana-ey Christians, particularly older believers, confess that they not only have seen many healings, but also have personally experienced God's healing touch in the past. In interviews they testified, "When a family member gets sick, we pray for healing, and God answers our prayer." The healing experience also makes the Pentecostal Christians an encouragement to non-Christian members; especially when they are sick, they often want to seek the help of the God who heals.

An average Kankana-ey community lacks many basic provisions. There is no electrical power source and, in some places, there is not even an adequate water system. There is no medical service whatsoever, except in large villages where a health worker may be found, but without a supply of suitable medicine. Therefore, if anyone is ill, people either wait for a natural recovery or carry the patient many mountain miles to reach a hospital or a clinic, which adds to their hardship. Their farming barely sustains their living. In remote villages cash income is not known. Thus, bringing the sick to the hospital and buying medication is difficult. It is not unusual to find a sick baby crying all by himself or herself, while other family members are all in the field. The last resort is performing a ritual. However, this very dearly costs the afflicted family. Against this background, it is no wonder that healing from the Holy Spirit is so routinely sought among Kankana-ey Pentecostals. The power experience leads them to the truth of and allegiance to God. The concrete mindset of the tribal people readily acknowledges the power and goodness of God who works healing wonder "without cost."

3. Revelation

"Revelation" can mean, in one useful definition, communication by a spiritual being to humans. As in every religion, there are two kinds of divine communication to humans: voluntary and involuntary. In "voluntary communication," a message from a divinity is readily revealed to humans. In the involuntary mode, humans attempt to obtain a message from spirit beings by inducing them, often through ritual.

3.1 Native Kankana-eys

The native Kankana-eys worldview regards as real and powerful omens and signs. They are dreams, strange animals, moonblack and red birds, snakes, dogs and pigs. A disturbing or unusual dream signifies an impending accident or misfortune. When strange animals or birds enter a house, the native Kankana-eys believe that they may foretell of future occurrences for the family. Birds with red colors signify either bad or good luck, depending on their entering movements. A snake crawling inside a house may foretell good or bad luck as well. These incidents must be referred to the priest (*mankotom*) or the elders for prescription of necessary ritual. If the movement of the animal signifies bad luck, the ritual *pukkay* is required. It is intended to counteract bad luck or misfortune caused by offended spirits. The preferable sacrificial animal is a dog, the barking of which is believed to drive the evil spirits away.

The native Kankana-eys also believe that a pig wallowing in the mud in the morning is a sign of bad luck for the family. The pig should be butchered immediately. A dog barking and wailing at night indicates the presence of evil spirits or an imminent death in the community. The owner of the dog must offer a *madmad* (prayer) ritual to drive away the malevolent spirits. The same owner must invoke the protection of the *Kabunyan*, to keep the community from evil or misfortune (Igualdo 1989:333). If a person's clothes are immersed in river water, it is believed that a family member will be drowned. To dissuade spirits of such intent, ritual is performed.

The native Kankana-eys are particularly sensitive to dreams. Frequently, deceased ancestors reveal the future through dreams. If a family member has a bad or unusual dream, he or she should refer it to the priest (*mankotom*) for proper interpretation and prescription of ritual. If a person who plans to travel dreams of a trip on the night prior to travel, the individual should cancel the trip. If this warning is ignored, he or she will meet with an accident, or the planned business will not be successful. If a traveler meets a black bird flying across or opposite the way of travel, the person must return home, lest death be his or her fate.

The native Kankana-eys, like many other animistic groups, believe that there are built-in messages in certain phenomena. The omens hold profound significance, for they contain vital messages for the people's future welfare. Some omens and signs are universally understood, but there are others that require a professional interpretation as well as proper measures to counter impending misfortune; hence, the vital role of the priest.

3.2 Pentecostals

The Pentecostals share a basic theological orientation with traditional Christianity. The primacy of the written word as God's revelation is never questioned. However, they also believe in God's direct communication through various other modes. Reports of visions, audible messages, and dream are common. Also prophecy in public settings and speaking in tongues with accompanying interpretation are considered modes through which God reveals his will.

The Bible provides an ample amount of evidence that the above phenomena are Holy Spirit manifestations. The Book of Acts records that people saw visions and prophesied after Pentecost. After being baptized in the Holy Spirit, people tended to speak in tongues and prophesy (Ac. 8). Verse 12 of Acts 8 remarks on signs and miracles manifested after the Pentecostal experience. Acts 5:1-10 observes that Peter, by the spirit, foretold the deaths of Ananias and Sapphira. Peter's foreknowledge is understood by today's Pentecostals as God's special revelation in this specific context. It can be identified with the gifts of discernment and prophecy. The Holy Spirit was with him so that he was able to exercise the gifts of God for ministry. Acts 10:9-16 describes a vision of Peter's. The account of the vision is detailed. The experience directly dealt with Peter's bias against the Gentiles. It further substantiated revealed truth (v. 15).

Paul experienced similar works of God. Acts 27:23-24 tells of the angel of God speaking to Paul, revealing God's plan for him. Vision, prophecy, and dreams were frequently used media for God to communicate to Paul his specific will and plan. When Paul had the Macedonian call, he immediately understood it as God's revelation. All these accounts share several commonalties which are also observed by Pentecostals. First, direct revelation is never intended to replace the written word of God. The early church cherished as God's inspired revelation what we today call the Old Testament. Frequently, direct revelation serves to affirm the principles revealed in the written word. Second, the occasions of direct revelation recorded in the Bible are very specific. As in the case of the Macedonian call, often the Spirit directs choices between what seem to be equally acceptable options. Today's Pentecostals distinguish themselves not merely by *remembering*, but especially by *believing* what is written about such work of the Spirit in the Bible. "Prophetic words," accordingly, are often "waited upon" in Pentecostal public services. Pentecostals believe that God's specific communication for specific contexts is accessible, and this is in addition to the written revelation.

3.3 Kankana-ey Pentecostal Christians

If a Kankana-ey Christian has a horrible dream, for example, one in which a dead father appears and expects something from the family, the individual, upon waking, often remains shaken by what he or she has seen in the dream. In such circumstances Kankana-ey Christians often seek the help of pastors to pray for "deliverance" from the fear. Incidents like these occur particularly among new Christians. Their immediate need is to be strong enough to resist old influences. It takes time to instruct the believer disturbed by the above dream that the "father" is not one's own father, but rather is a disguised evil spirit trying to intimidate the family. Taking the authority of the name of Jesus and claiming God's protection is a prayer theme often heard among these believers. Mature Christians see such cases as a means of testing their faith. They perceive evil dreams as attempts of the enemy to destroy their faith. The spiritual dynamic is recognized as spiritual warfare in which they must fight against the devil, with the power of God. So upon waking from nightmares, they immediately "check their spiritual state."

In fact, many Kankana-ey believers have come to the Lord through deliverance from evil dreams. Some dreams have such a powerful effect that an individual cannot take any food or sleep for several nights. When one experiences the power of God delivering him or her from the effect and fear of the omen, that person in fact, becomes free once-for-all.

Worldview and previous religious orientation provide fertile soil for new spiritual experiences. Reports from the field frequently indicate that numerous people see visions as they are in prayer. This phenomenon seems to occur especially among persons who have experienced the baptism of the Spirit. Some speak in tongues, and others are "slain in the Spirit." During these moments, they recall, extraordinary peace fills their beings and is often accompanied by visions, fragrance, and/or the audible voice of the Lord. During the prayer time in a church worship service, it is not unusual for several members to raise their voices and either prophesy or speak in tongues, with other members interpreting.

The Kankana-ey Pentecostals appear to have more experiences of this kind than other Christians, perhaps on account of the dual influences of native animism and Pentecostalism. They view God's work in a way that is exceedingly immanent.

4. Spiritual World

Belief in the spiritual world clearly is evident in Kankana-ey practices concerning life after death. The spirit world is not just a theological subject, but a reality one has to reckon with constantly.

4.1 Native Kankana-eys

The native Kankana-eys believe that there is a hierarchy of deities, and that the deities all have different effects on the human world. A deceased person is believed to join the other spirits in the skyworld. When A*dika-ila,* the supreme being, summons the soul, the body becomes lifeless (Sacla 1987:60).

As discussed in Chapter 4, the native Kankana-eys distinguish between the spirits of people who have long been dead and those who have recently died. The spirits of those who are long dead are called *Ap-apo*, the second highest god rank in the Kankana-ey spiritual world. These spirits are believed to live with *Kabunyan* and to make trips from the skyworld to the earth, to the underworld, and back. The spirits of recently deceased humans are called *Kak-kading*. They stay on the earth. During rituals, a host family offers and pours a few drops of wine to recognize these spirits' presence in the ritual (Sacla 1987:17-18).

The native Kankana-eys believe that some spirits also live in the underworld. They are called *Anito*. They are of particular interest, since they are responsible for all the misfortune. *Anito* denotes certain groups of spirits. The particular living places of some of these groups of spirits, I already mentioned in Chapter 4, are as follows (Bagamasped and Hamada-Pawid 1985:103). *Pinad-eng* live in the forest, and are known as owners of wild pigs and chickens. They are spirits to whom hunters offer sacrifices for successful hunting. *Tinmongao* dwell in the mountains and are called mountain spirits. They ruthlessly inflict sickness and injury on people who trespass on the spirits' living place. Victims should offer sacrifice to soothe the spirits' anger. *Penten* dwell in water, and are called water spirits. They are believed to be spirits of those people who have died frantically by accident or by drowning. They cause rivers to swell when people cross during rainy days. *Butat-tew* live in caves, and are the spirits who group themselves at night and misguide humans from their way. They suddenly appear and disappear. *Ampasit* also live in caves. They usually are malevolent spirits and have power to steal people's souls. They mislead people traveling at night.

Since the native Kankana-eys believe in life beyond death, on the fifth day of a funeral, relatives and friends give *opo* (contributions), which can include money, all kinds of fruits, and jars of wine for the dead person to take along on the journey to the skyworld (Anima 1977:88). The priest (*manbunong*) announces to the spirits of the deceased ancestors, who are waiting for this occasion in the skyworld, the names of those who give contributions. The Kankanaeys believe that if the spirits do not receive *opo*, anyone among the attendants may die or become sick. In such fear they attempt to give ample *opo*. Because of their capability to bless or harm, the dead spirits are treated as living, conscious beings.

4.2 Pentecostals

The Pentecostals also believe in life after death. However, they do not believe that the deceased ones become spirits who affect human life; nor do they treat the deceased ones as objects of worship.

The Bible reveals that the spirit world is reality. There are angels as well as evil spiritual beings often referred to as demons, evil spirits, or simply, enemies. The angels serve God and execute his will. They are primarily "messengers," as the Hebrew word מלאך indicates. However, they are also involved in human (especially believers') lives in various ways. The Bible appears to say that each one of God's children has guardian angels. The angels are God's army (2 Ki. 6:17).

The Scriptures are clear that the evil spirits and demons cause physical and mental illness, although there are also other causes of the same maladies. On many occasions, demons recognized the Lord. They even pled with him not to cast them out (Mk. 5:9-11). This behavior clearly illustrates that some diseases are caused by evil spirits or demons. They also create disturbances in the believer's life, especially in spiritual life (e.g., Dan. 10:13).

Today's Pentecostals, unlike some other Evangelical Christians, take seriously the reality of the spiritual world. They regularly "rebuke" the activity of the adversaries. They literally take authority in the name of Jesus and verbally pronounce their commands against them. In this sense, the Pentecostals often engage in overt spiritual warfare. In their thinking, this same "power" is closely linked with the experience of Spirit baptism. A favorite passage of Pentecostals is Luke 10, in which Jesus commissions the seventy. The Lord simply commands them to "heal the sick" (v. 9). When the seventy return, they report, "Lord, even the demons submit to us in your name" (v. 17). The link between the healing ministry and the submission of demons is clear.

Yet, among Pentecostals, the casting out of demons is not limited to healing. Any disturbance in daily or spiritual affairs may be treated as hindrances or harassments of the enemy. In a public or private setting, whenever a prayer request is shared, people naturally rebuke the activity of the enemy. Their awareness of the spiritual world and its influence distinguishes Pentecostals from other Christians. Accordingly, they expect the Holy Spirit – but not necessarily the angels – to "protect" them from all evil.

4.3 Kankana-ey Pentecostal Christians

Consciousness of the spiritual world and its effect upon human affairs is more evident among Kankana-ey Pentecostals than among other Pentecostals. This feature probably stands out because of their animistic background. They are particularly conscious of potential retaliation wrought by evil spirits, especially for the offense of abandoning the old allegiance and servitude to the spirits. These believers thus feel that they need added protection of the Lord. This orientation is well attested in their responses to curses, as discussed above.

A common testimony heard from Kankana-eys is that they have been deceived by the evil spirits. When they thought they were offering sacrifices to their ancestral spirits, it was in fact, evil spirits who pretended to be their ancestors. This realization sets in with their new biblical orientation, and it drives new Christians to "hate and curse" the old spirits. Christians in general grow to pay much less attention to the deceased ones. So, they do not necessarily bury the dead within the premises of the house, the practice expected of non-Christian family members. The dead are regarded as having departed the living once-for-all. Furthermore, the believing family members do not go through the complex funeral process. The traditional funeral requires at least a week-long sacrifice, and this entails an enormous economic burden.

However, they remain aware that they are surrounded by hostile powers, and they frequently claim power in the blood of Jesus for protection. Several frequently enunciated terms, such as the "blood of Jesus," the "cross," and the "power of the Holy Spirit" are pronounced with a sort of magical expectation. Perhaps in this behavior is seen the influence of the word "spirit" as it used to represent a lower deity who makes contact with human beings. Due to this orientation, these people often pray *to the Spirit*.

Their assurance of life after death is significant. The animists live with perpetual fear of the unknown future, especially that which occurs after death. The possibility of becoming an *Anito* haunts them. Large amounts of sacrifice are offered to secure a favorable future for the non-Christian Kankana-eys. In contrast, the Christians enjoy the security of a guaranteed future. Because of their poor living conditions, they put great emphasis on eternal life in heaven. This is their supreme hope.

In summary, this chapter has compared and theologically analyzed worldview contours of the native Kankana-eys and the Pentecostals across four primary religious categories: God (blessing and curse), Holy Spirit (healing), revelation, and the spiritual world. The Kankana-ey Pentecostals have been examined as a third religious group which has been profoundly influenced by both belief systems.

The former two groups share many worldview features. Both are clearly conscious about the spiritual world. Their religions, therefore, reflect the immanence of spiritual beings. God or gods and the Spirit or spirits are intimately involved in human affairs. They are not only worshipped but also expected to intervene in daily human situations. Both groups expect the spirit beings to bless, curse, heal, and solve problems, and often their expectations are met through their religious devotion, although the Pentecostals would term this "faith." The similarity of basic religious worldviews between the native Kankana-eys and the Pentecostals may explain the active and aggressive success of the Pentecostal churches in this region.

Conclusion

This section will discuss missiological implications, recommendations, and concluding remarks.

1. Missiological Implications

I would like to reflect on what I have learned through the study and also through my ministry with the Kankana-eys. The main emphasis of the Assemblies of God ministry among the Kankana-ey people has been evangelism and church planting. The evangelistic activities of the mountain workers are easily characterized by their enthusiasm to communicate the gospel and affection toward people. Their strong dedication cannot be explained in human terms. It must be the divine calling which empowers them to endure personal sacrifice and to risk their own lives in order to spread the Word of God among the animistic people. Their trust in God's resources and power was evident in their day-to-day life. When they visited villages that practiced headhunting as their cultural tradition, they, as strangers, had to encounter a perilous moment. At such moments, they looked to the Lord for his help and protection. Their testimonies are filled with God's miracles.

Through reading Vanderbout's personal letters and material related to various mountain workers, I was challenged by the degree of dedication and commitment. The loss of a soul became a reality and they were determined to proclaim the living Word of God among the pagan people. Without such adamant will to win the souls, there would not now be successful ministry in the mountain. It is apparent that when people desire to do God's work, he moves his hand and accomplishes his will.

It is a special blessing that God has constantly raised young and old to spread his good news. Often, especially in the early years, they were not adequately trained for evangelism. Their empirical experience with God's reality left a strong conviction that others had to be rescued from eternal condemnation. It is God who raises his workers. However, we have to carefully find ways to encourage people to be and to remain committed to the work of the Lord.

When the twelve disciples were commissioned (Acts 1:8) by Jesus, they had a great burden to share the gospel with non-believers. Many times, they were persecuted by their own people, both Jews and the Gentiles. But that did not quench the burning desire to preach the gospel to the people. Communicating the Word of God was an urgent thing for them to do.

A related point of observation is that, throughout its history, the Assemblies of God never had an overall program to evangelize the Igorot tribes. It was basically through dedicated individuals that this ministry continued. When a missionary left the mountains, for instance, normally there was no plan to replace him or her. Humanly speaking, the Assemblies of God never had a comprehensive plan for the Cordillera region.

One reason is that the initiative came from outsiders – that is missionaries. Limited resources were often pointed to as the major reason. However, it appeared that some national key leaders in the mountains had not worked together. It took a third party, often a missionary, to bridge this fragile relationship. Some say that this was due to different tribal backgrounds among the leaders. Traditionally, their ancestors lived extremely insecure lives. Headhunting was widespread and one could easily become a prey to this senseless practice. This naturally led to extreme suspicion. For this reason, a missionary's role was critical. This means that when the missionary loses a bigger picture of God's work, he or she can easily make already existing divisions/factions worse among the national leaders.

This by no means underestimates the importance of the work of the majority of dedicated "grass-root level" pastors and workers. The living conditions in the mountains cannot be compared with that of the more civilized and "Christianized" lowlands. When a worker returns to the mountain after his or her Bible school education, this indicates a great determination and passion for his or her own people. It is a totally sacrificial work. When my husband and I visited some of the mountain churches, we observed that a few pastors did not even have a suitable place for their families to live. There is no water system or electricity. Their only desire is to shepherd flocks and win souls. One worker had eleven children, but only two survived. I believe that in order to bring the souls to Christ, missionaries and local pastors should make a sincere commitment: the commitment to God as well as to his people. And these "front-line" pastors should be encouraged as much as possible.

Through our ministry they have been assisted in two ways. The first is educational assistance. Mountain children can receive only their elementary education in their own community. For a secondary education, they have move to a bigger town. This involves not only losing a valuable work force, either to work in the garden or to take care of his or her younger siblings, but also spending a formidable amount. To these virtually "cashless" mountain societies, renting a room, paying for tuition and fees, extra clothes and food are beyond their reach. Our educational assistance program places pastors' children as the first priority.

This extends to college level. The second is medical assistance. When there is a medical need, such as hospitalization and medicine, we normally assist pastors. These two programs have been proven far more effective and less risky than handing out monetary assistance on a regular basis.

The mountain ministry requires a lot of endurance and perseverance. The animistic people are tightly bound to their traditional belief system. They easily reject other religions without even hearing their messages. The Roman Catholic Church, the pioneer of mountain ministries, lost many priests because of persecution. Native people burned many churches and mission stations. It took quite a long period of time before the gospel found receiving hearts. When my husband and I started our ministry among these people, we had to first of all, build a meaningful mutual relationship with the tribal people. They are reserved and introverted. Thus, it take much patience to wait for the hearts to become receptive.

Church planting has been an effective way of spreading the gospel. The mountain workers, after personal evangelism, normally open a home Bible study. The initial contact is normally made through the extended family network. Often, a nearby established church conducts such evangelistic activities. After a period of teaching, a house church is established. New believers and interested people gather together in a small place and have regular Sunday services.

The church planting was one ministry that my husband and I were involved within the mountains. We learned that the presence of a physical building had a varied significance. First of all, in a pagan community, a church building is a visible reminder that God is in the midst of the people. Often, native people comment that they never had even a humble structure to store instruments for pagan sacrifice. Once a member of the Jehovah Witnesses group commented, "Your God is bigger than ours because your church building is bigger than ours." Secondly, in the minds of the people as well as of the Christian workers, a house church is dispensable; that is, it can be discontinued any moment. However, once a building is erected the chance for discontinuity is much less. The building also expresses the presence of a group of God's people. Encouraged by such a notion, we will continue to build not only the spiritual body of Christ, but also visible and physical buildings in unreached communities throughout the mountains. It is not unusual for a new congregation that has completed its church building to reach out to nearby communities with the gospel.

The Assemblies of God did not think through and work out contextualization. By God's grace, an ideal contextualization just happened with the message of the power. As discussed in Chapter 3, through the manifestation of God's power, the Kankana-eys came to Christ by experiencing healing, casting out demons, and being baptized in the Holy Spirit. They were converted through personal experiences with God. Thus, the power was a catalyst in their conversion.

When I stepped into ministry among these people I learned that they perceived that deities have power to heal and bless. They are also believed to be responsible for the welfare of the living and they are active in human affairs. Community and rituals constantly reinforce many of Kankana-ey beliefs. This is a result of not yet knowing the one true God. Thus, the responsibility of Christians is to convince them about the true God who can meet their felt-needs as the source of healing, blessing and, ultimately, salvation. The God whom Christians worship has unconditional love, and he lavishly gives it to bless his people. In God, human beings find beneficence, happiness, prosperity, and solutions for various needs.

Fulfilling ritual requirements is exacting for the Kankana-eys who are subsistence commoners. Frequently, they borrow money from their relatives or friends to pay for the expenses of a compulsory ritual. Otherwise, according to their traditional belief worse things happen. They are, in fact, in constant fear of the deities. I feel an urgency for Christians to bring the gospel of love and liberation. Paul says in Romans 5:8, "God has demonstrated how much he loves us by sending Christ to die for us while we were still sinners." Jesus is the demonstration of God the Father. The way Jesus loved is the way the Father loves. The way Jesus has forgiven is the way the Father forgives.

The news of the gospel must be preached to the Kankana-ey tribal people who are in the bondage of darkness and are controlled by belief in false spirits. My personal role as a gospel bearer is to continue revealing the power of God to help free these people from the bondage of obligation (performing ritual), and to invite them to find true life and joy in the salvation of Christ.

2. Recommendations

Based on findings of this study, I would suggest the following recommendations:

2.1 Power Ministry

Ministers, church workers, and missionaries of the Assemblies of God should continue their unique and successful approach: the demonstration of the Holy Spirit's power in their ministry. The efficacy of power encounter in the ministry of the Assemblies of God is apparent. Through the divine power of God displayed in healing of various sicknesses and diseases, ministry was established and souls were brought to Christ.

As indicated in Chapter 3, in the earliest stage of the ministry (1950-1969), power demonstration was beyond the description of human words. The pastors' prayers were so intense that the sick were often healed instantly. The earnest prayer of God's people moved God's hand on many occasions. However, after a certain period of time, the intensity of the manifestation of God's power was not the same as it had been, although churches were continually establishing and growing.

During the period of 1970-1990, the mountain churches were pioneered and grew, more or less, through Bible study. Young pastors, after being trained in Bible school, began to teach the Word of God among the congregations in the church. As discussed in Chapter 3, there is an obvious distinction between first and second era. In the earliest period of time the power of God was intensely manifested throughout the Benguet Province and other mountain provinces; but in the latter period, the manifestation of God's power, although continually demonstrated, subsided. Why did the manifestation of the power of God not continue with the same intensity? I conjecture that, in the first period of time, Vanderbout's influence on the mountain pastors was great. She trained older and younger people to be future ministers in the mountain church. She not only trained them but also took them to villages and conducted open-air services. She was obviously used by the Holy Spirit as the power of God was demonstrated in revival meetings. However, after Vanderbout left the Assemblies of God, although there were preeminent pastors, there was no such person as Vanderbout, whose life was entirely given to God and empowered by the Holy Spirit.

This poses a great challenge to the current generation of workers. The workers and pastors of the former generation did not receive adequate training. In fact, most of them received only one-month of short-term training. Yet, their effectiveness and commitment was mind-boggling. The newer breed of workers has received not only high school education but also proper Bible and theology training in established Bible schools. These workers seem more intellectual and better equipped to teach the Bible. This may work ideally for the contextualization process: manifestation (power-encounter) first and Bible teaching (truth-encounter) following. However, as the emphasis on the miraculous work of the Spirit decreases, the expectation of the people also diminishes. One suspected reason is their training environment. The older leaders never left their own environment, while the younger ones moved away from the mountain culture to the radically different lowland, where the major denominational Bible school was located. This seems to point to the need for a training program and a facility within the mountain region. As the younger workers normally expect that some from the outside take care of the "manifestation" aspect, the role of missionaries such as ourselves becomes important.

Through an evaluation of the ministry of the Assemblies of God among the Kankana-eys, the mountain pastors and workers should renew their awareness of the manifestation of God's power as a crucial element in the spread of the gospel and as an essential means by which the Assemblies of God laid its foundation and achieved great success in its ministry.

2.2 Mobilization of Laity

Most of the legendary workers in the mountain were "lay people." At conversion, they were farmers and family men. The success story of the Assemblies of God does not come from Vanderbout alone. There were many faithful and persevering national workers. Their zeal for evangelism and church planting produced fruits seen today. Only some of them later attained the status of clergy.

Even today the mountain church pastors and workers should encourage and help lay people to continue to seek and expect God not only to allow them to experience the work of the Holy Spirit through healing and miracles, but also to use them for the expansion of God's Kingdom. As the demarcation between clergy and laity becomes clearer, there is great hesitance on the part of the lay people to be actively involved in ministry which is sometime misunderstood to be the prerogative of the clergy.

Past experiences tell us that workers coming out of the lay group exhibit far more serious commitment than those who finish high school and enter the Bible school. For this reason, the newly started Cordillera Ministry Training Center by a national leader is timely. Sunday School teachers, deacons and young people come for a week to receive training as well as encouragement to continue God's work.

2.3 Women's Involvement

I want to encourage female pastors and church members to be effective in the ministry. According to Kankana-ey culture, the male has a voice to say his opinion and lead the community. However, for strange reasons, there are many dedicated and wonderful female workers and pastors, even though they seem to have a limitation in attaining a leadership beyond a local church setting. This encouraging phenomenon may have happened because Christianity was viewed as "different" from their traditional cultural values. It is also possible that Vanderbout, a female missionary, set a good role model through her effective and accepted ministry. Many mountain male pastors submitted themselves to her leadership, and received training from her. It was particularly significant within a male dominated society such as this. Why would it be possible? According to my observation, through the study, she was led by the Holy Spirit. When Vanderbout arrived in Tuding which was known as a notorious and criminal village, she had settled down in that place and immediately went to work. Some local pastors opposed her starting the ministry in such an area. But Vanderbout knelt down on her knee and attempted to hear God's voice and followed only his will. This scene connotes what a prayerful and obedient woman she was. When she obeyed his will, miracles took place. Vanderbout was empowered by the Holy Spirit during her ministry in the mountains. That was key to her welcome and acceptance by the village people and becoming an effective woman. During my interview with church members in Benguet Province last June-July in 1995, I noticed that the majority of interviewees were female. They actively responded to my interviewing questions. I would encourage the female pastors and the congregation to be effectually used for God's Kingdom and expand his work. The role of the woman in the church is as important as the male in the congregation.

2.4 Contextualization

So far, with God's help, the Assemblies of God has produced an acceptable model of contextualization. Its radical appeal to the power of God precluded the possibility of syncretism from the very beginning. This is well substantiated in the comparison of three worldviews: the worldview of native Kankana-eys, Pentecostalism, and Kankana-ey Pentecostals. On the other hand, it was not active in presenting the Christian gospel in a native form. Many forms are religiously tainted. Even with careful planning, an "experiment" can have a destructive consequence. Christianity still remains an "import." With their theological maturity and a new breed of young leaders, an attempt can be made to construct a "Kankana-ey Pentecostal theology." One possible area is rereading the Scripture, especially the Old Testament through native eyes. The Book of Exodus, for instance, shows many parallel concepts with the Kankana-ey worldview, such as the land, God's miracle, liberation, a new God, God's people, God's care, human leadership, power struggle, and others. They can produce a simple work such as this within their own context.

2.5 Social Work

The Pentecostals are traditionally known as unconcerned with social involvement. The Assemblies of God mountain ministers and missionaries should be concerned for developing social work. The Assemblies of God has neglected the social dimension of the Christian message and life. However, the mountain ministry, in particular, commends a holistic approach. In a simple theory, one can preach only when a living human is around. With a high mortality rate, it is important to save physical lives before one can introduce God's eternal life. There are several possible areas the Assemblies of God can begin as a cooperative work among nationals and missionaries.

Government medical service cannot reach people in remote communities. There is no other social service agency except the church. A local church can be a center for social services. In other parts of the Philippines, a Christian group established a co-op system to make over-the-counter medicines available to the people at a reduced cost. The church can be a place for a medical ministry. There are dedicated medical people in our city who can donate their time as long as there is a supply of medicines. Maintaining a medical outreach team to minister to the mountain people is a strong possibility. Personally, we will continue our assistance to Christian workers, pastors and their families in times of medical need.

Helping Christian youth to receive secondary education has a twofold consequence. First, receiving the four-year high school education means pushing forward the point of marriage, resulting in having fewer children than their parents had. An average number of children in the household ranges between eight to sixteen. Secondly, the secondary education means a wide-open possibility for the future.

In the past six years, we were able to help about thirty to forty children receive a high school education. This is a joint effort between local churches, families and missionaries. There are graduates who are already in colleges and Bible schools. To expand this ministry, we are pioneering in two towns where children can attend high school, while housed in the dormitory facility of the local church.

2.6 Family Planning

Family planning is an urgent agenda hotly debated between the Roman Catholic Church and the government. In the past, when it comes to a family planning policy, the ineffectiveness of the government met a strong opposition from the

Catholic authority. The annual national population growth rate is over 3% and in the mountain region that can be more than double.

In the mountains, the issue is more complicated. They have myths surrounding contraceptive measures. This will take a medical education. To counter the powerful Catholic influence, the matter should be treated from a theological and biblical perspective. A Christian body can coordinate work among local government, Christian medical volunteers, pastors, and missionaries to produce a new model for family planning.

2.7 Environmental Issues

Environmental concerns are not limited to developed countries. Indiscriminate logging has caused massive erosion. The traditional slash-and-burn farming brought landslides and dried out water sources. Although a total log ban is in effect, small scale logging and burning can easily threaten a community.

In the past, all the government programs failed some due to the corruption of government officials and others simply due to a program unfitting to the mountain settings. This was further hindered by the presence of the Communist rebels in the mountain area. As the peace and order situation improves and the effect of environmental abuse becomes evident, it is becoming time for Christians to come up with a new Christian approach to environmental issues. This can include a biblical basis on what it means to be stewards of God's world. With the help of local government and non-government organizations (NGOs), new alternative farming methods, new plants and trees can be introduced. Naturally a local church will be the center. This, as well as a Family Planning program, can provide a good avenue for developing ecumenical relationships.

2.8 Community Services

There are numerous ways to improve daily life. One essential need of many communities is securing a clean water supply. Often a good water source is present. It takes simple technological guidance and assistance in building material, such as pipes, tie wires, joints, cement and iron bars. In one community, the church submitted a proposal to the village and they received it as a gift from the Christians. There is no doubt that this would open up many opportunities to witness Christ to pagan villagers. They will work as a village to build the system. Improvement of trails and building or repairing hanging bridges can not only serve as an expression of Christian love and concern, but also as an opportunity to share God's goodness, as the whole community will spend many days on the project.

Probably, it is not justified to say that the Pentecostals were not concerned for social work. Vanderbout, for instance, did not begin her ministry in preaching or healing. She visited many humble homes, native villages, and cared for their physical wounds. In fact, she opened one children's home as an expression of Christian love. However, Pentecostal social involvement was entirely dependent upon individual aspiration. There has been no programmatic approach as a body.

2.9 Cultural Sensitivity

The Assemblies of God workers of non-Cordilleran origin and missionaries should learn the culture and customs of the Kankana-ey tribal people in order to develop more effective approaches with the gospel. Often the workers and missionaries neglect to learn native culture and customs but are quick to preach the gospel. They should learn the culture and customs prior to sharing the Word of God so that there will be effectiveness in their proclamation of the gospel.

As discussed in Chapter 4, the Kankana-eys are shaped by a distinctive religious practice which can be considered one of the most significant parts of their culture. The Kankana-ey tribal people operate with an underlying assumption that spirit beings (including deceased spirits) are intimately involved in their daily activities and are closely associated with all their affairs. The spirits obtain power to fulfill wishes of living kin and to resolve problems. The Kankana-eys view the world and respond to the world on the basis of these deep-level convictions.

I conjecture that only ministers who know the worldview of these people and their belief system can effectually share the gospel and bring people to Christ. The more mountain workers develop such sensitivity, the more they will be able to preach a relevant message, a message not transcendental but immanent, which can penetrate the hearts of the people hungry for the experience of the living God.

2.10 Evangelistic Challenge

As mentioned above, the rapid social change in some communities and eventually in the entire mountain region in a near future indicates that the "golden hour" for evangelism may soon come to an end. There are hundreds of small communities in remote mountains which do not have even one single Christian. I know that not many people are willing to go to mountain villages to evangelize because of the involvement of much time and hardship. The key then is the mobilization of laity as above discussed. They are mobile and many are zealous to win souls. At the same time, with a radical change around the corner, Christian groups need to study their strategies seriously. Some villages already exposed to "civilization" or an urban culture can be a model.

2.11 Growth in Understanding the Word of God

We have already observed that the power of the Spirit and the Word of God are two pillars that together, have resulted in the unprecedented success of the ministry of the Assemblies of God among the Kankana-eys. The mountain church pastors and missionaries need to stay concerned for the church members' growth in the Word of God. I believe that the church members should grow in the knowledge of God's truth, and this growth should parallel their experience with power encounter. Through learning the Word of God, they will grow in their faith. The church should offer a regular Bible study to teach the Scriptures. Experiencing power encounters alone will not engender Christian maturity. A balanced message, the divine power, and the truth should all be preached and exercised.

2.12 Missionary Involvement

It is obvious that the Assemblies of God has succeeded among the Kankana-eys, but not among other tribal groups. For instance, among the adjacent Ibaloi tribe, the Assemblies of God had no established congregation until the early 1990s, and this tribe is spread around the Baguio area where missionaries, including Vanderbout, were stationed. This seems to point to the idea that only when there is a consistent interest among leaders, does the ministry bear fruit. It is especially critical that missionaries exert much concentrated effort to win people groups. For the Kankana-eys, there has been almost uninterrupted missionary presence. Several decades later this has made a radical difference.

My prayer is that the marvelous success story of the Assemblies of God among the Kankana-eys may be duplicated in the future in other tribal regions including Bontocs, Ibalois, Kalanguyas, Ifugaos and Kalinga-Apayaos. I also pray that we will be used to accomplish this victory for God.

3. Concluding Remarks

In concluding the research, this study has focused on the history of the Assemblies of God ministry among the Kankana-ey tribal people in the Benguet Province of the northern Philippines, from its inception to the present. The study has further attempted to discover how the Assemblies of God approached these animistic people with the gospel. The process identified the element of the gospel (a theological approach) stressed in the ministry, evangelism and church planting methods in the mountains.

The first chapter described the sociopolitical contact of the mountain people with the outside world, from the earliest period. The mountain people were first discovered by the Spanish, and they became known through the Spaniards, to the Americans. The discovery of the mountain people not only factored into the development of a social and political system but also provided opportunities for outsiders to spread the gospel among the mountain people.

The second chapter dealt with the ministry of Christian groups other than Assemblies of God in the northern Philippines. There are four main groups in the study: the Roman Catholic Church, the Episcopal Church, the United Church of Christ in the Philippines, and the Baptist Church. These Christian groups have been actively involved in social work and have established effective ministries in mountain regions. The first three groups strongly stressed the social aspect of ministry – establishing schools, hospitals, clinics, and orphanages through which they have attempted to share the gospel.

The third chapter dealt with the ministry of the Assemblies of God among the Kankana-ey tribal people. The initial ministry was started by the American woman Elva Vanderbout. She was whole-heartedly involved in the ministry, together with local workers. The power of the Holy Spirit was revealed in her evangelism. In revival meetings sick people were healed by divine power. Such events laid forth an avenue by which pagan people were brought to Christ. During the earliest time of her ministry (1950-1969), mountain churches were established by power encounter – healing. In the later period (1970-1990), churches were established by both power and truth encounters. Trained young leaders pioneered churches through Bible study. Bible study provided the village young and old folks not only learning the experience of the truth but also fellowship and evangelistic opportunity to reach out to neighbors. This activity was necessary for churches to grow.

The fourth chapter discussed the religious practice of the Kankana-ey tribal people. The discussion included three main categories: "Spirit Beings," "Roles of the Priests," and "Thanksgiving and Healing Rituals." In the first category, I analyzed how the Kankana-eys perceived the spirit beings, their characteristics, and their power capacity. This analysis assisted in describing the worldview of the Kankana-eys. In the second category, I analyzed various roles of the priests who mediate between humanity and divinity. The third category covered rituals of thanksgiving and healing. The Kankana-eys perform rituals on two main occasions: to express their gratitude and to obtain cures for the sick.

The fifth chapter discussed the principalities and the power. Satan attempts to control the world and people's lives. Its primary role is to make people to fall into sin and overthrow them into darkness. But God's power, which is greater than the power of darkness is able to bring people into the light. Converted people commit their lives to God and keep their relationship with him. The Scriptures noted in this section reveal that God's truth is often displayed in his power. Accordingly, the truth is not to be taken merely in terms of head knowledge, but rather through knowledge closely related to our lives. Those who are in his light live according to the truth which God has taught. Allegiance encounter should follow after a conversion to Christ. New allegiance means a total change from darkness to light and whole commitment to God.

In the sixth chapter I dealt with power encounter. The study traced the demonstration of God's power recorded in the Old Testament and the Gospels. The power of God was manifested in different occasions to reveal who he was. Jesus Christ began his public ministry with the power encounter. He not only displayed the power of the Lord but empowered his disciples with divine power for the purpose of expanding the Kingdom of God.

The seventh chapter dealt with Kankana-eys' ethnic theology. Findings here were based on interviews within several key Assemblies of God churches in Benguet Province. I investigated the people's understanding of God, the Holy Spirit, revelation, and the spiritual world, as well as their faith and practice which had developed through daily experiences.

The last chapter presented a worldview comparison, from a theological perspective among three groups: the native Kankana-eys, the Pentecostals, and the Kankana-ey Pentecostal Christians. The study included an analysis of each group's view of God, the Holy Spirit, revelation, and the spiritual world. This analysis was presented with conviction that the findings would enhance the delivery of the gospel to the Kankana-eys.

The approach of the Assemblies of God stands in contrast to the other Christian groups surveyed in Chapter 3. The latter started their ministries through social works. These groups believed that education was significant to train young people in the mountain for future leadership in church and government. They further perceived that through education, the gospel would be shared among young people and, eventually, their parents. They also considered that showing social care was necessary for needy people who would not have received such benefits from the government. They started hospitals, clinics, and orphanages My experience in the mountain ministry verified that there were many villages where not even a single clinic existed. Many people resorted to consulting with the village priest whenever they faced sickness. This normally required them to offer ritual. It was for reasons such as this that other Christian groups thus attempted to preach the word of God indirectly through social ministry.

In contrast, however, the Assemblies of God preached the gospel directly, with manifestations of God's power. The power was eminently displayed in salvation and healing meetings. Sick people were healed by the scores and gave their hearts to Christ. The Holy Spirit moved among the people in mighty ways so that many experienced the baptism in the Holy Spirit. As a result of power encounter, house churches were established in various regions.

As has been observed, each group approached and established the ministry in the mountains in their own distinctive way. Non-Pentecostal groups provided social care for people's physical needs. This ministry became foundational for them, and their approaches continue even today. However, Pentecostals in the mountains, namely the Assemblies of God, began their ministry with a power message and with power manifestations. The gospel directly penetrated the hearts of these people.

It is clear that the core of the gospel message that the Assemblies of God presented was the "power" of God to heal the sick and cast out dark powers and spirits. As this study has demonstrated, such power was revealed from the very beginning of Vanderbout's ministry. She cast out evil spirits by the power of the Holy Spirit. The power of the Holy Spirit was experienced among the people who attended her open-air revival meetings. The documented accounts remarkably resemble those recorded in the Book of Acts. Besides the "power" message, Vanderbout and the mountain workers were also faithful to the call of God to proclaim the gospel. Vanderbout and her ministry team were not content to see a few works set up and churches built, but they enthusiastically reached out further and deeper into mountain villages with a burden to save souls that were under the bondage of darkness. This attitude characterized the mountain pastors, even after the time of Vanderbout's departure.

According to Kraft (1991a:7), Jesus regularly demonstrated power when he associated to people outside his inner circle. At the same time, he focused on the teaching of truth with those who had already committed themselves to him. Kraft (1991a:4) further stresses that "allegiance encounter" should be made after the initial conversion through either power or truth encounter. People need ongoing teaching and challenges to serious commitment and obedience gained through continued encounters in all three dimensions. Thereby, they are enabled to grow in their relationship with God and with fellow believers.

The true success of the Pentecostal message is not due to the occurrences of supernatural phenomena alone. Fortunately, in the Kankana-ey region, constant ministerial care has been present through the work of various missionaries and national church leaders. Upon the initial power-encounter, the Kankana-ey Pentecostals have further flourished and made full commitments – that is they have experienced full "allegiance-encounter." This is evidenced in their abandoning of their former allegiance to traditional spirits and deities. They have firmly pledged themselves to their new allegiance to the newfound God, the Savior.

References Cited

Aigbe, Sunday: "Pentecostal Mission and Tribal People Groups." In *Called and Empowered.* Murry Dempster, Byron D Klaus and Douglas Petersen, eds. Pp. 165-179. Peabody, MA: Hendrickson. 1991

Anderson, Gerald H.: *Studies in Philippine Church History.* Ithaca and London: Cornell University Press. 1969

Anderson, N. T.: "Finding Freedom in Christ." In *Wrestling with Dark Angels.* C. Peter Wagner and Douglas Pennoyer, eds. Pp.125-159. Ventura, CA: Regal Books. 1990

Anima, Nid: *The Mountain Province Tribes.* Quezon City, Philippines: OMAR Publications. 1977

Bagamaspad, A. and Z. Hamada-Pawid: *A Peoples'History of Benguet.* Baguio, Philippines: Baguio Printing and Publishing Co. 1985

Bangsaliw, Tacio: Personal Interview with Author. Mankayan, Benguet, Philippines, May 16. 1994

Barnett, Milan L.: "Subsistence and Transition of Agricultural Development Among the Ibalois." In *Studies in Philippine Anthropology.* Mario D. Zamora, ed. Pp. 299-333. Quezon City, Philippines: Alemar-Phoeniz Press. 1967

Barrows, David P.: "Memoirs." Unpublished Paper. Berkely: Bancroft Library, University of California. 1873-1954

Batley, Don H.: "The Holy Spirit: Energy of God for Mission." *International Review of Mission* 75: 152-157. 1986

Beals, Ralph L and Harry Hoijer: *An Introduction to Anthropology.* Quezon City, Philippines: JMC Press. 1971

Berger, Peter L.: *The Sacred Canopy: Elements of a Sociological Theory of Religion.* New York, NY: Anchor Press. 1980

Bethel Bible College. *Kalawili: Yearbook* 17 (1): 1-23. 1991

Bolislis, Paquito: "A Study of the Social Customs and Practices of the Isnegs of Upper Apayao." M.A. Thesis Baguio Central University, Baguio City, Philippines. 1967

Braver, Raymond: *Partners in Mission.* Iloilo, Philippines: ABC Publications. 1988

Bugtong, Ben: Personal Interview with Author. Tuding, Itogon, Benguet, Philippines, May 29. 1994

Bureau of Non-Christian Tribes: *Report of the Chief*. Manila, Philippines. 1902
Bureggemann, Walter: *I and 2 Samuel*. Louisville, KY: John Knox Press. 1973
Busacay, Johnny: Personal Letter to Author. Atok, Benguet, Philippines, March 14. 1990
Cabatan, Juan: Personal Interview with Author. Liwang, Bakun, Benguet, Philippines, May 20. 1994
Cadangan, Reynaldo: Personal Interview with Author. Tuding, Benguet, Philippines, March 12. 1989
Catipon, Leonora A.: "Palali Assembly of God Church." Philippines Mountain Churches, MIS 590, Class Research Paper. Baguio, Philippines: Asia Pacific Theological Seminary. 1991
Caput, Antonio: Personal Letter to Author. Mankayan, Benguet, Philippines, May 29. 1994
Caput, Leoraldo: Personal Letter to Author. Tuding, Benguet, Philippines, March 15. 1993
Carino, M. L.: "Discourse as Power: A Critical Analysis of Selected Texts Presenting Notions of the Igorot as the Other." M. A. Thesis Ateneo de Manila University. 1988
Carson, D. A.: *The Gospel according to John*. Grand Rapids, MI: Eerdmans. 1991
Casino, Tereso C.: "The Relevance of the Christian Concept of God to the Cordilleran's Search for Identity as a People." Doctor of Sacred Theology Dissertation. Asia Baptist Graduate School of Theology. 1992a
–: "The Cordilleran Cañao." Unpublished Paper. Baguio City, Philippines. 1992b
Catholic Directory. Manila, Philippines: Catholic Trade. 1976
Cayso, Tita: Personal Letter to Author. Bakun, Benguet, Philippines, March 30. 1993
Chidoro, J.: Personal Interview with Author. Lamut, Benguet, Philippines, August 15. 1991
Clapp, Walter C.: "Some Bontoc Problems and Possibilities." *The Spirit of Missions* 70: 647-650. 1905
Cobble, James F.: *The Church and the Powers*. Peabody, MA: Hendrickson. 1988
Continguey, Edward: Personal Letter to Author. Abatan, Benguet, Philippines, May 15. 1994
Continguey, Marcelina: Personal Letter to Author. Baguio, Philippines, May 17. 1994
Craddok, Fred B.: *Luke*. Louisville, KY: Westminster/John Knox Press. 1990

Cundall, Arthur E.: *Judges and Ruth*. Downers Grove, IL: InterVarsity Press. 1968
Cushner, Nicholas P.: *Spain in the Philippines*. Quezon City, Philippines: Ateneo de Manila University Press. 1970
Dalnnan, Richard: "Some Bontoc Problems and Possibilities." *The Spirit of Missions* 70: 467-650. 1905
Dayaoen, Pilion: Personal Letter to Author. Buguias, Benguet, Philippines. January 21. 1977
Deats, Richard L.: *Nationalism and Christianity in the Philippines*. Dallas, TX: Southern Methodist University Press. 1967
Delson, Marcelino T.: *The Philippine Cordillera and Its People: Review and Synthesis*. Baguio, Philippines: AJ Printing Press. 1988
De Mas, Sinibaldo: *Informe Sobre El Estado De Las Filipinas En 1842*. Madrid: Poblacion. 1843
–: *German Travellers on the Cordillera*. William H. Scott, trans. Manila, Philippines: The Philippines Book Guild. 1975
De Raedt, Jules: "Religious Representations in Northern Luzon." *Saint Louis Quarterly* 2 (3): 245-340. 1964
Devries, Simeon J.: *I Kings*. Waco, TX: Word Books. 1985
Dozier, Edward P.: *Mountain Arbiters*. Tucson, Arizona: University of Arizona Press. 1966
Dumia, Mariano A.: *The Ifugao World*. Quezon City, Philippines: New Day Publishers. 1979
Dunn, James D. G.: *Romans 9-16*. Dallas, TX: Word Books. 1988
Earle, Ralph: *Mark*. Grand Rapid, MI: Zondervan. 1957
Early, J. C.: "Home of the Luzon Highlanders." Unpublished Paper. Michigan Historical Collection, Bentley Library. 1918
Esperanza, T. C.: "The Assemblies of God in the Philippines." M.A. Dissertation. Fuller Theological Seminary. 1965
Filson, William R. and A. L. Santonia: "The Philippine Episcopal Church." Philippines Mountain Churches, MIS 590, Class Research Paper. Baguio, Philippines: Asia Pacific Theological Seminary. 1991
Firmantes, Lizette: Personal Interview with Author. Baguio, Philippines, October 15. 1991
Folkmar, Daniel: "The Administration of a Philippine Province." In *American Colonial Policy and Administration*, Pp. 79-119. Philadelphia, PA: American Academy of Political and Social Science. 1907
Fry, Howard T.: *A History of the Mountain Province*. Quezon City, Philippines: New Day Publishers. 1989

Furer-Haimendorf, C.: "Priests." In *Magic, Witchcraft, and Religion: An Anthropological Study of the Supernatural.* Arthur C. Lehmann and James E.Myers, eds. Pp. 93-105. Mountain View, CA: Mayfield Publishing. 1989
Gardner, Richard B.: *Matthew.* Scottdale, PA: Herald Press. 1991
Gowing, Peter G.: *Islands under the Cross.* Manila, Philippines: National Council of Churches Pub. 1966
Gray, John: *I and 2 Kings.* London: SCM Press. 1970
Gundry, Robert H.: *Matthew.* Grand Rapids, MI: Eerdmans. 1982
Halsema, James J.: *Bishop Brent's Baguio School.* Baguio, Philippines: Brent School. Pub. 1988
Hamlin, E. J.: *Inheriting the Land.* Grand Rapids, MI: Eerdmans. 1983
Hawthorn, Gerald F.: *Philippians.* Waco, TX: Word Books. 1983
Henry, Rodney L.: *Filipino Spirit World.* Manila, Philippines: OMF Literature. 1986
Hiebert, Paul G.: *Konduru.* Minneapolis, MN: University of Minnesota Press. 1974
Hiebert, Paul G., and Daniel R. Shaw: *The Power and the Glory.* Pre-publication manuscript. 1993
Hick, John: *The Myth of God Incarnate.* Philadelphia, PA: Westminster Press. 1977
Hobbs, Herschel H.: *An Exposition of the Gospel of Luke.* Grand Rapids, MI: Baker. 1966
Hobbs, T. R.: *2 Kings.* Waco, TX: Word Books. 1985
Holmes, Arthur F.: *All Truth Is God's Truth.* Grand Rapids, MI: Eerdmans. 1977
Infante, Teresita R.: *The Woman in Early Philippines and among the Cultural Minorities.* Manila, Philippines: University of Santo Thomas. 1968
Igualdo, Lolito T.: "The Social World of the Kankana-eys." D.Ed. Dissertation. Baguio Central University. 1988
Inio, Tito: Personal Interview with Author. Goldfield, Benguet, Philippines, August 23. 1987
Personal Interview with Author. Goldfield, Benguet, Philippines, February 13. 1991
Personal Interview with Author. Goldfield, Benguet, Philippines, March 15. 1993
Ironside, H. Allan: *Gospel of Luke.* Neptune, NJ: Loizeaux Brothers. 1968
Jamieson, Robert: *Genesis-Deuteronomy.* Grand Rapids, MI: Eerdmans. 1945
Jenks, Albert E.: *The Bontoc-Igorot.* Manila, Philippines: Bureau of Printing. 1905
Joines, K. R.: "The Bronze Serpent in the Israelite Cult." *JBL* 87: 245-256. 1968

Jowers, Clyde: "Mindanao Baptist Bible School." In *Gleanings from the Reaping*. Statistical Report for 1965. 1964
Joyner, Russell E.: "The One True God." In *Systematic Theology: A Pentecostal Perspective*. Stanley M. Horton. ed. Pp. 117-144. Springfield, MO: Logion Press. 1994
Kane, Samuel E.: *Thirty Years with the Philippine Headhunters.* New York: Grosset and Dunlap, n.d., Reprinted from *Life and Death in Luzon.* 1933.
Kantzer, K. S. and Carl F. H. Henry: *Evangelical Affirmations.* Grand Rapids, MI: Zondervan. 1990
Keesing, Felix M.: *The Ethnohistory of Northern Luzon.* Stanford, CA: Standford University Press. 1962
Keil, C. Friedrich and F. Delitzsch: *Joshua, Judges, Ruth.* Translated by James Marthin. Grand Rapids: Eerdmans. 1950
Keon, Ma Aurora R.: "Preliminary Reflections towards Historical Perspective on Some Mountain Peoples of Northwestern Luzon, Philippines." *Baguio Tech Journal* 12 (1): 1-14. 1981
Klein, Ralph W.: *1 Samuel.* Waco, TX: Word Books. 1983
Kraft, Charles H.: *Christianity in Culture.* Maryknoll, NY: Orbis Books. 1979
"Allegiance, Truth and Power Encounters in Christian Witness." Unpublished Manuscript. Pasadena, CA: Fuller Theological Seminary, School of World Mission. 1991a
"What Kind of Encounters Do We Need in Our Christian Witness?" *Evangelical Missions Quarterly* 27 (4): 258-265. 1991b
Worldview for Christian Witness, MB 525, Class Syllabus. Pasadena, CA: Fuller Theological Seminary, School of World Mission. 1994
Power Encounter, MR 570, Class Syllabus. Pasadena, CA: Fuller Theological Seminary, School of World Mission. 1994
Lambrecht, Francis H.: "Apostolic Vicariate of the Mountain Province." *Historical Note* 11 (1-2): 141-148. 1980-81
Lee, C. L., M. S. Ponce and J. Y. Yoon: "The United Church of Christ in the Philippine Mountain Ministry." Philippines Mountain Churches, MIS 590, Class Research Paper. Baguio, Philippines: Asia Pacific Theological Seminary. 1991
Lowery-Palmer, Alma: "Yoruba World View and Patient Compliance." Ph.D. Dissertation. Department of Anthropology, University of California. 1955
Lua, Norma N.: *Fiction in the Traditional Kankanay Society.* Baguio, Philippines: Cordillera Studies Center. 1984
Luzon Bible Institute. *Horn: Yearbook* 15 (1): 1-21. 1994
Ma, Wonsuk: Personal Interview with Author. Pasadena, CA. April 13. 1994

Maddela, Thomas P. and Emilio S. Tolentino: "Igorot." *Journal of Northern Luzon* 12 (2): 130-131. 1972

Malek, Sobhi W.: "Islam Encountering Gospel Power." In *Called and Empowered: Global Mission in Pentecostal Perspective.* Murray A. Dempster, Byron D. Klaus, and Douglas Petersen, eds. Pp. 180-197. Peabody, MA: Hendrickson. 1991

Marino, Bruce R.: "The Origin, Nature, and Consequences of Sin." In *Systematic Theology: A Pentecostal Perspective.* Stanley M. Horton, ed. Pp. 255-289. Springfield, MO: Logion Press. 1994

Martin, Ralph P.: *2 Corinthians.* Waco, TX: Word Books. 1986

McDowell, J. and D. Stewart: *Understanding the Occult.* San Bernardino, CA: Here's Life. 1982

Moltmann, Jürgen: *The Church in the Power of the Spirit: A Contribution to Messianic Ecclesio-logy.* San Francisco, CA: Harper & Row. 1977

Monroe, Remigio E.: "Igorot Dances Associated with Rituals and Ceremonies: Analysis and Interpretation." Doctoral Thesis. Baguio Central University. 1987

Morris, Leon: *The First Epistle of Paul to the Corinthians.* Grand Rapids, MI: Eerdmans Publishing Co. 1989

Moss, C. R.: *Nabaloi Law and Ritual.* Berkeley, CA: University of California. 1920

Mowinckel, Sigmund: *The Psalms of Israel's Worship.* Vol. 1, Translated by D. R. Ap-Thomas. New York, NY: Abingdon Press. 1958

Munger, Henry W.: *Christ and the Filipino Soul: A History of the Philippine Baptist, 1900-1945.* Iloilo City, Philippines: ABC Printing Center. 1967

Murray, John: *Epistle to the Romans.* Grand Rapids, MI: Eerdmans. 1973

Neil, Stephen: *A History of Christian Missions.* Middlesex, England: Penguin Pub. 1964

Nida, E. A. and W. A. Smalley: *Introducing Animism.* New York, NY: Friendship Press. 1959

Nineham, D. E.: *The Gospel of St. Mark.* New York, NY: Seabury Press. 1859

Packer, J. I.: "The Empowered Christian Life." In *The Kingdom and Power.* Gary S. Greig, and Kevin N. Springer, eds. Pp. 208-215. Ventura, CA: Regal Books. 1990

Pacyaya, Alfredo G.: "Acculturation in Sagada." In *Acculturation in the Philippines: Essays on Changing Societies.* Peter Gowing and William Scott, eds. Pp. 123-140. Quezon City, Philippines: New Day Publishers. 1970

Phelan, John L.: *The Hispanization of the Philippines.* Madison, Wisconsin: University of Wisconsin Press. 1959

The Philippines Atlas. Manila, Philippines: Fund for Assistance to Private Education. 1975

Phoon, Kum Yew: "Pudong Assembly of God Church." Philippines Mountain Churches, MIS 590, Class Research Paper. Baguio, Philippines: Asia Pacific Theological Seminary. 1991

Plummer, Alfred: *An Exegetical Commentary on the Gospel According to St. Matthew.* Grand Rapids, MI: Eerdmans. 1953

Pomerville, Paul A.: *The Third Force in Missions.* Peabody, MA: Hendrickson Pub. 1995

Posey, Jesse Earl, Jr.: "A Historical Study of Baptist Mission in the Philippines, 1900-1967." Th. D. Thesis. New Orleans Theological Seminary. 1860

Reed, Robert R.: *City of Pines: The Origins of Baguio as a Colonial Hill Station and Regional Capital.* Berkeley, CA: Center for South and Southeast Asia Studies, University of California. 1976

Regpala, Ma Elena R: "Culture as Weapon: Lessons from American Colonialism." *Cordillera Quarterly* 11 (2): 5-8. 1986

Remus, Harold E.: "Miracle (NT)." In *The Anchor Bible Dictionary.* Vol. 4. David Noel Freedman, ed. Pp. 856-869. New York, NY: Doubleday. 1960

Reyes, Angelo J. and Aloma J. De Los Reyes: *Igorot: A People Who Daily Touch the Earth and the Sky.* 3 vols. Baguio City, Philippines: Cordillera Schools Group. 1978

Reynolds, Hubert and Fern B. Grant: *In the Isneg of the Northern Philippines.* Dumaguete City, Philippines: Silliman University, Anthropology Museum. 1973

Rheenen, Gailyn Van: *Communicating Christ in Animistic Contexts.* Grand Rapids, MI: Baker Book House. 1991

Ricardo, Osio: Personal Interview with Author. Abatan, Benguet, Philippines. May 15. 1994

Rowley, H. H.: "Zadok and Nehushtan." *JBL* 58: 113-141. 1939

Russell, Susan: "Ritual Persistence and the Ancestral Cult among the Ibaloi of the Luzon Highlands." In *Changing Lives Changing Rites: Ritual and Social Dynamics in Philippine and Indonesian Uplands.* Susan Russell and E. C. Clark, eds. Pp. 17-41. Ann Arbor, MI: University of Michigan. 1989

Sabay, A., S. Y. Lee and J. Tan: "Survey of Christian Works among the Igorots Done by the Roman Catholic Church." Philippines Mountain Churches. MIS 590, Class Research Paper. Baguio, Philippines: Asia Pacific Theological Seminary. 1991

Sacla, Wasing D.: *Treasury of Beliefs and Home Rituals of Benguet.* Baguio City, Philippines: BCF Printing Press. 1988

Saliw-an, John: Personal Interview with Author. Tuding, Itogon, Benguet, Philippines. May 15. 1994

Sasaki, Masaaki: Personal Letter to Author. Tokyo, Japan, May 21. 1990

Sato, Y., S. W. Choi and B. Setiawan: "The Ministry of Anglican Church among the Igorot." Philippines Mountain Churches. MIS 590, Class Research Paper. Baguio, Philippines: Asia Pacific Theological Seminary. 1959

Schumitsch, Charlotte: "Missionettes in the Philippines." *Pentecostal Evangel*. Springfield, MO, March 25. 1962

Scott, William H.: "Cultural Changes Among Igorots in Mining Companies." *Church and Community* (January-February): 27-30. 1967

On the Cordillera. Manila, Philippines: MCS Enterprises. 1969

"Igorot Responses to Spanish Aims: 1676-1896." *Philippine Studies* 18 (4): 695-717. 1971

History on the Cordillera. Baguio, Philippines: Baguio Printing and Publishing Co. 1974

"The Forbidden Mountain." *Filipino Heritage* 5 (6): 1128-1129. 1978

The Discovery of the Igorots. Quezon City, Philippines: New Day Publishers. 1987

A Sagada Reader. Quezon City, Philippines: New Day Publishers. 1988

Shaw, R. Daniel: *Kandila*. Ann Arbor, MO: University of Michigan Press. 1990

Simpson, J. D.: "Deception: Satan's Chief Tactic." In *Wrestling with Dark Angels*. C. Peter Wagner and Douglas Pennoyer, eds. Pp.115-123. Ventura, CA.: Regal Books. 1990

Skivington, Samuel R.: "Baptist Methods of Church Growth in the Philippines." M.A. Thesis. Fuller Theological Seminary. 1977

Smith, Robert H.: *Matthew*. Minneapolis, MN: Augsburg. 1989

Snider, Theodore M.: *The Continuity of Salvation*. Jefferson, NC: McFarland. 1942

Soriano, Juan B.: "Pentecost in the Philippines." *Pentecostal Evangel*. Springfield, MO, August 7. 1948

Spradley, James P.: *Participant Observation*. Fort Worth, TX: Harcourt Brace Jovanovich College Pub. 1980

Steyne, P. M.: *Gods of Power*. Houston, TX: Touch Pub. 1992

Sturgeon, Inez: *Give Me This Mountain*. Oakland, CA.: Hunter Advertising Co. 1960

Tabora, Flora D.: "Some Folk Beliefs and Practices among the Mountain People of Northern Luzon." *SLU Research Journal* 9 (3-4): 494-513. 1978

Tippett, Alan R.: "The Evangelization of Animist." In *Let the Earth Hear His Voice*. J. D. Douglas, ed. Pp. 21-35. Minneapolis, MN: World Wide. 1973

Vanderbout, Elva: Application for Appointment as Missionary. Springfield, MO, April 1, 1946
"Report on Trip to the Alsados." *The Missionary Challenge.* Springfield, MO, April. 1954a
"A Work of Mercy in the Philippines." *Foreign Field Report.* Springfield MO, July. 1954b
"Salvation-Healing Revival in Baguio City, Philippines." *Pentecostal Evangel.* Springfield MO, June 15. 1955
Personal News Letter. Springfield MO, May. 1957
"Talubin Christians Re-Enact Conversion." *The Missionary Challenge.* Springfield, MO, March. 1958a
"Here and There." *Midland Courier.* Vol. XI, No. 40. Baguio, Philippines. January 26. 1958b
"Salvation-Healing Meetings in Mountain Province." *The Missionary Challenge.* Springfield, MO. February. 1958c
Personal Letter to the Foreign Mission Department. Springfield, MO. August. 1959
Personal Letter to the Foreign Mission Department. Springfield, MO. August. 1961
"A Westward Move." *Our Missionary.* Springfield, MO. August. 1962
Personal Letter to the Foreign Mission Department. Tuding, Baguio, Philippines. February 17. 1966
Vanoverbergh, Morice: "Prayers in Lepanto-Igorot as It Is Spoken at Bauko." *UMJEAS.* Jan. 2: 14. 1953
"Kankana-eys Religion." *Anthropos* 67: 73. 1972
Verana, Cecilia: "New Tribes Mission." Philippines Mountain Churches, MIS 590, Class Research Paper. Baguio, Philippines: Asia Pacific Theological Seminary. 1991
Vicente, John: Personal Interview with Author. Lamut, Benguet, Philippines. 1991
Wee, Viviene: "Religion and Rituals among the Chinese of Singapore: An Ethnographic Study " M.A. Thesis. University of Singapore. 1973
Well, David F.: *God the Evangelist: How the Holy Spirit Works to Bring Men and Women to Faith.* Grand Rapids, MI: Eerdmans. 1987
Wiber, Melanie: "The Cañao Imperative: Changes in Resource Control, Stratification and the Economy of Ritual Among the Ibaloi of Northern Luzon." In *Changing Lives Changing Rites: Ritual and Social Dynamics in Philippine and Indonesian Up-lands.* Susan Russell and E. C. Clark, eds. Pp. 45-62. Ann Arbor, MI: University of Michigan. 1988

Wilson, Laurence L.: *The Skyland of the Philippines*. Baguio, Philippines: Baguio Printed Bookman. 1961

Wimber, J. and K. Springer: *Power Points*. San Francisco, CA: Harper San Francisco. 1991

Wink, Walter: *Naming the Powers*. Philadelphia, PA: Fortress Press. 1992

Worcester, Dean C.: "The Non-Christian Peoples of the Philippine Islands." *National Geographic*. 24: 1251ff. 1913

The Philippines, Past and Present. 2 vols. New York, NY: Macmillan. 1914

Yacuan, George: Personal Interview with Author. Baguio, Philippines. October 20. 1991

Zakovitch, Yair: "Miracle (OT)." In *The Anchor Bible Dictionary*. Vol. 4. David N. Freedman, ed. Pp. 845-856. New York, NY: Doubleday. 1992

Subject Index

Aaron 168
Abigail 168
Abinoam 166
Abra 36; 37; 38
Adam 151; 152; 178
Adika-ila 104; 108; 112; 113; 219; 229
adversary 147
agriculture 42; 43
allegiance 145; 149; 154; 155; 158; 159; 160; 161; 163; 225; 231; 245
allegiance encounter 154
altar 74; 150
Ambiong 97
amen 215
ancestor 78; 132; 136; 137; 138; 140; 141; 208; 209
animist 155
animistic 114; 224; 226; 231
animists 78; 103; 213; 221; 231
Anito 56; 106; 108; 112; 113; 126; 127
anthropological perspective 145
Ap-apo 105; 108; 112; 113; 114; 115; 129; 229
Assemblies of God 73; 74; 75; 78; 85; 86; 87; 89; 90; 91; 95; 96; 97; 145; 187; 224; 233; 234; 235; 236; 237; 238; 239; 240; 242; 243; 244; 245; 246
Augustinians 45; 46; 47
Azazel 145
Baal 149; 150

bad luck 83; 106; 109; 110; 116; 119; 125; 211; 226
Baguio 33; 34; 37; 40; 42; 48; 52; 57; 58; 59; 68; 70; 75; 80; 82; 89; 224; 243
Bakun 89; 94; 95
ballad 127; 128; 129; 130
baptism 46; 63; 155; 223; 228; 230
Basig 90
battle 146; 147; 166; 167
bay-yog 125; 127; 129; 130; 140
Belial 146; 147
belief 63; 92; 103; 107; 135; 140; 150; 156; 164; 188; 191; 194; 196; 197; 199; 201; 202; 203; 206; 208; 210; 215; 218; 232; 236; 242
Benguet 34; 35; 37; 39; 41; 42; 47; 48; 52; 64; 68; 69; 70; 80; 89; 187; 223; 224; 237; 239; 244; 245
Benguet Province 37; 39; 68
Bethany 173
Bethel Bible College 87
Beto 94
biblical perspective 145; 187; 241
Binabulayan 94
blessing 103; 115; 117; 126; 127; 128; 129; 136; 137; 139; 141; 160; 169; 187; 188; 189; 191; 193; 194; 209; 213; 215; 216; 218; 232; 236
blood of Jesus 180; 183; 203; 221
bolo 134
Bosal-lan 134; 136; 140; 141
Brent School 53; 57; 58; 59
Buguias 89; 96; 97

259

camote 123; 133
Canaanites 166
canonical 54; 55
centurion 171
charism 179
charisms 179; 180
Christianity 46; 63; 99; 154; 160; 163; 187; 198; 220; 227; 238; 239
church planting 57; 65; 67; 69; 71; 85; 96; 99; 233; 238
commission 34; 54; 158; 163; 223
commonalties 213; 227
componential 107; 113; 116; 119; 135
componential analysis 112; 113; 118; 140; 141
conquest 32
contextualization 48; 57; 145; 235; 237
Cordilleran 31; 32; 33; 38; 51; 52; 56; 64; 242
Cordillerans 32; 35; 61; 66
crucifixion of Christ 178
curse 187; 195; 196; 197; 200; 213; 214; 219; 220; 221; 231; 232
Dagupan 38
Damascus 152
darkness 74; 76; 78; 145; 153; 155; 177; 207; 210; 236; 245; 246
dasadas 127
daughter of Jairus 172
Davao 68
David 35; 156; 167; 168
dawdawak 134; 140
Deborah 166; 167
deities 56; 104; 105; 128; 129; 135; 213; 214; 215; 222; 229;236; 247
deliverance 160; 173; 228
delivered 45; 78; 167
demoniac 176
demon-possessed 93; 175; 176

demon-possessed man 175
demons 146; 147; 151; 153; 175; 176; 177; 183; 230
devil's work 146
devils 176
Dipat 132; 136; 140; 141
disciples 155; 173; 174; 176; 223; 233; 245
doctrine 49; 138
domain analysis 107; 135
domains 107; 110; 112; 113; 116; 118; 119; 135; 140
dream 99; 112; 117; 120; 140; 165; 168; 174 204; 207; 211; 226; 228
Egypt 165; 168; 174
elementary 49; 60; 76; 234
elements 65; 76; 113
Elijah 149; 150; 169; 170
Elisha 164; 169
encounter 76; 116; 148; 149; 152; 155; 159; 160; 162; 176; 217; 233; 237; 243; 244; 245
encounters 148; 152; 159; 163; 187; 243; 244; 246
Enoch 146; 169
Episcopal 41; 51; 54; 56; 57; 60; 61; 62; 244
Episcopal Church 51; 53; 62
Episcopalians 51; 53; 57; 60; 61; 62
ethnic theology 187; 213; 245
ethnology 35
evangelism 46; 49; 57; 62; 65; 68; 70; 72; 73; 77; 79; 87; 93; 99; 213; 233; 235; 238; 242; 244
events 116; 121; 122; 149; 152; 211; 244
evil 76; 93; 132; 137; 146; 147; 148; 151; 152; 175; 177; 180; 196; 197; 198; 207; 208; 211; 220; 226; 230; 231

evil power 209
evil spirits 146; 208; 209; 230; 231
existential knowledge 182
experiential truth 159
factors, 173
fallen angels 146
farming 42; 43; 188; 217; 241
fellowship 71; 173; 181; 182; 184
female respondents 188; 192; 195; 198; 203; 206; 209
Filipinos 31; 34; 45; 57; 59; 60
fortune 115; 117; 120; 213; 214
Franciscans 46
freedom 150; 153; 172; 174; 176
Galilee 151; 153; 174; 176
Gentile mission 176
Gentile territory 176
Gentiles 163; 227; 233
Gerasa 176
God's blessing 187; 191; 194; 216; 218
God's faithfulness 215; 217
God's glory 173
God's goodness 191; 194; 204; 242
God's love 183; 230
God's people 147; 166; 235; 237; 239
God's power 74; 80; 81; 96; 98; 145; 159; 160; 170; 177; 183; 187; 197; 221; 223; 224; 235; 237
God's sovereignty 170
God's truth 145; 153; 183; 243; 245
God's word 152; 167; 221
goddesses 104; 112; 126; 127; 128
gods 92; 107; 110; 115; 116; 122; 126; 128; 130; 131; 132; 145; 146; 164; 168; 187; 214; 215; 217; 218; 219; 232
Goldfield 98
good luck 105; 110; 122; 126; 129

good news 78; 96; 154; 155; 163; 178; 183; 198; 200; 230; 233
gospel 32; 45; 46; 57; 61; 64; 65; 66; 67; 68; 69; 73; 76; 79; 81; 91; 95; 96; 146; 153; 163; 175; 177; 183; 195; 199; 220; 223; 236
Gospels 170; 171; 223; 245
government 33; 34; 36; 37; 38; 42; 43; 53; 62; 81; 240; 245
guilt 193; 204; 219
guilty 104; 218; 219; 220
healing 66; 80; 82; 90; 91; 95; 99; 103; 108; 114; 117; 118; 121; 129; 130; 132; 134; 145; 160; 163; 145; 161; 163; 164; 201; 202; 203; 213; 219; 221; 222; 223; 225; 232; 235; 238; 242; 244; 246
healing rituals 121; 140
heaven 85; 148; 156; 169; 209; 210; 211; 244; 231
Hebrew people 168
Hebrews 174
Holy Spirit 74; 76; 77; 78; 81; 84; 94; 95; 99; 152; 177; 198; 200; 201; 202; 203; 206; 210; 213; 220; 221; 222; 223; 224; 227; 244; 245
hunting 39; 85; 104; 109; 128
Ibaloi 59; 64; 243
Ibalois 47; 104; 243
Ifugao 37; 47; 48; 49; 96; 104
Igorot 31; 33; 40; 131
illness 94; 1-6; 1-9; 112; 113; 115; 117; 137; 146; 195; 203; 218; 222; 230
Ilocano 38; 59; 64; 66; 70
indigenous 33; 39; 56; 63; 137; 138
indigenous music 56
institutions 52; 86; 89; 121; 138; 146
integration 159

261

Israel 149; 150; 163; 164; 165; 166; 168
Jairus 172; 173
Jericho 166
Jerusalem 149; 173; 223
Jesuits 46
judges 166
justice 74
justification 180; 182
Kaang 95
Kabunyan 120; 237
Kak-kading 105; 1-8; 113; 229
Kalinga-Apayao 37; 46; 48; 91
Kankana-ey Pentecostal 213; 216; 217; 220; 221; 224; 228; 231; 239; 245
Kankana-eys 73; 104; 105; 108; 111; 126; 128; 129; 132; 135; 138; 140; 141; 145; 209; 210; 219; 222; 229; 231; 233; 235; 236; 238; 242; 243; 244; 245
Kapangan 50; 99
Kingdom of God 146; 163; 171; 175; 223
knowledge of God 145; 156; 157; 243
La Trinidad 34; 35; 47; 64; 97; 98
Lamut 97; 98
Lazarus 170; 173
leadership 40; 53; 56; 64; 67; 69; 70; 71; 87; 98; 121; 138; 165; 167; 238
life and death 163; 169; 170
liturgical 54; 55
liyaw 127
Longboy 94
Luzon Bible Institute 83; 87; 88; 90
Maeya 107; 108; 113
Makedse 106; 1-8; 113
maksil 134; 140

male respondents 190; 193; 196; 199; 202; 204; 205; 207; 209; 210
manbunong 93; 114; 116; 118; 119; 122; 125; 126; 128; 130; 133; 134; 140; 214; 222; 230
Mankayan 89; 90
mankotom 115; 116; 122; 125; 133; 226
mansib-ok 115; 116; 118; 119
master 95; 149; 169; 174
maturity 96; 145; 153; 154; 157; 158; 161; 221; 243
medium 40; 70; 132; 179
messengers 84; 167; 230
Messiah 151; 170; 176
messiahship 151
messianic role 170
Methodists 51; 63
mining 34; 35; 43; 128; 136; 139; 140; 188; 192; 193; 194; 195
miracle 80; 82; 164; 169; 170; 173; 175; 239
misfortune 92; 103; 106; 110; 112; 115; 117; 119; 132; 194; 213; 226; 229
misfortunes 115; 139
Moses 165; 168; 169; 170
Mountain Province 35; 36; 37; 42; 54; 81
myth 146
Naaman 164
Nabal 167; 168
New Testament 158; 165; 170; 181; 223
Non-Christian tribes 35; 36; 40
non-Christians 47; 210; 211
non-Pentecostal 45; 73
northern Luzon 31; 32; 37; 39; 43; 45; 51

Old Testament 147; 149; 152; 156; 158; 163; 183; 223; 227; 239; 245
omens 105; 114; 115; 119; 125; 133; 137; 204; 205; 226
pagan festivals 71
pagan mountain people 33
pagan practices 48; 66; 204
pagan priests 46; 224
pagans 198; 200; 205; 220; 224
Pakde 133; 136; 140; 141
Palili 97
Papasok 93
Paul 62; 114; 147; 152; 155; 156; 177; 178; 180; 181; 183; 215; 227; 236
Pauline literature 177
Pauline theory 178
peace-pacts 38; 39
Pentecost 77; 78; 224; 227
Pentecostals 213; 215; 216; 218; 219; 220; 222; 223; 225; 227; 230; 232; 239; 240; 242; 245; 247
perception 134
personal encounter 148
Pharaoh 165; 168
Philippines 31; 34; 36; 38; 40; 45; 46; 51; 53; 57; 59; 62; 64; 65; 67; 68; 74; 75; 83; 84; 86; 88; 223; 240; 244
pigs 105; 106; 121; 123; 125; 131; 177
Potok 126; 134; 140; 141
power encounter 79; 145
power of Christ 148; 163; 177; 183; 199
Presbyterians 51; 63
priests 46; 48; 52; 54; 60; 81; 103; 114; 116; 118; 119; 121; 125; 166; 210; 235; 245

principalities 145
prophetic words 227
prophets 149; 150; 169
Pudong 99
reconciliation 178; 181; 183
recruitment 39; 87
resurrection 55; 173; 177; 178; 181; 182; 183; 206
righteousness 156; 180; 182; 219
rituals 56; 94; 103; 105; 108; 114; 116; 118; 119; 121; 123; 127; 129; 133; 134; 137; 140; 145; 191; 197; 214; 217; 229; 245
role of encounters 145
Samuel 97; 147; 167
Satan 95; 146; 148; 151; 153; 170; 175; 208; 245
Satanic 148; 153; 160; 161; 205; 207
Son of God 63; 146; 152; 171; 177
Southern Baptist 67; 68; 70
sovereignty 170
thanksgiving rituals 141
three encounters 159; 160
tribes 32; 33; 37; 52; 66; 85; 104; 234
truth encounter 149; 154; 246
Tuding 76; 78; 79; 80; 83; 88; 90; 92; 97; 223; 239
underworld 103; 105; 107; 209; 229
United Church of Christ in the Philippines 63; 64; 244
war 34; 52; 58; 63; 76; 89; 165
worldview 70; 155; 213; 219; 220; 222; 232; 239; 245
worship 55; 66; 78; 126; 152; 164; 168; 174; 209; 218; 222; 228; 230; 236
wrath 106; 128; 180; 183

Scripture Index

Genesis
3:17-18   220
5:24   169
6:1-4   146
15   150
19   150
19:26   167
21:1-2   212
25:21-26   169
26:10   219
30:22-24   169

Exodus
3   150
3:19   156
7:3   168
7-11   168
9-11   168
12:29   168
12:31-32   168
14   169
19   150
22:1   220
32:1-35   165

Leviticus
10:1-2   167

Numbers
11:1-3   167
11:4-34   167
12   163
21:4-9   136; 165
21:5-6   165

22:22   147
27:12-23   169

Deuteronomy
7:9-10   219
7:9   215
7:12-13   158
32:4   215
33:12   216
34:9   139

Joshuah
3-4   169
5:10   166
6   166
6:1   166
6:9-15   166

Judges
1-3   166
4:1-15   166
4:7   166
4:14-15   167
6   150
13   150
13:2-24   169

1 Samuel
1:11-20   169
6:19-21   167
25:1-38   167
25:3   167
25:10   168
25:38   168

29:4	147	19:20	149
		20:3	164
2 Samuel			
6:6-9	167	1 Chronicles	
		21:1	147
1 Kings			
5:4	147	2 Chronicles	
11:14	147	4:7	166
13:4	163	26:16-26	167
13:24-25	167		
13:28	167	Job	
17:17-24	169	1, 2	147
18:23-24	150		
18:25-29	150	Psalms	
18:29	150	11:5	220
18:39	150	14:1	167
18:34-38	149	34:12	158
		51	220
2 Kings		72:2	219
2	169	82:6-7	146
2:8	169	89:2	215
2:9-14	169	89:8	215
2:11	169	91:16	158
2:11-12	169	94:12	220
2:13	169	95:8-11	220
4:8-10	169	100:5	216
4:14-17	169	103:3-5	158
4:17	169	145:8-9	216
4:32-37	169		
5	163; 164	Isaiah	
5:5	164	14	155
5:10	164	42:6	163
5:11	164	53:4	171; 223
6:17	230		
13:20-21	139	Lamentation	
17:26	167	3:22	215
18:4	165		
19:1-35	149	Ezekiel	
19:5-7	149	28	155
19:6	149		

Daniel
10:13   230

Amos
1:4   150
1:7   150
1:10   150
1:12   150
1:14   150

Zechariah
3:1   147

1 Enoch
6:3   146
8:1   146
8:3   146
8:4   146
9:2-3   146
9:6   146
9:7   146
10:4   146
10:11   146

Jubilees
1:20   146
10:7   146
10:11   146
11:5   146
12:20   146
15:33   146
17:16   146
19:9   146
23:29   146
40:9   146

Matthew
3:16   223
4:1-11   151
4:3   152

4:5   152
4:8   152
5:39   156
5:43   156
5:44   156
6:33   156
8:1-4   171; 223
8:3   171
8:3-5   171
8:5-13   171
8:6-7   171
8:7   171
8:8   171
8:10   171
9:32-33   147
12:9-13   171; 223
12:22-37   175
12:24   147
12:28   146
12:43-45   147
14   175
14:15-21   170
20:28   171; 223
26:28   171; 223
28:19   163

Mark
1:12-13   170
1:23-26   170; 175
1:23   147
1:23-26   170
1:24   147
1:29-34   171; 223
1:34   170
1:40-42   171; 223
2:1-12   171; 223
3:1-6   171; 223
3:11   170
3:22-30   146
5:1-20   175

267

5:1-11	176	9:1	183
5:4-5	176	9:1-6	174
5:5	176	9:10-17	174
5:7	176	9:11	175
5:8, 9	147	10	230
5:9-11	230	10:1-2	223
5:11-13	176	10:1-9	171; 223
5:13	147	10:9	223; 230
5:42	170	10:17	230
6	175	10:38	173
6:30-44	170	11:14-15	175
6:31	175	11:20	146
6:37	175	19:8	220
6:45-51	170	22:42	158
7:31-37	172		
7:32	172	John	
7:34	172	1:5	155
7:35	172	2:1-11	174
8:1-9	170	4:46-54	171; 223
16:15	163	5:19-20	151
		6:38-40	157
Luke		6:69	176
4:1-19	79	8:12	155
4:14-15	153	8:32	150; 153
4:18	170	9:17	171; 223
4:33-36	175	11:1-16	172; 173
4:33	175	11:1-46	170
4:35	176	11:40	173
4:37	176	12:1-8	173
5:12	147	12:3	173
5:12-13	151	12:15	174
7:11-16	172	12:22	174
8:26-39	175	12:25	173
8:26	175	12:45	174
8:49-56	172	14:6-7	150
8:49	172	16:13	153; 154
8:53-55	173	16:15	153
8:56	170	16:17	153
9	175	17:3	157

Acts		5:10	181
1:7-8	158	5:12-18	182
1:8	223; 233	5:12	146
2:4	78; 224	5:14	146
2:40-47	220	5:17	146
5:1-10	227	6:4-11	182
6:8	152	6:4	182
6:10	152	6:8	182
6:15	152	8:17-18	182
8	227	8:19-22	220
8:12	227	8:20	220
9:20-21	152	12:1-2	179
10:9-16	227	12:9	179
10:15	227	15:19-20	178
13:14-42	152		
13:22	156	1 Corinthians	
13:45-47	152	1:18	118; 177
13:50-51	152	1:24	177
14:17	216	2:4	183
16:11-15	155	3:2	157
17:1-3	152	5:6-10	179
17:5-8	152	5:14	177
17:16-33	152	6:3	146
18:1	152	10:11	220
18:5f.	152	11:10	146
18:12-13	152	13	179
24:10-16	152	13:4-7	179
25:23-26	152	15:35-58	157
27:23-24	227		
28:17-29	152	2 Corinthians	
		3:18	157
Romans		4:4	147; 156
1:4	117	4:7-11	182
1:16	177; 178	5:14-17	183
1:18	220	6:15	147
1:20	177	11:3	147
2:13	157		
5:1-5	180	Galatians	
5:1-2	180	2:19-20	182
5:8	178; 216; 236		

Reference	Page
1 Thessalonians	
3:5	147
5:23-24	215
2 Thessalonians	
2:3	147
Ephesians	
1:3	148
1:4	148
1:13	154
1:18	148
1:20	177
1:21	148
2:2	147
2:6	148
2:7	148
3:10	145
4:30	148
5:8	155
5:16	148
5:27	148
6:8	148
6:11	147
6:12	146; 147
Philippians	
3:8	181
3:10	181
4:13	177
Colossians	
1:3	156
1:5-6	156
1:10	156
1:19	181
1:24	182
2:3	181
4:1	156
1 Timothy	
4:1	153
4:6	153
4:13	153
2 Timothy	
2:13	215
Hebrews	
5:12-13	157
10:23	215
12:5-17	220
1 Peter	
3:18	183
5:8	147
2 Peter	
2:4	146; 147
James	
2:10	219
2:18	157
2:26	157
3:13	157
1 John	
1:9	215
3:8	146
Jude	
6	146
Revelation	
16:14	147

Appendix

List of Visited Churches for Interview

Ambiong Assembly of God Church. Ambiong Benguet Province, Philippines. June, 1995.
Buguias Assembly of God Church. Abatan, Buguias Benguet Province, Philippines. June, 1995.
Baguio Assembly of God Church. Baguio City, Philippines. July, 1995.
Bakun Assembly of God Church. Longboy, Benguet Province, Philippines. July, 1995.
Goldfield Assembly of God Church. Goldfield, Benguet Province, Philippines. July, 1995.
Itogon Assembly of God Church. Saddle, Benguet Province, Philippines. July, 1995.
Lamut Assembly of God Church. Lamut, Benguet Province, Philippines. July, 1995.
La Trinidad Assembly of God Church. La Trinidad, Benguet Province, Philippines. July, 1995
Liwang Assembly of God Church. Liwang, Benguet Province, Philippines. July, 1995.
Mankayan Assembly of God Church. Mankayan, Benguet Province, Philippines. July, 1995.
Masalin Assembly of God Church. Masalin, Benguet Province, Philippines. July, 1995.
Papasok Assembly of God Church. Papasok, Benguet Province, Philippines. July, 1995.
Sipitan Assembly of God Church. Sipitan, Benguet Province, Philippines. July, 1995.
Takadang Assembly of God Church. Takadang, Benguet Province, Philippines. July, 1995.

Questions for Interview (Translated from the Kankana-ey original)

God
(blessing)

1. If your crops and plants are destroyed by a strong typhoon so that there is no way to recover, what did you normally have done when you were not yet Christian and what would you do now?
2. If in spite of hard work, your production of gold was still disappointingly low, what would have done when you were a pagan, and what would you do now?

(curse)

1. If your uncle died due to illness, according to Kankana-ey tradition, the funeral is to be accompanied by a series of rituals. All family members, relatives, friends and neighbors are expected to attend them. If in this situation you decided not to go but to stay at home, and as result they severely cursed you, What would be your attitude? What would you do to counteract the cursing?
2. Consider the following hypothetical scenario: When you try to evangelize your pagan neighbor, she shows her interest in knowing the Gospel. However, her father, being a staunch pagan, curses you, as well as his daughter. What do you do?

Holy Spirit

1. If you had a little baby who started coughing and the cough became so severe that the baby suffered a whole night with cough and fever, what would do?
2. You have been ill for a long period of time when village people and relatives visit you. Many of them are non-believers and encourage you to return to your roots in the old belief system and its practices. They believe it to be a quicker way to recovery. Presented with this attempt at persuasion, what would be your response?

Revelation

1. One day when you are about to leave for a trip, you see a strange animal crawling in your way, an event which is commonly considered a bad omen. What do you do?

2. When you plan to visit your sister's home, you have a terrible dream the previous night. Would you go on the trip or not? If you needed to go, what would you do?

Spiritual World: After death

1. Before your conversion, in a ritual the priest would say that an ancestor's spirit had come. Now what do you think it was that had come?
2. Where do you think all the deceased spirits are now?